BUILDING BRIDGES:

Case Studies in Collaborative Governance in Canada

EDITED BY

CLAUDE M. ROCAN

INVENIRE

Invenire is an Ottawa-based "idea factory" specializing in collaborative governance and stewardship. Invenire and its authors offer creative and practical responses to the challenges and opportunities faced by today's complex organizations.

Invenire welcomes a range of contributions – from conceptual and theoretical reflections, ethnographic and case studies, and proceedings of conferences and symposia, to works of a very practical nature – that deal with problems or issues on the governance and stewardship front. Invenire publishes works in French and English.

This is the thirty-eighth volume published by Invenire.

Invenire is associated with La Maison Gouvernance and publishes a quarterly electronic journal, found at *www.optimumonline.ca*, which reaches more than 10,000 readers.

Editorial Committee
Ruth Hubbard
Daniel Lane
Gilles Paquet (chair)

The titles published by Invenire are listed at the end of this book.

BUILDING BRIDGES:

Case Studies in Collaborative Governance in Canada

EDITED BY

CLAUDE M. ROCAN

Invenire
Ottawa, Canada
2018

© Invenire 2018

Library and Archives Canada Cataloguing in Publication

Building bridges (Ottawa, Ont.)
    Building bridges : case studies in collaborative governance in Canada
/ Claude M. Rocan, editor.

Includes bibliographical references.
Issued in print and electronic formats.
ISBN 978-1-927465-46-2 (softcover).--ISBN 978-1-927465-47-9 (PDF)

    1. Public administration--Canada--Decision making--Case studies.
2. Intergovernmental cooperation--Canada--Case studies. 3. Public-private
sector cooperation--Canada--Case studies. 4. Case studies. I. Rocan,
Claude, editor II. Title.

JL86.D42B85 2018   352.3'30971   C2018-903616-8
                                                C2018-903617-6

Published by Invenire
260 Metcalfe Street
Suite 2A
Ottawa, Canada K2P 1X0
www.invenire.ca

Cover design by Sandy Lynch
Illustration: © Aridha Prassetya | Dreamstime.com
Layout and design by Sandy Lynch

Printed in Canada by Imprimerie Gauvin

Distributed by:
Commoners' Publishing
631 Tubman Cr.
Ottawa, Canada K1V 8L6
Tel.: 613-523-2444
Fax: 613-260-0401
sales@commonerspublishing.com
www.commonerspublishing.com

TABLE OF CONTENTS

CONTRIBUTORS

Dr. Burton Ayles is a Canada Member of the Canada/Inuvialuit Fisheries Joint Management Committee (FJMC). This agency is responsible, with the Department of Fisheries and Oceans (DFO), for the co-management of fisheries and marine mammals in the Western Canadian Arctic. Prior to joining the FJMC in 1998, Burton was a research scientist and then senior regional Director with DFO. His recent focus has been on the development of co-management of fisheries in the Canadian Arctic.

Robert Bell, a biologist and educator, moved to Aklavik in 1969, one of the six communities in Canada's western Arctic that were negotiating a comprehensive land claim. The communities of the area were being overwhelmed by hydrocarbon exploration both in the Mackenzie Delta and the offshore. Their land claim goal was to achieve some control over the land and resources upon which they depended. He later chaired the resulting Canada/ Inuvialuit Fisheries Joint Management Committee (FJMC) for 15 years, retiring in 2009.

Dr. Redmond (Red) Clarke was born in England and educated at Cambridge University and the University of Manitoba. He worked for the Department of Fisheries and Oceans on environmental assessment, fisheries, habitat and oceans management and the implementation of land claims settlements, especially in the Arctic. After retiring, he was briefly an interim member of the Fisheries Joint Management Committee and then has helped it develop fishery management plans. He is an enthusiastic bird-watcher.

Derek Cook has over 30 years of community development experience in the government, academic and non-profit sectors. Currently he serves as the Director of the Canadian Poverty Institute at Ambrose University. Prior to this appointment, he worked for many years in local government, including his role as Executive Director of the Calgary Poverty Reduction Initiative. Derek holds a M.Sc. in Planning from the University of Guelph, a B.A. in Political Studies from McGill University and is a Registered Social Worker (RSW) in the province of Alberta.

Anna J. De Hart, B.A. (Honours Psychology, York University), M.A. (Conflict Studies, Saint Paul University/University of Ottawa) has more than 25 years of experience in public service at both federal and provincial levels in the areas of policy analysis, public consultation, human resources, training and evaluation. She also has a Diploma in Adult Education (St. Francis Xavier University) and an ADR Certificate through CIIAN. Prior to returning to university, Ms. De Hart worked in healthcare.

Robyn Dryden is the Network Coordinator for the Gang Action Interagency Network, a Winnipeg based organization, working on grassroots solutions to the city's gang problem. Robyn has a Bachelor of Arts in Criminal Justice and Conflict Resolution Studies from the University of Winnipeg and is currently working on her Masters in Conflict Analysis and Management at Royal Roads University.

Suzanne Garon, PhD, is a sociologist and full professor at the School of Social Work of the University of Sherbrooke, Quebec, Canada. She is also a regular researcher at the Centre for Research on Aging, where she teaches in the Ph.D. program in gerontology. She is the principal investigator in the implementation and evaluation of the Age-Friendly Cities and Communities program in Quebec (AFCC-QC) and the director of the WHO Collaborating Center on Age-Friendly Environments.

Kristin Hynes worked as a Fisheries Resource Specialist for the Canada/Inuvialuit Fisheries Joint Management Committee (FJMC) from 2012 to 2018. Prior to her work at the FJMC, Kristin studied benthic invertebrates for her M.Sc. research at the University of

Manitoba and the Department of Fisheries and Oceans (DFO). Kristin is currently working for Alberta Environment and Parks as an Invertebrate Monitoring Biologist, based out of Edmonton.

Dr. Gail Krantzberg is a Professor leading the Engineering and Public Policy Program at McMaster University. She has worked as a scientist and policy analyst on Great Lakes matters for government and academia for more than 30 years. She was the Director of the Great Lakes Regional Office of the International Joint Commission (IJC). She has authored six books and over 190 scientific and policy articles on ecosystem quality and sustainability.

Tere Mahoney is a conflict and social policy practitioner, with an interest in operationalizing systems-change for vulnerable populations. Assisting both on the ground and through policy in the areas of poverty reduction, disability, ethno-political conflict and Indigenous issues, she has worked extensively with public participation, collective impact, process design, digital storytelling, qualitative research and systems thinking methodologies. In her practice she assists clients to build their capacity for conflict, with an aim to reduce one of the larger impediments to collaborative social change. She is also a visual artist and writer.

John Noksana, Jr. has been an Inuvialuit member of the Canada/Inuvialuit Fisheries Joint Management Committee (FJMC) since 2015. He is an active subsistence hunter and fisher and has served on several local regional and international resource management boards/agencies, including the Tuktoyaktuk Hunters and Trappers Committee, the Inuvialuit Game Council and the Inuvialuit/Inupiat (Alaska/Canada) Whaling Commission. Representing the Inuvialuit, he is able to ensure that their rights as Indigenous peoples are protected and their traditions and the environment maintained for future generations.

Mario Paris is an Assistant Professor at the School of Social Work at the Université de Moncton, New Brunswick. His research interests are in community building and aging. He studies the Age-Friendly Cities and communities program in Quebec, as well as on the national and international levels. He is also interested in community housing arrangements for older adults.

Claude M. Rocan (Ph.D) held policy/advisory positions with the Government of Saskatchewan and the Government of Canada at the senior professional and executive levels. From 2008-2010, he was a Visiting Fellow with the Graduate School of Public and International Affairs at the University of Ottawa. He is the author of *Challenges in Public Health Governance: The Canadian Experience* (Invenire Books 2012). He is currently an independent researcher and writer specializing in collaborative governance.

Dr. Wanda Wuttunee, Professor in Native Studies at the University of Manitoba, focuses on teaching and research on Indigenous business leaders and their efforts to benefit home communities. She is also interested in mainstream business/community partnerships that work to enhance vibrant, sustainable and healthy Indigenous communities. Her non-Indigenous students have insight and tools to be allies in shaping the future engagement of Indigenous communities in Canada. She received the Indigenous Faculty Excellence: Trailblazer in 2018.

"Kindness affects more than severity."

From Aesop's Fable, *The Wind and the Sun*

INTRODUCTION

Since a highly influential article was published in 1973, much has been said, and written, about "wicked problems," to the point that it seems a little common-place to refer to them. And yet, they represent an enormous and unavoidable challenge to modern society. Rittel and Webber, and many scholars since, made a crucial distinction between 'tame' problems and 'wicked' problems. Problems are 'tame' when they can be solved with increased knowledge or resources attributed to them. Scientific goals, such as sending humans to Mars, or finding a cure for a pernicious disease, are obviously very complicated, but are solvable with increased knowledge and technological advancements. Sooner or later, brilliant minds will find a solution to these problems. 'Wicked' problems, on the other hand, are of a different order. They are not amenable to solutions through technical expertise or administrative measures (Head 2008). Increased knowledge is of course necessary in addressing such problems, but it is not sufficient. Jon Kolko has offered four reasons for what makes a problem 'wicked': incomplete or contradictory knowledge; the number of people and opinions involved; the large economic burden they imply; and the interconnected nature with other problems (Kolko 2012).

How to end poverty is a classic example of a wicked problem and reflects all of Kolko's categories. Despite a vast body of literature on the topic, the question of what constitutes the root causes of poverty is still hotly debated. Indeed, there are even different views of what constitutes poverty. Ending poverty would certainly require considerable financial resources, although, at the global level at least, perhaps not as much as many might suppose (WHO 2008), which itself is a point that is contestable.

Finally, and perhaps the most critical point, the issue of poverty is inextricably connected to many other policy areas, such as race relations, justice systems, economic opportunity, public health, education, housing and so on.

Poverty is perhaps the most glaring example of a wicked problem. But the same points can equally be made about many other issues that bedevil modern societies. In fact, most societal problems in our times *are* wicked problems (Rittel and Webber 1973; Head 2008). To make matters worse, because of their depth and breadth, there is no final, conclusive solution to wicked problems, no way to resolve them once and for all. Probably the best that can be hoped for, through persistent efforts, is to tackle these issues in ways that mitigate the negative consequences and produce more productive results for society, with the full knowledge that there is no "silver bullet" that will put these issues to rest forever (Head 2008). At best, they can be re-solved – repeatedly (Rittel and Webber 1973). The challenge is in how to achieve these outcomes.

Collaboration is key – but how?

The reality is that, because of their inter-connectivity with other issues, wicked problems can only be addressed through the joint efforts of a wide group of players. Many of the problems we face today require approaches that mirror the complexity of the issues themselves – they will need to be multi-faceted, multi-disciplinary, and multi-dimensional (Lasker *et al.* 2001: 185). No one player, governmental or otherwise, has the knowledge, resources, or even the understanding to deal with these issues on its own. What is required is collaboration on a broad scale, involving a wide array of participants from various sectors in society so that the contributions of all significant interests can be brought to bear. Unfortunately, this is much easier to state in the abstract than it is to accomplish on the ground. How does one weave together the participation of a large number of diverse and often contradictory interests to tackle a societal problem? What mechanisms can be used to achieve the level of collaboration that is needed?

The nature of the issues to be confronted in our age puts much pressure on our governance systems. It has often been pointed out that the classic hierarchical model of government is ill-suited to addressing wicked problems (Goldsmith and Eggers 2004: 180).

The 'silo-ed' nature of government bureaucracies typically are not sufficiently innovative and flexible to respond to issues that cross sectoral lines. Of course, governments still have a major role to play in setting public policy. They have the public mandate, the resources, and the accountability mechanisms to set public policy. What is different is that governments are now part – but just a part – of complex sets of interactions involving many groups and interests. Increasingly, complex problems are dealt with "in a setting of mutual dependencies" (Koppenjan and Klyn 2004: 5). So, if not government, who is at the controls? Several observers have noted that in the modern context no one is in charge, or at least not *fully* in charge (Paquet 2009: xvii; Hubbard and Paquet 2010: 4; Denhardt and Denhardt 2000: 553; Salamon 2002: 2). To put it another way, we live in a world where many are somewhat in charge (Agranoff 2007: 187). This is, as Kettl puts it, "pluralism on steroids" (Kettl 2009: 11).

How, then, does society function in these circumstances? Increasingly, public issues are dealt with through networks. Networks have indeed become "the intellectual enterprise for our era" (Kahler 2009: 2). In fact, they are not just the *intellectual* enterprise, but also the *practical* enterprise. We have gone past the point where one actor, particularly the state, has the levers necessary to fully address a complex public policy issue. Unilateral approaches end in failure and indeed often prove counter-productive as they typically trigger resistance from those not involved (Koppenjan and Klyn 2004: 9). Instead, what is increasingly common is a strong level of involvement of various actors on a particular issue. Governments at various levels, non-government organizations, unions, private sector bodies, professional groups, and citizens groups can play a strong role in giving a voice to constituencies that might be affected, or at least have an interest in a matter under consideration. This fosters a high level of inter-dependence, with the various players depending on each other to achieve common objectives. At the same time, however, each player is autonomous in its own right, reporting to an independent authority, whether a state entity, board of directors, community of shareholders, or other structure.

Allow me to recount a personal experience. In a previous capacity as Director General of the Centre of Health Promotion at Health Canada and subsequently at the Public Health Agency of Canada, I had responsibility for a wide range of files, including child health, falls prevention, family violence prevention, physical activity promotion, mental health promotion, healthy aging, and several others. What was striking to me, as someone who had spent several years in more conventional bureaucratic structures, is that in each case the issue was being managed by a network. These networks typically included other federal departments that had an interest in the issue, one or more provincial public health agencies or departments, representatives of professional associations in the health sector, national Indigenous associations, voluntary sector organizations and university researchers. To add to the complexity, there were often also representatives from other policy sectors which had an interest in the issue, such as environment, transportation, agriculture, sports, to name only a few.

From a governance point of view, what was, and remains, intriguing to me is that it can quite accurately be said that no one was completely in charge, or the converse, that many were somewhat in charge. Each player was accountable to a separate authority. Government representatives answered to their home departments, VSO participants answered to their board of directors, and so on. Funding was obviously an important factor, and the agency that provided funding for the project in question clearly had a significant voice in the decision making. But other participants also had resources that they brought to the table, such as subject-matter expertise, research capacity, outreach capacity, and organizational infrastructure, among others, which made them important partners in the process and helped to level the playing field. Each member, as a part of the network, contributed to the work involved, and participated in making decisions as part of that group. Overhanging the networks was an implicit recognition that each individual organization was dependent on the efforts and resources of the other participants in the network to achieve its objectives as a part of that group. Although bureaucracies were involved, this was clearly a departure from the traditional bureaucratic model.

Public health is in no way unique in this type of governance. In fact, management by network of this type is quite typical of how the public enterprise now functions. On the one hand, this is a very positive development. It provides a dynamic setting with a high potential for creativity and innovation. The joining of resources, both material and intellectual, can open the door for innovations that might not otherwise be feasible. At the same time, it is also fraught. Parallel to its positive features, it also holds the potential for conflicts between individuals and organizations that might be competing for power, visibility, funding and status. These tensions can easily lead to breakdowns and often do (Koppenjan and Klijn 2004: 209). There is nothing surprising in this. The question to be answered is how to realize the benefits of working collaboratively, while minimizing the potential risks. Given the potential risks and downsides, are collaborations even sustainable?

What do we call this?

The model of governing that will be dealt with in this book goes by many names. It has been called network governance (Agranoff 2007), network management (Herranz 2006), metagovernance (Sorensen and Torfing 2009), public value management (Stoker 2006), collaborative public management (McGuire 2006), New Public Service (Denhardt and Denhardt 2002) among others. (Admittedly, there are probably shades of differences between some of these terms, but these are not significant for our purposes.) In this book, we will use the term *collaborative governance*. For a working definition, we will draw from Ansell and Gash, who define the term as: "A governing arrangement when one or more public agencies directly engage non-state stakeholders in a collective decision-making process that is formal, consensus-oriented, and deliberative and that aims to make or implement public policy or manage public programs or assets" (Ansell and Gash 2008: 544). Our point is not to advocate on behalf of the concept. Collaborative governance is more than a theoretical concept. The reality is that it exists among us, despite the fact that its existence is not always fully recognized or understood. The inter-connectedness of issues, situated in what might be called the "knowledge era" (Agranoff 2007: 156), make it imperative that a diversity of players from across society be drawn into the public policy decision-making process.

"Horizontal governance" has also been used at times, but this term does not capture the complexity of the type of governance we will be examining. The collaborative arrangements that are presented in this book are places where hierarchical and horizontal management models meet. Agranoff describes networks as "overlays on the hierarchies of participating organizations" (Agranoff 2012: 135). Others have said the networks exist "within the shadow of hierarchy" (Scharf 1994: 37). Whatever imagery one wishes to use, the point to make is that collaborative models do not supplant vertical authorities – by necessity, they co-exist with them (McGuire 2006: 40; O'Toole 2010: 8). As can be seen from the case studies, operating in such an environment presents very specific challenges for those involved.

What this book is about

In this book we seek to learn more about how collaborative structures operate, what challenges they encounter, and how these are overcome. In other words, this book is meant to shed light on how collaborative governance functions from an experiential perspective. For this reason, this book should be of interest to both practitioners of collaborative governance as well as researchers. The literature on the phenomenon of collaborative governance is both extensive and impressive. Yet, there is still much to learn about this form of governing, as its application varies widely to reflect the circumstances involved. This book attempts to contribute to this knowledge through the presentation of case studies. Collaborative governance initiatives are necessarily situational, having to take into account multiple factors, including funding, capacity, leadership, internal composition, proximity to decision makers and many others. Several studies have attempted to provide general theories about the circumstances in which collaborative governance best functions (see for example Huxham and Vangen 2005). These are unquestionably useful. It is also not difficult to find lists of "dos and don'ts" for those who wish to enter into this governing territory (see for example Twyfords 2012). These can also provide guidance, although reference to generalized "success factors" should probably be approached with caution at this stage of our collective understanding of the topic.

Case studies, on the other hand, while narrow in focus, allow one to go deeper in understanding the 'granularity' to be found in actual experiences (Flyvbjerg 2006: 235). In essence, every initiative that follows this path can be seen as a "natural experiment," and as such presents a learning opportunity. Case studies provide a glimpse of the "moving parts" within a collaboration, which, without necessarily leading to hard conclusions about what works and what doesn't – a risky endeavour in itself – can serve to enrich our understanding of the phenomenon. They also provide the opportunity to capture and weigh those factors in the context of a particular set of circumstances.

The case studies

The case studies presented in this book are all based in Canada, and thus reflect the distinct characteristics of the Canadian context. Governance of the type dealt with here needs to situate itself within the context of the broader political community. The fact that Canada has a parliamentary system, based on the Westminster model, a federal system of government that is relatively decentralized compared to many other federations, the particular policies and programs we have at the federal, provincial/territorial and local levels, the political culture in place, all have a critical impact in shaping the governance arrangements that emerge. The regionalized nature of Canadian society is also an important factor, and for this reason the case studies are taken from various regions in Canada, including Quebec, Ontario, Manitoba, Alberta, and the North.

Another important factor in affecting the shape and 'colour' of collaborative governance is found in the policy sector involved. It seems at least reasonable to conjecture that a governance structure in the field of, say, policing, may not function in the same way as one in social service or economic development. Again, as an attempt to take into account this dimension, the case studies presented here are taken from diverse policy fields, including poverty reduction, crime prevention, healthy aging, environmental remediation, economic development, and fisheries co-management.

Each of the case studies represents a unique attempt to address a wicked problem through collaboration. Derek Cook and Tere Mahoney describe the structure and dynamics around the Calgary Poverty Reduction Initiative (CPRI). The CPRI brought together a broad-based coalition of governments, VSOs, private sector representatives, and citizens and was co-led by the Mayor of Calgary and the President of the United Way of Calgary and Area in an attempt to deal with a classic example of a wicked problem.

Robyn Dryden details the experience of the Gang Action Interagency Network (GAIN), which also took a broad city-wide approach, but focused on the specific issue of criminal gangs in Winnipeg, often called the "street gang capital of Canada." While the approach there was to focus on a more specific issue, gang activity, that issue touches on many other equally perplexing social issues that lead to criminal behaviour, such as poverty, housing, education, mental illness and addiction, inadequate family supports and so on. These issues, in turn, are reflected in GAIN's partnership model.

Gail Kranzberg's subject is participatory decision-making as it relates to the Remedial Action Plan (RAP) for the environmental recovery of Collingwood Harbour in Ontario. This study demonstrates an attempt to address the very large problem of environmental degradation by focussing on a relatively narrow geographic area, yet involving the major players that need to be implicated, such as federal, provincial, and municipal governments, industry, user groups, environmental activists, and other interested parties.

Mario Paris and Suzanne Garon, analyze the application of the Age-Friendly Cities and Communities model – a global framework initiated by the World Health Organization – using the lens of collaborative governance. In this case, the approach is to make communities more accessible to seniors with a province-wide framework that engages cities and municipalities to apply this framework to their circumstances, involving the relevant local actors as appropriate.

Wanda Wuttunee discusses six collaborations between First Nations communities and municipalities in the area of economic development, with particular attention to two collaborations: that involving the LSFN First Nation, the Municipality of Sioux Lookout and Kichenuhmaykoosib Inninuwug in Ontario, and the partnership of the Opaskayak Cree Nation, the town of The Pas, and the rural municipality of Kelsey, Manitoba. While the case studies presented by Wuttunee do not involve such a large number of organizations, they demonstrate approaches to achieve collaboration in instances where cross-cultural divisions are present and where the legacy of the *Indian Act* and residential schools, and related factors, needs to be acknowledged before progress can be made.

In a somewhat similar vein, the case study contributed by Burton Ayles, Redmond Clarke, Kristin Hynes, Robert Bell, and John Noksana deals with co-management of fisheries in the Western Canadian Arctic. In this case, a crucial component of bridging the cultural divide was to find a way to incorporate both Western scientific knowledge and the traditional knowledge of the Inuvialuit to fisheries management.

Each is fascinating and instructive in its own right, and together, these case studies provide a rich and diverse body of experiences that provide useful guidance for present and future practitioners of collaborative governance, as well as fodder for the development of hypotheses that can be used to guide further research on the subject. In addition, we include as an Annex a chapter by Anna De Hart discussing the challenge of assessing the collateral impact – both positive and negative – of primary and secondary players on collaborations, and the importance of taking these factors into account when conducting evaluations.

Our framework

To facilitate seeing common patterns and themes, a common analytical framework was used and applied by the authors in a way that suits the particularities of the case they are describing. This framework is drawn from Ansell and Gash (2008), and somewhat amended to suit our purposes.[1] It is represented in the graphic below:

FIGURE 1. Analytical Framework for Case Studies

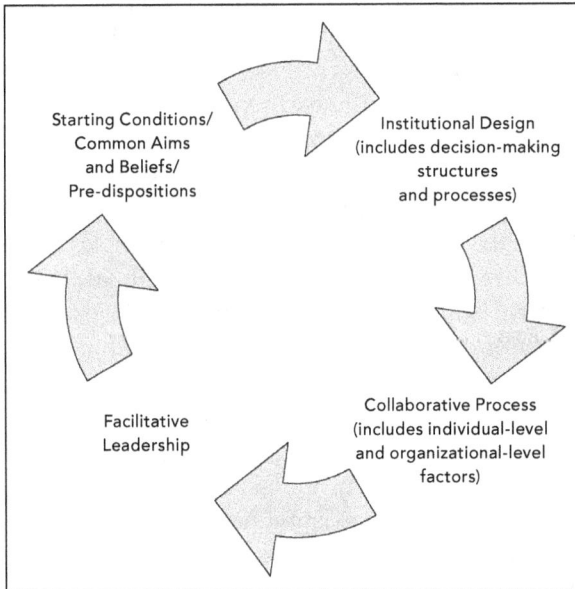

Starting Conditions/
Common Aims
and Beliefs/
Pre-dispositions

Institutional Design
(includes decision-making
structures
and processes)

Facilitative
Leadership

Collaborative Process
(includes individual-level
and organizational-level
factors)

[1] This framework was also used in Rocan 2012, and applied to a case study of the Canadian Heart Health Initiative.

As can be seen in the graphic, the framework covers four broad categories: starting conditions, institutional design, collaborative process, and facilitative leadership. Essentially, these categories provide a relatively simple and straightforward way to categorize the factors that are relevant to our topic. Below, we review each category to discuss what is meant and, to illustrate, suggest some relevant factors that pertain to each heading.

Starting conditions

Admittedly, this heading is rather self-explanatory, but nonetheless represents a dimension not to be overlooked. A structure built on a weak foundation is not likely to sustain over time. So what is this foundation? Elliott *et al.* refer to a level of "pre-disposition," characterized by a set of commonly-held values and beliefs (Elliott *et al.* 1998: 607). A part of this predisposition might be a common perception of a crisis or threat combined with the recognition by the key actors that they cannot achieve their objectives on their own, and that to succeed they will have to work with other parties (Innes and Booker 2003: 40; Agranoff 2012: 134). As an example, Robyn Dryden's article reports that the Gang Action Interagency Network in Winnipeg came out of a recognition that gang activity was a major problem in the city, and that no single government department or independent organization had the means to deal with it on its own. Moreover, there must be a shared sense of common purpose among the partners (Huxham 2003: 404).

Starting off without a clear set of objectives can easily lead to collaborative collapse, failure, or at the least, endless wheel-spinning. These objectives are often laid out in a foundational document that serves as the basis for a new collaboration. Ayles *et al.*, in their case study, demonstrate that the Inuvialuit Final Agreement, a comprehensive claims agreement, established the basis for the co-management of fisheries in the Western Arctic. Similarly, Wanda Wuttunee points to Friendship Accords as the touch-stones for the economic development agreements she describes.

Another key dimension is whether the parties have a history of working together, which, unless the experience is negative, can help to establish a pre-existing level of trust between the key participants. Other possible factors can also be added to the mix, such as financial or other incentives that can encourage parties to come together. As can be seen from the case studies that follow, how the above factors, and others, apply in real-life situations is highly variable. As with the other categories in this framework, there is no precise formula or road-map that inevitably leads to successful results. The situation will always be dynamic – priorities can change, individual actors can leave or be added to the team, and external factors could lead to parties reconsidering their participation. In this sense, there will be a need for collaborations to re-invent themselves periodically if they are to survive. That said, starting on a strong foundation provides a collaboration with a significant advantage.

Institutional design

This category refers to the basic "ground rules under which collaboration takes place" (Ansell and Gash 2008: 550). Essentially, what are the decision-making structures and processes within a collaboration? Many factors come under this heading. It can include rather "micro" yet basic questions such as frequency of meetings, establishing quorum, chairing of meetings and so on. The internal organization of the network is also of critical importance, as Dryden shows in her discussion of the importance of working groups to advance the work of the Gang Action Interagency Network. Such issues might be set out in a formal constitution or agreed to more informally among the members. There is also the question of what constitutes agreement among the members; is it arrived at by consensus or by some form of majority vote. Allied to this is the issue of how disagreements within the group are managed. Differences of view are unavoidable in any group, so it is crucial to have a way of addressing these so that the group can move forward. These can be addressed through formal conflict resolution mechanisms, or more informal mechanisms. Gail Krantzberg indicates that in the case of the Collingwood Harbour Remedial Action Plan, facilitated dialogue and debate was used to resolve conflicts when they arose.

The type of mandate each participant has from their 'home' organization is also relevant. In other words, does the network participant have delegated authority to make decisions or take positions on behalf of his/her organization (Agranoff 2012: 154)? As mentioned earlier, collaborative governance arrangements are composed of a number of representatives of independent authorities, each having its own decision-making structures. The relationship of the representative to his/her home organization can have a major impact on the functioning of a collaboration.

Can this person be assumed to speak for his/her organization? Does this person report back to his/her home organization to ensure its leadership and members are kept informed and "onside"? The confidence of the other participants will weaken if the individual cannot 'deliver' his home organization when it comes time to contribute resources or make important decisions. On a broader level, it is important to remember, as stated above, that a collaboration exists "in the shadow of hierarchy," and that to be successful, network members will need to manage carefully their relationship to the body or bodies to which they are vertically accountable. In their article on the Calgary Poverty Reduction Network, Derek Cook and Tere Mahoney explain the tensions between the Calgary Poverty Reduction Initiative Secretariat and the municipal bureaucracy in that city, and suggest that, in retrospect, more attention could have been paid to the need to 'manage upwards'.

Important as it is, especially when public funds are involved, vertical accountability is only one dimension of accountability as it applies to collaborations. To whom and how is a network accountable? As will be discussed in the Conclusion, accountability in a collaboration must be looked at through a different lens compared to a more hierarchical environment. The complexity of modern governance systems demands "more networked and varied forms of accountability" (Stoker 2006: 53). Krantzberg, for example, makes a crucial point in stating that both individual and group accountability were in evidence in the case study mentioned above. While less clear-cut in their accountability frameworks than is the case in more formal organizations, the way collaborations define their accountabilities can make an important difference in their internal functioning, and in how they are viewed by external actors.

The distribution of power between members within a network is another important factor which can affect the functioning of a collaboration. Inequality in influence can be driven, for example, by funding, access to decision makers, membership size, or myriad other reasons. This is often an issue when governments and voluntary sector organizations (VSOs) participate in a common initiative, especially when – as is often the case – the governmental party is providing the lion's share of the funding. Where multiple levels of government are involved, common in a federal state, VSOs can feel relegated to the role of spectators as governments vie for control of the process. Power imbalances can also be felt where for-profit and not-for-profit entities are included in the same network. Cook and Mahoney provide a vivid illustration of the tension that can arise when the interests of for-profit enterprises clash with those of organizations that are less powerful, and when senior leaders of both groups over-shadow the participation of representatives of vulnerable populations. In the case of the co-management of fisheries in the Western Arctic, on the other hand, Ayles *et al.* point out that while there were power asymmetries between the government bureaucracy and the Inuvialuit, the fact that potential areas of conflict were successfully resolved early in the process helped to build a climate of trust. Inequalities in power are common, and are not necessarily destructive to a collaboration, but it is important for leaders to be sensitive to the possible impact power inequalities may have on the network, and to look for ways to mitigate its impact (Huxham and Vangen 2005: 79).

Collaborative process

This category includes both institutional and organizational factors. It asks, not *how* does a collaboration work, but *what* makes it work? Essentially, it involves the dynamics at work within a network. Part of this is captured by Lasker *et al.'s* reference to "synergy," by which is meant "a process...so the group...can develop better ways of thinking about problems and addressing them" (Lasker *et al.* 2001: 186).

   Perhaps the core of this category relates to the measures, large and small, that are taken to keep a collaboration functioning and on track. It is widely acknowledged that collaborations are quite labour intensive (Koppenjan and Klijn 2004: 209; Huxham and Vangen 2005: 37). Once established, they cannot simply be put on "automatic pilot." Those in leadership roles need to be sensitive to changing circumstances, internal and external, and to make adjustments as necessary. As Huxham and Vangen put it, with collaborations there is a need to "nurture, nurture, nurture" (Huxham and Vangen 2005: 42).

   A critical factor consistently mentioned in scholarly studies of collaborative governance is the dimension of trust (Huxham 2003: 409; Deseve 2005: 134; Imperial 2005: 304; Agranoff 2004: 85). It is probably not realistic to expect that a complete and unqualified level of trust can ever be achieved. The fact that participants in a network represent organizations with varied priorities, objectives, resources, and so on suggests that a certain distance between individuals is to be expected. Many networks contain within them organizations which may be competing for market share, fundraising, or simply public profile, and it is to be expected that their members will naturally reflect these values. On the other hand, without some level of trust, it would prove difficult if not impossible to accomplish any meaningful objectives. The more complex the interactions that are involved, the more important it is for the actors to trust one another (Agranoff 2012: 90; Koppenjan and Klyn 2004: 72).

It follows from the above, therefore, that one of the constant demands of leaders of collaborations is to engage in *trust-building* activities. This can be achieved through a number of means. Helpful in this respect is the very process of building consensus around a shared vision, and through this exercise, facilitating mutual learning about the issues to be addressed and how these issues are perceived by the various members (Agranoff 2007: 121). Small incremental "wins," as observed by Paris and Garon with respect to the Age-Friendly Cities and Communities in Quebec, can also have a positive impact in increasing the level of trust within a network (Huxham and Vangen 2005: 170).

Another critical factor, intimately related to trust and trust-building, relates to the internal communication within the network. For a collaboration to function effectively, it is important that members feel that they are being kept up-to-date and are kept aware of all pertinent information. The sense that some members are hoarding information can be extremely corrosive in these situations, and can lead to speculation about hidden agendas and manipulation. On the positive side, knowledge-sharing as part of a "system of distributive intelligence" (Innes and Booker 2003: 48), beyond being essential to deal with "wicked problems," has the effect of strengthening the ties between members.

Finally, there is the question of the skill sets of the members of a collaboration. While this might have particular relevance for those in leadership roles, it applies to all participants in a network, regardless of their role. Working in a network is not the same as working in the more structured environment of a bureaucracy. In a sense, the command and control management style common in a bureaucracy is often the opposite of what is needed in an environment where participants operate more or less as equals. In the latter case, the skill set required emphasizes negotiation, mediation, trust-building and networking (which is not to imply that such skills are not also useful in a bureaucracy) (Goldsmith and Eggers 2004: 158). Given the fact that most participants in a collaboration are often part of bureaucracies in their 'home' organizations, there is an onus on them to learn to operate effectively in both environments. Since the rules of a bureaucracy are usually more clearly defined, there is the ever-present danger of transporting this style of management to a more 'horizontal' environment, with damaging consequences for the network (Teisman and Klijn 2002: 204). How members of a collaboration manage this duality can have a powerful impact on the sustainability of their enterprise.

Facilitative leadership

Again, this category of factors seems self-evident. Studies have found that leadership is the most often reported internal factor for a collaboration (Rousos and Fawcett 2000: 385). This is not surprising. Some form of leadership seems to be necessary in most forms of collective enterprise. Yet, on the surface this may seem somewhat contradictory to the notion that "no one is fully in charge." Perhaps for this reason, some have preferred to apply the term "stewardship" when applied to collaborative governance (Paquet 2008). Terminology aside, there will be a need for certain functions to be performed, so some form of role differentiation is needed.

Rather than ask who is in charge, it may be more fruitful to identify who has responsibility for which tasks (Agranoff 2012: 117). These can be seen as "positional players," whose position is defined, not by hierarchy but by their role in the enterprise (Huxham and Vangen 2000: 1169). At the most basic level, someone – though not necessarily just one person – will be needed to initiate a collaboration and to be the spear-head for it particularly in its early stages. There may also be a need for someone to speak for the group in a public setting, or in making representations to fora of policy makers.

There are also critical times where one or more players will need to take a more pivotal role. Someone may need to mediate a dispute between members, or break a deadlock that has occurred in the discussions. Counter-productive behaviours within the group, such as players who may be pursuing hidden agendas, or simply not contributing ('free riders'), may also have to be addressed. This may necessitate those in key roles having to switch – temporarily, one would expect – from a spirit of collaboration to more of an enforcement role, or what Huxham and Vangen have called "collaborative thuggery" (Huxham and Vangen 2005: 79).

In general terms, collaborations tend to exhibit some form of distributive leadership. Some members may be there to provide intellectual leadership for the group, others may apply their organizational or financial skills, while still others may be effective networkers with other groups. The ways in which these roles are incorporated into the enterprise, of course, can vary widely as the case studies presented here illustrate.

Furthermore, the leadership needs of a network can change as the collaboration evolves. Butterfoss *et al.* suggest four stages in the development of a collaboration: formation, implementation, maintenance, and accomplishment of goals or outcomes (Butterfoss *et al.* 1993: 322). Each stage of this development calls on a different type of leadership. One would expect that so-called "policy entrepreneurs" and "policy brokers" (Sabatier and Jenkins-Smith 1999) would be needed especially in the formative stage, while those with coordination and management skills might be needed in the latter stages. This suggests a need for individuals in key positions to engage in a process of continuous learning and adaptation (Stoker 2006: 49). There is some evidence of this in the Paris and Garon study. Alternatively, moving from different stages in a collaboration might also mean the need for leadership functions to change among individuals as the network evolves, depending on what skills are needed and the aptitude of those in key positions. As with most factors related to collaborative governance, there is no one formula to be followed that inevitably leads to success. There are a number of ways the leadership function can be distributed among the members to suit their changing needs. What is critical is that the style of leadership adjusts as the needs and circumstances of a collaboration evolve.

What follows

The above discussion was meant to describe the categories contained in the analytical framework used in this book and to illustrate some factors related to each category. It is clearly not meant to be exhaustive of the factors that might be included, nor are all factors mentioned accounted for in each of the case studies that follow. However, since the factors affecting the application of collaborative governance seem almost innumerable, the framework offered is helpful in categorizing them, and in turn finding parallels across studies. As the case studies demonstrate, each application of collaborative governance is unique, and each, in its own right, can be seen as a learning opportunity. Mark Imperial states that one learns to collaborate by collaborating (Imperial 2005: 305). To this can be added that one learns about collaboration through the experiences of those who use it or have used it as their governance model. As stated at the outset, wicked problems will not disappear – they are imbedded in the fabric of our society. Effective models of collaboration need to be developed to find approaches that best respond to these challenges. It is to be hoped that the models presented in these case studies shed light on the nature of the challenges themselves and how to respond to them.

Acknowledgements

I want to thank the many individuals who helped to make this book a reality.

First of all, I would like to thank the contributors for responding so positively to an initial email from a total stranger with an idea for a book, and for their hard work and dedication to deliver a quality product.

Special thanks to Gilles Paquet for his enthusiastic support for this project from the outset and throughout, for his insightful comments on the penultimate manuscript, and for his infectious love of books.

Thanks to Ruth Hubbard, for her helpful and constructive comments on the penultimate manuscript, and for guiding the book through its production stages.

Thanks also to McEvoy Galbreath and her team for their careful work in copy-editing this book and handling the myriad production elements with expert care.

And, as always, I am forever grateful to my wife, Anna, for her support, patience and encouragement.

References

Agranoff, Robert. 2004. "Leveraging Networks: A Guide for Public Managers Working Across Organizations," in John M. Kamensky and Thomas J. Burlin (eds.). *Collaboration: Using Networks and Partnerships*. Lanham, MD: Rowman and Littlefield.

Agranoff, Robert. 2007. *Managing Within Networks*. Washington, DC: Georgetown University Press.

Agranoff, Robert. 2012. *Collaborating to Manage: A Primer for the Public Sector*. Washington, DC: Georgetown University Press.

Ansell, Chris and Alison Gash. 2008. "Collaborative Governance in Theory and Practice," *Journal of Public Administration Research and Theory*, 18(4): 543-571.

Butterfoss, Frances Dunn, Robert M. Goodman and Abram Wandersman. 1993. "Community Coalitions for Prevention and Health Promotion," *Health Education Research*, 8(3): 315-330.

Denhardt Janet V. and Robert B. Denhardt. 2000. "The New Public Service: Serving Rather than Steering," *Public Administration Review*, 60(6): 549-559.

Denhardt Janet V. and Robert B. Denhardt. 2002. *The New Public Service: Serving, Not Steering*. Armonk, NY: M.E. Sharpe.

Deseve, G. Edward. 2009. "'Integration and Innovation' in the Intelligence Community: The Role of a Netcentric Environment, Managed Networks, and Social Networks" in Stephen Goldsmith and Donald F. Kettl (eds.). *Unlocking the Power of Networks: Keys to High-Performance Government*. Washington, DC: Brookings Institution Press.

Elliott, S.J., S.M. Taylor, R. Cameron, and R. Schabas. 1998. "Assessing Public Health Capacity to Support Community-based Heart Health Promotion: The Canadian Heart Health Initiative, Ontario Project (CHHIOP)," *Health Education Research Theory and Practice*, 13(4): 602-622.

Flyvbjerg, Bent. 2006. "Five Misunderstandings about Case-Study Research," *Qualitative. Inquiry*, (12)2: 219-245, http://journals.sagepub.com/doi/abs/10.1177/1077800405284363 [Accessed May 16, 2018].

Goldsmith, Stephen and William D. Eggers. 2004. *Governing by Network*. Washington, DC: Brookings Institution Press.

Goldsmith, Stephen and Donald F. Kettl (eds.). 2009. *Unlocking the Power of Networks: Keys to High-Performance Government.* Washington, DC: Brookings Institution Press.

Head, Brian W. 2008. "Wicked Problems in Public Policy," *Public Policy,* 3(2): 101-118.

Herranz, Joaquin Jr. 2006. *Network Management Strategies.* Evans School Working Papers Series. Seattle, Washington.

Hubbard, Ruth and Gilles Paquet. 2010. *The Black Hole of Public Administration.* Ottawa, ON: University of Ottawa Press.

Huxham, Chris. 2003. "Theorizing Collaboration Practice," *Public Management Review,* 5(3): 401-423.

Huxham, Chris and Siv Vangen. 2000. "Leadership in the Shaping and Implementation of Collaboration Agendas: How Things Happen in a (Not Quite) Joined-Up World," *Academy of Management Journal,* 43(6): 1159-1175.

Huxham, Chris and Siv Vangen. 2005. *Managing to Collaborate: The Theory and Practice of Collaborative Advantage.* London and New York: Routledge.

Imperial, Mark T. 2005. "Using Collaboration as a Governance Strategy: Lessons from Six Watershed Management Programs," *Administration & Society,* 37(3): 281-320.

Innes, Judith E. and David E. Booker. 2003. "Collaborative Policy-making: Governance through Dialogue," in Maarten A. Hajer and Hendrick Wagenaar (eds.). *Deliberative Policy Analysis: Understanding Governance in the Network Society.* Cambridge, UK: Cambridge University Press.

Kahler, Miles (ed.). 2009. *Networked Politics: Agency, Power, and Governance.* Ithaca and London: Cornell University Press.

Kettl, Donald F. 2009. "The Key to Networked Government," in Stephen Goldsmith and Donald F. Kettl (eds.). *Unlocking the Power of Networks: Keys to High-Performance Government.* Washington, DC: Brookings Institution Press.

Kolko, Jon. 2012. *Wicked Problems: A Handbook & a Call to Action.* Austin, TX: Austin Center for Design.

Koppenjan, Joop and Erik-Hans Klijn. 2004. *Managing Uncertainties in Networks.* London and New York: Routledge.

Lasker, Roz D., Elisa S. Weiss and Rebecca Miller. 2001. "Partnership Synergy: A Practical Framework for Studying and Strengthening the Collaborative Advantage," *The Millbank Quarterly*, 79(2): 179-205.

McGuire, Michael. 2006. "Collaborative Public Management: Assessing What We Know and How We Know It," *Public Administration Review*, 66 (special issue): 33-43.

O'Toole, Laurence J. Jr. 1997. "Treating Networks Seriously: Practical and Research-based Agendas in Public Administration," *Public Administration Review*, 57(1): 45-52.

O'Toole, Laurence J. Jr. 2010. "The Ties That Bind? Networks, Public Administration, and Political Science," *PS: Political Science and Politics*, 43(1): 7-14.

Paquet, Gilles. 2008. "Governance as Stewardship," *Optimum online*, 38(4): 14-28.

Paquet, Gilles. 2009. *Scheming Virtuously: The Road to Collaborative Governance*. Ottawa, ON: Invenire Books.

Rittel, Horst W.J. and Melvin M. Webber. 1973. "Dilemmas in a General Theory of Planning," *Policy Sciences*, 4(2): 155-169.

Rocan, Claude M. 2012. *Challenges in Public Health Governance: The Canadian Experience*. Ottawa, ON: Invenire Books.

Roussos, Stergios Tsai and Stephen B. Fawcett. 2000. "A Review of Collaborative Partnerships as a Strategy for Improving Community Health," *Annual Review of Public Health*, 21: 369-402.

Sabatier, Paul A. and Hank C. Jenkins-Smith. 1999. "The Advocacy Coalition Framework: An Assessment," in Paul S. Sabatier (ed.). *Theories of the Policy Process*. Boulder, CO: Westview Press.

Salamon, Lester M. 2002. "The New Governance and the Tools of Public Action," in L.M. Salamon (ed.). *The Tools of Government: A Guide to the New Government*. Oxford, UK: Oxford University Press.

Scharpf, F.W. 1994. "Games Real Actors Could Play: Positive and Negative Coordination in Embedded Negotiations," *Journal of Theoretical Politics*, 6(1): 27-53.

Sorensen, Eva and Jacob Torfing. 2009. "Making Governance Networks Effective and Democratic Through Metagovernance," *Public Administration*, 87(2): 234-58.

Stoker, Gerry. 2006. "Public Value Management: A New Narrative for Networked Governance?" *American Review of Public Administration*, 36(1): 41-57.

Takahashi, Lois and Gail Smutny. 2002. "Collaborative Windows and Organizational Governance: Exploring the Formation and Demise of Social Service Partnerships," *Non-Profit and Voluntary Sector Quarterly*, 31(2): 165-185.

Teisman, Geert R. and Erik-Hans Klijn. 2002. "Partnership Arrangements: Governmental Rhetoric or Governance Scheme?" *Public Administration Review*, 62(2): 197-205.

Twyfords Consulting. 2012. *The Power of Co: The Smart Leader's Guide to Collaborative Governance*. Wollongong, Australia: Twyfords.

WHO Commission on the Social Determinants of Health. 2008. *Closing the Gap in a Generation: Health Equity through Action on the Social Determinants of Health*. Final Report.

CHAPTER 1

The Power of Collaboration and the Collaboration of Power: Lessons from a Multi-sectoral Poverty Reduction Collaborative

By Derek Cook and Tere Mahoney

Introduction and context

Poverty in Calgary has always existed as an enigma. It could indeed be termed a condition of 'prospoverty' where persistent poverty has historically co-existed with relatively high degrees of general prosperity. The stubbornness of poverty in the face of strong economic growth has frustrated many people as it defies the normal prescriptions for reducing poverty, namely strong income and employment growth.

In 2010 Naheed Nenshi was elected Mayor of Calgary on the basis of a 10-point plan for the city. One of those 10 points was the creation of a poverty reduction strategy. This came to fruition in 2011 with the launch of the Calgary Poverty Reduction Initiative. Over the next three years, this initiative worked to produce a comprehensive strategy for poverty reduction using a collaborative governance model. This chapter explores the development of the Calgary Poverty Reduction Initiative and the lessons it provides about collaborative governance.

Analytical framework and methodology

An understanding of poverty requires an understanding of complexity. Stacey defines complexity according to the principles of certainty and agreement to distinguish between simple, complicated and complex issues (Stacey 2002). According to this framework, simple issues are one where there is technical certainty in terms of the action needed to resolve the issue as well as agreement among the actors on what needs to be done and how it should be done. Complicated issues are ones where either there is agreement among the actors, but little technical certainty about the process, or technical certainty about the process, but little agreement among the actors about how to proceed. Complex issues are ones where there is little agreement among the actors about how to proceed, as well as little technical certainty about the process required to address the issue. Poverty is such a complex issue.

As a key aspect of a complex issue is lack of agreement among the actors, conflict is an inherent aspect of resolving poverty. This is in part due to the range of actors involved and the competing interests they represent. Of particular importance are economic actors, political actors, civil society actors and those who experience poverty, exclusion and marginalization. Each actor brings a particular form of power to bear on the discussion about poverty and power differentials will affect the level of agreement on the best approach to resolving the issue. Conversely, those who experience poverty typically lack power and experience multiple levels of disadvantage given the inter-sectionality of the root causes of poverty which increases the complexity of the issues around which agreement is required.

Senior and Swailes identify five different types of power: positional power, expert power, referent power, reward power and coercive power (Senior and Swailes 2016). Persons who are marginalized typically lack access to most (or all) of these sources of power, so have little ability to influence decisions about how to approach issues such as poverty. Consequently, economic, government and civil society actors often employ their various sources of power to forge agreement on strategies but which do not jeopardize their own self-interests. Anti-poverty strategies therefore run the risk of becoming negotiated trade-offs between powerful economic, government and civic interests that may or may not respond to the real needs of people experiencing poverty.

More importantly, this process of strategic development mitigates against systemic change. Systems are comprised of boundaries within which actors engage in relationships governed by structures and rules that maintain the core purpose of the system. The purpose of the system is itself informed by the paradigm that undergirds all aspects of the system's functions. Thus the power to define who and what is within and outside of the system, the power to influence the rules of interaction, and the power to define the purpose of the system is critically important. Any effort to redefine these aspects will be resisted by those for whom the system provides benefits. Consequently, reaching agreement on a complex issue that arises as a consequence of the properties of the system will be difficult and inherently conflictual.

The way in which these various interests and inherent conflicts are managed will affect the resilience of the system itself. The tendency in systems is to seek to gain certainty or agreement. Certainty is often sought through the application of expert knowledge and the reliance on consultants and best practices to arrive at technical solutions that might reduce risk and avoid conflict. To increase the likelihood of technical solutions being developed the scope of the initiative is often constrained to simplify the problem. This enables the efficient allocation of resources by articulating linear cause and effect relationships between measurable inputs and outputs. Conversely the search for agreement in the absence of technical certainty can lead to efforts to limit the range of actors and interests involved thereby reducing the risk of conflict. Involving senior leaders who can exercise power over the process and actors can also drive agreement. Resilience theory suggests that both strategies for moving out of the realm of complexity are counter-productive.

Resilience theory suggests that the resilient systems are characterized by a high level of diversity with power distributed through a horizontal network of empowered actors. Such a system provides for effective but loose integration of the system components, informed by well-developed feedback loops that provide real-time information to this network of actors who have the ability to act on the information received and adjust quickly to changes in the environment. Such systems rely on a high degree of trust between the actors which allows for a high tolerance of dissent which, in turn, enables risk taking and the creative resolution of conflicts. Such systems are not necessarily efficient, and in fact often exhibit significant redundancy. However, such systems are highly resilient due to their ability to foster innovation by bringing diverse perspectives to the table and to productively manage conflict and risk that leads to new solutions.

Given the complexity of many of the pressing issues currently being faced, there has been growing recognition that hierarchical models of governance are ill-suited to the demands of our complex problems. In response, collaborative models of governance have emerged that are more aligned with the principles of resilience articulated above. In particular, the Constellation model of governance and the Collective Impact approach to addressing complex problems are proving to have some success.

The Constellation model of governance is designed for multi-stakeholder partnerships, enabling them to work together to achieve a shared outcome on an issue without the need to establish a new organization. The constellation is typically organized around a shared issue (magnetic attractor) which brings partners together. Governance is provided by a Stewardship Group that creates a shared vision. The Stewardship Group provides guidance and direction to 'constellations' that are "self-organizing action teams that operate in cooperation with a broader strategic vision. The structures and initiatives of the collaboration take the form of 'constellations' – clusters of activity in which a subset of the partners voluntarily participate. Constellations can be formal projects, occasional and opportunistic initiatives, or committees that guide particular aspects of the partnership" (Surman 2006: 6). Work is managed by a Secretariat that is ideally positioned within a third party.

The Constellation model of governance is similar to the Collective Impact approach to social change. Recognizing that, when dealing with complex issues, the coordinated action of multiple actors will be required, the Collective Impact approach is a strategy for facilitating such coordinated action. Similar to the idea of a "magnetic attractor" in the Constellation model, Collective Impact speaks to the need for a common agenda which provides a shared vision for change. Collective Impact also requires a shared measurement system and continuous communication among the partners. Partners engage in mutually reinforcing activities that drive toward the outcomes articulated by the shared vision and embedded in the shared measurement system. Similar to the Secretariat of the Constellation model, Collective Impact requires an independent backbone organization that facilitates the collaboration (Kania and Kramer 2011).

Both the Constellation model of governance and the Collective Impact approach to social change reflect many of the key principles of resilience. Both rely on loosely integrated horizontal networks of empowered actors. Diversity of participation and perspectives is desired. Both rely on internal feedback systems that monitor and allow the system to respond to changes in the environment. Through distributed leadership, trust among the partners is maintained, providing better opportunities for conflicting viewpoints to be resolved. The diversity of participation and distributed leadership also creates important redundancies in the system that provides stability to the network in the face of sudden changes in leadership or conditions.

The degree to which the system is in fact resilient, however, will be determined by how diverse it proves to be, in effect, how broadly or narrowly it defines the boundaries of the system. The narrower the boundaries, the greater the initial degree of trust may be, but this will mitigate against the important inclusion of diverse perspectives necessary for innovation. The degree of trust present in the system will also determine how power and leadership are either concentrated or distributed, which will either promote or inhibit risk taking and dissent, also necessary for innovation. Finally, the ability of the collaboration to reach a shared vision will ultimately determine its success. Reaching a shared vision among diverse interests may ultimately require a paradigm shift that is less likely to occur among a homogenous group with centralized power. The critical aspect therefore in achieving system change through a collaborative process will be creating a coalition broad enough to challenge existing paradigms, while building trust among actors that allows for new paradigms to emerge.

The Calgary Poverty Reduction Initiative

Background

In 2011, the City of Calgary in partnership with the United Way of Calgary and Area launched the Calgary Poverty Reduction Initiative (CPRI). The purpose of the CPRI was to develop a community-based strategy to significantly reduce poverty in Calgary and enhance the well-being of all Calgarians. The driving force behind the initiative was the newly elected mayor, Naheed Nenshi, who had campaigned on a 10-point plan of action, one of which was to develop a poverty reduction strategy for the city.

In partnership with the United Way, a Stewardship Group was formed in early 2012 based on a Constellation Model of governance. The Stewardship Group included representatives from all three orders of government, the business sector, academia and non-profit organizations. A Secretariat was subsequently established to coordinate the initiative under the direction of the Stewardship Group. Over the next 15 months, an extensive community engagement process was executed leading to the development of the initiative's shared vision, goals, strategies and outcomes. The vision of the CPRI was: "A community where no human being is deprived of the resources, means, choices and power to acquire and maintain self-sufficiency while being able to be an active participant in society" (City of Calgary 2013).

This vision was a positive restatement of the definition of poverty adopted by the Province of Quebec in Bill 122 (2002), *An Act to Combat Poverty and Exclusion*. Emerging from an 18-month consultation and engagement process, the CPRI articulated four goals that were believed to be foundational to achieving the vision of the initiative. Those four goals were:

- All Calgary communities are strong, supportive and inclusive.
- Everyone in Calgary has the income and assets needed to thrive.
- Everyone in Calgary can easily access the right supports, services and resources.
- All Aboriginal people are equal participants in Calgary's prosperous future.

These goals informed a range of strategies intended to produce the following outcomes. First, at the highest level, the initiative aimed to cut the poverty rate in half within 10 years. That would result in a poverty rate of 5 percent in 2023 compared to the 10 percent rate that existed at the time the strategy was adopted in 2013. Secondary outcomes focused on reducing vulnerability to poverty by ensuring that 90 percent of the population was above 125 percent of the poverty line, while also aiming to raise public awareness and concern about poverty.

Starting conditions

Poverty in a boom and bust economy

Poverty in Calgary has proved to be stubbornly persistent. Despite periods of record-setting economic growth, the poverty rate has never dropped below around 10 percent. Poverty also tends to be episodic rather than chronic, with people more commonly cycling into and out of poverty rather than there being an entrenched pattern of generational poverty. In contrast to other places, poverty in Calgary is also predominantly characterized by working poverty, as the majority of those in poverty work at least part-time, part-year, with many being employed full-time.

The challenge of poverty in Calgary is exacerbated by the boom and bust economic cycle which creates a high degree of vulnerability. During boom periods, the cost of living tends to rise disproportionately with wages leading to increased financial stress. This is exacerbated by growing income disparity which has resulted in fairly stagnant average income for the bottom 90 percent of the population. Consequently, the inflationary impact of the boom economy results in reduced savings and increased debt, leaving people more vulnerable to the bust cycle.

The boom and bust economy also tends to result in high levels of in-migration during the boom. Not only does such in-migration add to the inflationary impact on goods such as housing, it also creates a large segment of people prone to social isolation. Lacking traditional informal support networks, such newcomer populations are socially vulnerable to personal and financial shocks. This vulnerability is most acutely experienced among traditionally marginalized populations including recent immigrants, indigenous persons, visible minorities, persons with disabilities and lone-parent families, but extends beyond to a much wider swath of the population as well. As a result, the experience of, and vulnerability to, poverty is broad and belies a simple distinction between poor and non-poor.

Poverty as a wicked problem

Poverty is a classic 'wicked' problem. First of all, poverty is difficult to frame as competing definitions often stymie well-intentioned efforts to take positive action. Debates over absolute and relative measures reflect deep-seated assumptions about the causes and impacts of poverty as well as, often, the characteristics of those living in poverty. In the case of the CPRI, there was an inherent bias towards action and away from formal research and theoretical debates. In an initial meeting between the CPRI Executive Director and the Mayor[1], Mayor Nenshi stressed that he was interested in mobilizing the community to effect immediate change, not in creating a plan that would sit on the shelf. Consequently, little time was spent debating the definition of poverty, but rather consensus quickly emerged to adopt the Quebec definition articulated in Bill 122, *An Act to Combat Poverty and Social Exclusion.*

Not only is poverty difficult to frame, the relationship between cause and effect is unclear – the second defining feature of a 'wicked' or complex problem. Indeed, lack of clarity on the definition of poverty will produce a lack of clarity on cause and effect. In the case of Calgary, the disconnect between cause and effect was perhaps sharper given the failure of traditional poverty approaches to make an appreciable dent in the problem. Not only had strong economic and employment growth not reduced poverty in a substantive way, anecdotal and statistical evidence seemed to suggest that it had, in some respects, made it worse. Neither had decades of social services programs and social work interventions succeeded in reducing poverty. Once again the Mayor stressed in an initial meeting with the CPRI Executive Director that as a community we have been reasonably good at alleviating the effects of poverty, but have made almost no progress on ending it.[2] We must, he argued, do something differently to attack the root causes of poverty. Gaining a new understanding the root cause therefore became a central focus of the CPRI.

The third defining feature of wicked (complex) problems is that there is no obvious right or wrong answer, which is unquestionably true in the case of poverty. One's position on what must be done will emerge from one's unique understanding of the definition and cause of poverty, which is itself often reflective of one's social position. Consequently, agreement on poverty strategies is often frustrated by social conflict and power dynamics. In order to move constructively beyond such

[1] Personal communication in meeting between Mayor Nenshi and CPRI Executive Director, January 2012.

[2] *Ibid.*

power dynamics and inherent social conflict, a new shared understanding of poverty would need to be developed that could bring the various community interests together.

Finally, success in addressing complex problems like poverty is inherently hard to measure as there is often no objective criteria. This is extremely problematic in a political context where politicians and civic officials are pressed to demonstrate the effective use of tax dollars within a prescribed election cycle. This is further complicated by the fact that municipalities control very few of the major policy levers that could make a significant difference. In the case of Calgary, this limitation is even more acutely felt given the very limited formal role ascribed to municipalities by the *Municipal Government Act*, the provincial legislation that governs municipalities in Alberta. Consequently, any successful action would require participation from multiple partners, none of whom on their own could effect significant change, nor be able to claim credit for whatever change emerged from such collective action.

To balance this, Mayor Nenshi suggested that what was required was an approach that aimed to produce quick wins where possible while simultaneously working for longer term systemic change.[3] His direction was also to engage both individuals and communities to take ownership, while focusing on using our existing resources better in areas where we do have the opportunity to influence. This approach would require bringing diverse perspectives, sectors and stakeholders together to achieve collective impact based on a shared vision and new understanding of poverty. This approach was reflected in the governance model that emerged.

History of poverty reduction efforts

The Calgary Poverty Reduction Initiative was not the first coordinated effort to address poverty in Calgary. The City of Calgary had played a leading role in efforts to address poverty for many years through its Social Services Department.[4] The Social Services Department has historically engaged community social workers who work out of area offices in disadvantaged neighbourhoods across the city to undertake community

---

[3] *Ibid.*

[4] Subsequently renamed the "Community and Social Development" Department and later the "Community and Neighbourhood Services" business unit.

development activities designed to reduce poverty. The Social Services department also administers the Family and Community Support Services (FCSS) program, a provincial initiative that provides funding to municipalities to distribute to non-profit organizations for preventive social services.

Poverty prevention has long been a focus of FCSS funding for the city. In addition to funding non-profit organizations to address poverty, FCSS also funded internally a Social Policy and Research Unit within the city that was instrumental in providing data and analysis about poverty and related social conditions that informed social planning within the city and the broader community. Through this unit, the city also participated as one of the founding members of the national Urban Poverty Project, led by the Canadian Council on Social Development, which obtained and disseminated important poverty data from Statistics Canada to the community.

The United Way of Calgary and Area has also been an important partner in poverty reduction over the years. In addition to providing funding for services aimed to alleviate poverty, in the early 2000s the United Way began to take a more strategic approach aimed to address the systemic causes of poverty. In 2004, the Sustained Poverty Reduction Initiative was launched which brought together a range of organizations, including the city, to develop a more coordinated systemic approach to poverty reduction. In its 2005 report by the Sustained Poverty Reduction Initiative, the United Way stated "It will take a concerted effort to affect the rates and intensity of poverty in Calgary. We need comprehensive solutions that address the underlying conditions that create and perpetuate poverty" (United Way of Calgary 2005: 8).

The Sustained Poverty Reduction Initiative resulted in two key strategic investments by the United Way. The first was to establish a Sustained Poverty Reduction Committee, chaired by former provincial finance minister Jim Dinning and Nancy Laird, a senior VP from a Calgary-based multinational energy company. The Sustained Poverty Reduction Committee developed a six-point action plan to reduce poverty that focused on building public awareness; reducing policy barriers; increasing the availability of non-market, affordable housing; supporting healthier and more stimulating early childhoods;

building stronger neighbourhoods; and promoting economic well-being (United Way of Calgary 2005: 9).

The second strategic action undertaken through the Sustained Poverty Reduction Initiative was to invest in the organization Vibrant Communities Calgary (VCC). Vibrant Communities Calgary was formed in 2002 as part of the national network of Vibrant Communities organizations established by the Tamarack Institute with the objective of reducing poverty nationwide. The objective of VCC was to bring together a diverse group of community leaders and service agencies who would work collaboratively to reduce poverty in Calgary. VCC emerged as an important voice advocating for policy change, most significantly in advancing a living wage policy for the City of Calgary which came close to adoption in 2009. VCC was also instrumental in preparing an influential report, *The Cost of Poverty*, which was released in 2010 and estimated the total cost of poverty to the province of Alberta.

The other significant predecessor of the CPRI was the Ten Year Plan to End Homelessness. Starting in the early 1990s, The City of Calgary, through the Social Policy and Research Unit, began conducting bi-annual counts of homeless persons. Upon the release of the 2006 Homeless Count, a group of business leaders, philanthropists and non-profit leaders met to discuss ways of addressing the problem. Based on a strategy that had proven successful in New York City, this group proposed to the United Way that Calgary should pursue the development of a Ten Year Plan to End Homelessness. Jointly this group approached the Mayor who endorsed the proposal and established the Calgary Committee to End Homelessness. Launched in 2007, this committee was led by a senior business leader and included representatives from business, government, the non-profit sector, faith communities and the Aboriginal community. Developed over the winter of 2007, the official Ten Year Plan to End Homelessness was released in 2008.

Institutional design

It was in the context of this history of collaboration and strategic action that the Calgary Poverty Reduction Initiative was launched. These initiatives shared several key features. First, the initiatives tended to be driven from the top rather than spurred from the bottom. This typically involved leadership from a senior government or business leader, working in partnership with the United Way and the city. Secondly, such initiatives sought the involvement of a broad coalition of stakeholders including business, government and the non-profit sector. Thirdly, each recognized the importance of addressing systemic causes rather than just focusing on alleviating the conditions and symptoms of poverty. Finally, each was based on sound research and analysis of the problem, often framed in both the human and economic cost of inaction.

The Calgary Poverty Reduction Initiative bore many of these same features. Indeed, the impetus for launching the CPRI was partly buoyed by the success of such collaboration in spurring action, as well as driven by an acknowledgement of the fact that, despite such initiatives, poverty remained as intractable as ever. It was the hope of Mayor Nenshi that a plan to end poverty might emerge that mirrored the Ten Year Plan to End Homelessness.

One of the differences between previous initiatives and the CPRI was that the CPRI emerged from the leadership of the Mayor. Where previous initiatives had been endorsed by the Mayor, this initiative was formed and directed by the Mayor himself. This fact provided credibility to the process that allowed the CPRI to gain support from others in the community who may have otherwise been skeptical. Similar to other initiatives, however, the CPRI quickly moved to establish a broad-based coalition of actors who brought both influence and diverse perspectives to the table.

Organizational development

In 2011, a steering committee was struck to begin work on the development of the CPRI. This committee was led by a former business leader who had previously worked on the development of the Ten Year Plan to End Homelessness. A proposal was brought to City Council in mid-2011 which received approval and funding to proceed. At that point the United Way of Calgary and Area proposed to join the initiative as an equal partner and matched the funds provided by City Council. As a joint partnership, an organizational model emerged that recognized and balanced the interests of the two partners.

The organizational model that emerged was based on the Constellation model of governance. This model establishes a

Stewardship Group that coordinates a loosely knit 'constellation' of independent groups that provide information and advice to the Stewardship Group. As a joint partnership, both the city and the United Way appointed equal numbers of representatives to the Stewardship Group. The Stewardship Group was jointly co-chaired by two leaders, one appointed by the city and one by the United Way. Similar to other initiatives, the leadership of the CPRI fell to two people with senior leadership experience in both the business and non-profit sectors.

This diverse Stewardship Group oversaw the operation of the initiative's Secretariat which was the small staff team charged with the task of strategy development. In order to avoid undue influence by any one of the two partners, the CPRI was established as a quasi-independent unit that was under the direction of both the city and the United Way. While the Secretariat staff in the end were employees of the city, the CPRI was set outside of the normal bureaucracy and reporting relationships, with staff reporting through the Stewardship Group jointly to the Mayor's Office and the President of the United Way.

As a broad collaborative, the Stewardship Group included representation from key sectors across the community. This included elected officials from all three orders of government, business leaders, academia, the non-profit sector and the Aboriginal community. Initially, however, there was no representative on the Stewardship Group who represented the interests of people living in poverty. This reflected a typical pattern of top-down leadership also manifested in the initiatives that preceded the CPRI.

Calgary, in fact, does not have a strong history of grass roots organizations. Marginalized populations have not historically been well organized, and their interests have been articulated more through social service and community organizations. In 2006, however, a movement had started to organize low-income people through a project spurred by the Calgary District Labour Council and the Alberta College of Social Workers. With initial funding from the United Way, this new advocacy group, *Poverty Talks*, aimed to empower low-income people to speak and advocate for themselves. In 2008, this group had produced their own anti-poverty plan. Once funding from the United Way expired, Vibrant Communities Calgary offered to support the fledgling group with administration and facilitation. It was to this group that the CPRI turned to gain representation, from persons with a lived experience of poverty, on the Stewardship Group.

With the Stewardship Group established, the Constellation network remained to be established. The network itself was organized partly around important policy domains that had been identified by Torjman in the influential paper, *Poverty Policy* (Torjman 2008). In addition to policy domains, there were also key population groups that required representation and inclusion. The policy domains that emerged were housing, food security, employment, justice, health, and neighbourhoods. The population groups that emerged were women, immigrants, persons with disabilities, Aboriginal persons, seniors, and children and youth.

The approach to establishing the Constellation Groups was to identify a key community leader in each domain, and then allow the leader to assemble the group of people that they felt it was important to work with. The Constellation Group was co-chaired by that community leader along with a representative from the Stewardship Group. This ensured that there was good communication between the Constellation Groups and the Stewardship Group, while also ensuring that the members of the Stewardship Group were invested in the process. The Constellation Groups were provided with a discussion guide and broad objectives, but given considerable autonomy to conduct their own process to provide the input they deemed relevant. Providing this level of autonomy was important both for generating new ideas, as well as gaining important buy-in from the Constellation Groups to the process.

The Constellation network itself represented a broad and diverse cross-section of the community, with 13 groups representing over 200 stakeholder individuals and organizations. Support for the Constellation Groups and the process was also gained by turning leadership of the Constellation process over to natural leaders from within the respective sectors (domains). This ensured that there would be support later in the process once the strategy moved from development to implementation.

Strategy development

As a diverse collaborative, one of the key first steps in the process was building trust and a shared vision among the Stewardship Group. Members of the Stewardship Group did not have experience working with each other, and represented sectors that may have competing interests. Moreover, in the history of efforts to address poverty, there has been a tendency for different interests to assign blame; poverty activists may point to business or government action (or inaction) as the source of poverty, while business interests may see people living in poverty as primarily responsible for their situation. Clearly the attribution of blame would not create a productive dialogue.

The attribution of blame reflects deeper differences in the understanding of the definition and root causes of poverty, which are informed by differing paradigms. In order to come to a shared understanding of poverty and the way forward, a paradigm shift among the members of the Stewardship Group and the rest of the collaborative would be required. Such a shift would not occur by one understanding dominating the other, but by creating a new understanding that shifted all perspectives.

A new shared understanding emerged by shifting the conversation from poverty to a broader discussion of vulnerability. This was possible by acknowledging, first of all, that all interests in the collaborative are part of the problem, all are similarly part of the solution and that all benefit from a solution. This shifted the conversation from a focus on "helping" a portion of the population defined as "poor" to one of understanding the sources of vulnerability that can lead to poverty. Furthermore, the adoption of a broad holistic definition of poverty that addressed more than just the material (financial) dimension also facilitated this shift. While this provoked some deep conversation about whether or not the collaborative should focus its efforts on those most deeply impoverished, the consensus that emerged was that a broader view would be more productive. This resulted in the development of the following key messages:

- *We need to do it differently.* The CPRI wants to move beyond the traditional approaches to solving poverty, as these have not successfully addressed the root causes to date;
- *We believe change is possible.* We have the will, the resources and the precedent to make a difference;
- *We are all vulnerable.* There are many degrees and dimensions of poverty and we all experience some. We all need to increase our resilience to crises in order to prevent poverty;

- *We all benefit.* When we invest in Calgarians' resilience we not only increase our own resilience, we also live in a city that is enriched;
- *There is enough for all.* In a resource-rich, committed city like Calgary we believe there is enough for everyone to have decent quality of life;
- *We will discover the answers together.* Through a deliberate multi-sectoral, collaborative approach, we come to see that poverty directly or indirectly impacts all of us, so we must all be part of the solution (City of Calgary 2013: Internal Report).

The foundational concepts of universal vulnerability and the rejection of scarcity were critical to shifting the understanding of poverty within the Stewardship Group, allowing for a new shared understanding to emerge. This new understanding then informed the Constellation Group discussions.

Just as the Stewardship Group brought together diverse interests that required the development of a shared understanding, the Constellation network was similarly diverse. With Constellations organized around specific interests and demographic groups, the challenge was to facilitate the development of shared goals that spanned the specific interests of the individual Constellation. While the organization of the Constellation around a specific issue was important for gaining initial involvement, an overarching poverty reduction strategy would need to transcend the specific interests to create goals and strategic directions that reflected those interests but articulated a broader vision.

Developing the broader vision was accomplished by supporting each Constellation to develop goals specific to their area of interest and expertise. At the end of this process, the individual Constellations were brought together for a large gathering of all of the Constellations where the individual goals were shared. At the large gathering the connections between these goals were identified, and that allowed for the emergence of common goals that spanned the Constellations.

Once these goals were articulated and refined, each Constellation then embarked on the development of recommendations that would meet the overarching goals in the context of their own specific area of interest. At the end of this process, the large Constellation network was gathered together again to share their specific strategies. These were once again shared and common strategies began to emerge that addressed the interests of multiple Constellations. Through this process the initial generation of 200 potential strategies from the individual Constellations was refined to a manageable number of 50. These 50 strategies were subsequently evaluated on the basis of feasibility and impact to produce the final suite of 18 distinct strategies, grouped under four common goals, that formed the poverty reduction strategy presented to City Council.

In May 2013, the Stewardship Group unanimously endorsed the final strategy which was then presented to City Council and the Board of the United Way for approval. The strategy received unanimous approval from City Council and the United Way. This was a significant achievement given the disparate positions of members of City Council and of the United Way. The fact that the strategy effectively spanned both the right and the left of the political spectrum is evidence of the success of the strategy development process and the collaborative leadership that guided it.

Analysis

Success factors

Using a resilience and complexity framework, there were a range of factors that contributed to the success of the CPRI. The first critical factor was the distribution of power through a horizontal network of empowered groups. Conferring leadership of the Constellations to recognized leaders in the respective sectors was critical to gaining the support of the community for the process. This was enhanced by empowering those leaders to assemble the stakeholders that they felt were important to engage, rather than prescribing such membership and participation from the CPRI leadership.

By constructing the network based on existing relationships, a level of trust was introduced into the process at the outset which would be critical for risk and innovative thinking. Through the process of developing a shared vision by connecting Constellation Groups with each other, that initial level of trust was expanded as relationships across sectors began to develop. This also extended to the Stewardship Group as they established relationships with the Constellation network.

The strategy of establishing a Stewardship Group member as a co-chair of each Constellation also provided for a balance of power and facilitated effective communication between the Constellation and the Stewardship Group. This had the advantage of ensuring that the 'big picture' was represented at the Constellation level, as well as bringing the richness of the Constellation discussions to the Stewardship Group table. This connection proved to be critical later in the process when decisions needed to be made around the refinement and selection of goals and strategies.

The Constellations were further empowered to facilitate discussions and manage their own process in the manner that was most relevant to them. The CPRI leadership provided administrative support and guidance, but allowed the Constellations to respond to the overall goals and objectives of the CPRI in their own unique way. This respected and leveraged the diversity of the membership within and across Constellations.

The diverse composition of the Stewardship Group and the Constellation network aligns with a second feature of resilient systems which contributed to the success of the initiative. Diversity increases the resilience of systems by introducing new and different perspectives to the discussion. At the Stewardship Group level, the multi-sectoral make-up of the team enabled critical thinking and dialogue across sectors. At the level of the individual Constellation team, there was a challenge in ensuring diverse representation as sector leaders were empowered to assemble their own teams. This could have led to narrower perspectives. The inclusion of a Stewardship Group member on the team, however, balanced this risk. Further, the diversity of the Constellation network as a whole provided a counter-balance to the potentially narrow focus of Constellation Groups organized around specific interests. The process of assembling the entire network and facilitating dialogue across Constellations capitalized on the specific knowledge of the individual Constellations while leveraging the diversity of the network as a whole.

Shared leadership of a diverse network allowed the network to be flexible and adaptive, capable of responding quickly to changes in the political and community environment. Through this network, a feedback mechanism was established which is a third critical element in resilient systems. The structural connection between the Constellations and the Stewardship

Group allowed for information to flow from the community to the Stewardship Group for decisions and actions. Further, the empowered nature of the Constellations allowed them to act on information flowing from the community or from the Stewardship Group without significant delays in process by the need for hierarchical approval. The fact that the initiative was itself organized as a quasi-independent body outside of the normal hierarchical bureaucratic reporting structures also facilitated this organizational nimbleness.

As an initiative focused on systems change, perhaps the most important factor that facilitated the success of the CPRI was the ability to change the narrative and thereby challenge the paradigm. As paradigms are the underlying structures that inform systems, system change requires some level of paradigm shift. This is essential from a complexity standpoint as well as the forging of agreement in the context of lack of certainty can reduce the level of complexity. Forging agreement is ultimately a political process that requires a shared understanding of the issue in order to move forward. That shared understanding of the issue, in turn, requires the various stakeholders involved to see their interests reflected in the agreed-upon action. Facilitating a shared understanding that reflects the interests of a broad stakeholder network requires a move away from narrowly defined interests based on a competitive narrative to a new narrative that articulates a notion of the common good.

There were two key shifts in the narrative about poverty that enabled progress. The first was moving from a focus on a narrowly defined group of "poor" to a more broadly-based concept of universal vulnerability, as articulated in the key message "my neighbour's strength is my strength." The second was a movement away from the language of scarcity to the language of abundance, as articulated in the key message "there is enough for all." These key messages focused on envisioning an inclusive positive future state that benefitted the entire community rather than on programs and services targeted to a limited few. Further, the shift away from scarcity to abundance reduced the conceptual limitations imposed when poverty reduction strategies are conceived in terms of the reallocation of limited resources. These two shifts enabled the conversation to be inclusive, overcoming the us/them paradigm that feeds a competitive zero-sum game approach to systems change.

Challenges

While the CPRI was largely successful in achieving its stated objective of developing a community-based poverty reduction strategy to significantly reduce poverty in Calgary, it experienced significant challenges in doing so. Some of these challenges were overcome through the collaborative design, while others proved to be more entrenched and may limit the long-term effectiveness of the strategy in meeting its poverty-reduction goals. These entrenched challenges provide insight into the limits of collaborative initiatives.

The first challenge to be overcome was a certain level of cynicism and fatigue in the community. As described in the previous sections, the CPRI was not the first coordinated effort to address poverty. Indeed, one of the key reasons for initiating the CPRI was that previous efforts had not made measurable progress and it was felt a new approach was required. One of the key differences with the CPRI as opposed to previous efforts was the level of political support it enjoyed, being an initiative of the Mayor. This provided a degree of credibility and trust that the resources and political capital, necessary to act on any resulting strategy, would be forthcoming. This allowed many stakeholders to suspend their cynicism to engage with the CPRI.

The second factor that allowed the initiative to move beyond the cynicism and fatigue was the reframing of the issue to engage the community in a different conversation about poverty. This, however, required the initiative to challenge entrenched understandings of poverty. Such entrenched understandings were not only the established popular myths about poverty, but also established beliefs among those in the social service sector. For many, the move to a more universal understanding of poverty was challenging, and conflicted with their understanding of their mission of serving the most vulnerable. In particular, the effort to personalize the experience of poverty that was critical for moving beyond an "us/them" narrative was difficult.

Challenging the us/them paradigm also challenged the competitive context that exists within the social service system. The current funding framework encourages competition between agencies, as well as between interests. As Fineman has noted, the competition between vulnerable populations and the groups that represent their interests mitigates against the articulation of a narrative that outlines the shared experience of oppression and the underlying systemic cause (Fineman 2010).

While the CPRI was able to achieve limited success in moving from specific to shared interests, the interests of specific groups and organizations remained powerful and influenced expectations about the ultimate output of the strategy. For some engaged in the process, the expected outcome was the creation of new programs or services for which they expected they may be funded to deliver. The ultimate strategy that focused more on systemic change as opposed to programs and services was challenged by some.

Differing expectations also reflected power imbalances within the initiative. Power imbalances were experienced at the Stewardship Group level as well as within and across the Constellation network. Power was first manifested through the selection of the Stewardship Group itself. As the power to appoint rested jointly with the Mayor and the President of the United Way, this process determined, from a systems perspective, the boundaries of the system by establishing which interests would have more influence and which would be excluded. While there was an attempt to achieve sectoral balance, the fact that the process was not open affected the dynamics of the initiative as certain groups, who felt they had a legitimate place at the table, were excluded.

Those who were selected, moreover, were all senior leaders in their respective organizations and sectors. This reflected a long-standing history of recruiting senior leaders from the business and non-profit sectors to champion and lead such change initiatives. While this strategy aims to ensure senior commitment to implementing change recommendations, it also implicitly reinforces the power dynamics that are one of the root causes of poverty. Significantly, the initial selection of Stewardship Group members did not include anyone with a current lived experience of poverty. It was at the insistence of the Secretariat that a representative with lived experience was added to the Stewardship Group. Even so, the single representative at the Stewardship Group table did not exercise considerable influence in discussions as they did not represent an organization or constituency with power.

The influence of power was most strikingly apparent in the negotiation process near the end of the project leading to agreement on a final strategy. Despite the fact that the issue of income inequality was prominent in discussions at the Constellation level, there was resistance to including reference to it in the final strategy document. A draft version of the strategy identified the reduction of income inequality as one of the three overarching goals of the initiative. Although there was support from the majority of the members of the Stewardship Group for such a goal, a key member was opposed due to fears that the focus on inequality would offend their own board which was itself comprised primarily of senior business leaders. Despite efforts to find compromise wording, the partner ultimately demanded that all references to income inequality be removed from the strategy or they would publicly withdraw their support from the initiative. As this would have likely derailed the entire initiative, references to inequality were removed as demanded.

A final challenge faced by the initiative was the difficulty of managing a diverse collaborative network in the context of a highly bureaucratic and risk-averse organization. Although the Stewardship Group and Secretariat were established as a quasi-independent organization, their obvious close affiliation with both the City of Calgary and the United Way resulted in close oversight by both organizations over the activities of the project. This was complicated by the fact that the Secretariat itself possessed no independent power apart from the relationships it had established with the Constellation network, while navigating often conflicting directions from key partners with their own organizational interests. This led to occasional tension between the two sponsoring partners and set up the potential for conflicting directions, complicated by blurred lines of accountability particularly with the Secretariat. In this context, the opportunity to attempt to exert informal influence over the process was present.

Such informal influence was occasionally brought to bear in an attempt to mitigate perceived risk, particularly within the administration of the respective partners. This led to a focus on the creation of linear logic-models that could clearly articulate the relationship between strategy inputs and outputs, leading to measurable outcomes. This risk mitigation approach, however, is contrary to innovation and the construction of resilient systems and communities. What is required is the trust and structure that supports risk taking and the generation of demonstration activities rather than the replication of best practices. This, however, creates risk and the collaboration needs to incorporate the resilience principles that enable it to assume such risk.

This search for programmatic technical solutions reflects the tendency to deal with complexity by treating a complex problem as complicated, capable of being solved with the right technical knowledge. The effort to reduce complexity is also manifested on the axis of agreement by attempting to circumscribe the boundaries of which interests and represented in order to narrow the possible range of disagreement and more readily gain consensus. The power of collaboratives, however, is to work in the space of complexity, not to reduce it, but to create a path forward without coming to agreements that are too narrow or solutions that are too simple.

Lessons learned

Based on this review of the process, we suggest that several key actions could have enhanced the effectiveness of the initiative, particularly with respect to the Stewardship Group and its relationship with the Secretariat and the Constellation network. First, more focused effort on educating and supporting the Stewardship Group through the transition to implementation would have strengthened the initiative overall. More attention could have been paid by the Secretariat to 'managing upwards' rather than its priority focus on continued mobilization and support of the grassroots Constellation network. A critical aspect of the work of the Secretariat is to be the bridge between the grassroots and the leadership and this bridging function could have been more effective through more intentional efforts.

Secondly, greater use of external sources of support for coaching and mentoring could have improved the effectiveness of both the Stewardship Group and the Secretariat. The presence of a neutral third party to provide objective guidance may have strengthened relationships across the governance structure. Further, this could have provided an important community of practice for the Secretariat who functioned in relative isolation. For those engaged in leading poverty reduction initiatives, such work takes a unique toll due to their high personal investment and dedication as well as the seeming intractability of the problem.

Greater peer support may have enhanced the effectiveness of the Secretariat and leadership.

Thirdly, greater clarity of leadership could have mitigated against some of the conflict that inevitably arose. While the establishment of the initiative as a quasi-independent body had the advantage of removing it from some of the constraints of hierarchical bureaucracy, this structure was not sustainable in the long-term. Further, lack of clear authority and lines of accountability created confusion that hindered progress. In the end, a top-down process that aimed to engage the grassroots community suffered from this tension which was exacerbated by the lack of clear accountability and authority.

Finally, more attention needs to be paid to the way advocates work with people living in poverty who are often fighting the demons of isolation and shame, among others. While it is important to include persons with a lived experience of poverty through all stages of the process, the incredible weight of poverty as a negative phenomenon that needs to be 'fixed' by others with more privilege often serves to maintain structural inequality and reinforces shame through patronizing attitudes that keep the disconnect enduring. Authentic engagement of persons with a lived experience of poverty demands that such persons be given true power in the process, not just a token seat at the table.

Conclusion

Poverty is and remains a persistent and complex issue for which no single technical solution readily presents itself. Typical of wicked problems, efforts to address them are often stymied either by attempts to forge agreement by limiting the range of stakeholders and/or exercising power over the process. Alternatively, efforts to address poverty can be stymied by attempts to treat them as complicated (as opposed to complex) problems, amenable to technical solutions. This leads to a narrow focus on a limited set of issues and a focus on best practices. Neither the attempt to force agreement or define technical solutions, however, respects the reality of the complexity of the issue. Collaborative governance models offer promise to the extent that they can bring diverse interests together to forge agreement on innovative strategies.

Applying the principles of system resilience provides a framework for assessing the strength of the collaborative, particularly with respect to the dimensions of power and conflict management. Resilient systems are characterized by horizontal networks of empowered stakeholders with leadership distributed across the network. Such systems are based on functional trust relationships rather than hierarchical power relationships. Such networks are diverse, allowing for the adoption of multiple perspectives, and tolerant of dissent. Such diverse networks provide important environmental information and feedback that an empowered network is adaptive enough to respond to in a timely manner. Systems so organized tend to be resilient to disruptive changes in the environment and operate effectively in situations of extreme complexity.

The Calgary Poverty Reduction Initiative demonstrated many of the characteristics of resilient systems. The initiative was structured around a diverse horizontal network of stakeholders based on the Constellation model of governance. The informal structure which relied on existing leadership in the community leveraged those trust relationships to foster innovative solutions. The ability to shift the narrative further facilitated the development of a shared vision and shared strategies that transcended narrow interests. At the same time, however, the reality of managing such an empowered collaborative in the context of risk-averse bureaucracies, with their own vested interests, limited the overall impact of the initiative. It remains to be seen whether the power of the networks that were established can lead to effective implementation of innovative solutions based on a new narrative, or whether the interests of key organizations and their stakeholders will override that narrative and further perpetuate the *status quo*.

References

City of Calgary. 2013. "Enough for All: Unleashing Our Communities' Resources to Drive Down Poverty in Calgary," *Final Report of the Calgary Poverty Reduction Initiative*. Calgary, AB: City of Calgary.

Fineman, M. 2010. "The Vulnerable Subject and the Responsive State," *Emory Law Journal, Vol. 60, Emory Public Law Research Paper, No. 10-130*, https://papers.ssrn.com/sol3/papers.cfm?abstract_id=1694740 [Accessed May 3, 2018].

Kania, J. and M. Kramer. 2011. "Collective Impact," *Stanford Social Innovation Review,* Winter 2011.

Senior, B. and S. Swailes. 2016. *Organizational Change* (5th ed.). Harlow, UK: Pearson Education Ltd.

Stacey, R.D. 2002. *Strategic Management and Organisational Dynamics: The Challenges of Complexity.* (3rd ed.). Harlow, UK: Prentice-Hall.

Surman, T. 2006. *Constellation Collaboration: A Model for Multi-organizational Partnership.* Toronto, ON: Centre for Social Innovation.

Torjman, S. 2008. *Poverty Policy.* Ottawa, ON: Caledon Institute of Social Policy.

United Way of Calgary and Area. 2005. "Sustained Poverty Reduction: The Case for Community Action." Calgary, AB: United Way of Calgary and Area.

CHAPTER 2

The Gang Action Interagency Network of Winnipeg

By Robyn Dryden

Introduction

The Gang Action Interagency Network (GAIN) is a Winnipeg-based organization, working on grassroots solutions to the city's gang problem. It is comprised of over 180 government, law enforcement, and community-based organizations and representatives. Eight years ago, out of the success of the Sexually Exploited Youth (SEY) Coalition, which brought together organizations to fight the growing issue of sexual exploitation of youth, GAIN was born, with the hopes of attaining similar success to SEY, but with a focus on gangs. In its eight year history, GAIN has held various city-wide forums and both community- and youth-based consultations. In 2014 they released a report, *Community Assessment of a Gang Exit Strategy for Winnipeg*, which highlighted the importance of identity, belonging and healing, and expanding programming as the three crucial elements to combating gangs in Winnipeg. A multipronged approach, including prevention, intervention, and suppression, is required in order to tackle Winnipeg's gang problem.

With an estimated 1,400-1,500 active street youth gang members, the city of Winnipeg is widely considered the street gang capital of Canada. All young people can succumb to the pull of gangs, however, 58 percent of Winnipeg street gang members are of Indigenous descent and the number of newcomer members are growing. That being said, anyone can become susceptible to gangs and gang involvement. Identity and belonging, healing and expanding programming and resources were identified as ways to help young people both avoid and exit gang involvement. However, these areas are quite broad and touch on many services and programs throughout the city; as a result, a collaborative governance model is crucial to the success of both GAIN and its newly released gang strategy, *Bridging the Gaps: Solutions to Winnipeg Gangs.*

GAIN acts as a coordinating body for all gang-related information in the city of Winnipeg. Building off of its 180 partner organizations, GAIN enhances service alignment and collaboration through information and resource sharing. GAIN offers very few front line services, with the exception of a referral process for gang involved youth and a gang tattoo removal service, instead focusing on higher level issues, such as creating Winnipeg's first community led gang strategy. For the first seven years GAIN existed, it had no steady funding, instead founding members pushed GAIN forward off the sides of their desks. GAIN's first and only funding source was the Manitoba provincial government, through the Crime Prevention Branch. However due to shifting provincial priorities, the province of Manitoba cut GAIN's funding. Currently GAIN is applying for various grants and funding opportunities to ensure that they are able to retain the network's coordinator.

Starting conditions

Manitoba has long been considered the gang and murder capital of Canada, retaining the title for seven consecutive years. Youth in Manitoba continue to be incarcerated at a higher rate than other provinces. Many of these incarcerations are related to gang involvement.

Various organizations and individuals came together as a result of the violence and spike in youth incarceration and gang involvement. During the early 2000s Manitoba Justice Minister David Chomiak tasked Floyd Wiebe with starting Gang Awareness for Parents (GAP) because he felt there was a gap in educating parents about their kids getting involved in gangs. GAP was instrumental in helping to create GAIN and eventually the two organizations merged into one. As mentioned above, the Sexually Exploited Youth Coalition or

SEY was formed to create action around the issue of sexual exploitation and sex trafficking of youth in Manitoba. In 2002 the province of Manitoba launched the *Manitoba Strategy Responding to Children and Youth at Risk of, or Survivors of, Sexual Exploitation.* The second phase of that strategy saw the implementation of *Tracia's Trust,* a document which identified areas that require change and actions to enable that change to occur.

As these initiatives began to create positive change towards their goals, individuals who were working with and around the issue of youth gang involvement took note; they wanted to create similar success for gangs. As Winnipeg's non-profit community is fairly tight-knit, many of the people who were brought together in the early stages of GAIN had worked with each other previously. GAIN was created out of the passion that various stakeholders had around creating better options for the city's youth; there was no money attached to the organization and as a result many people worked off the sides of their desks to create action and propel GAIN forward.

Through public consultations in 2012 and 2013, which saw record attendance with 150 individuals participating, GAIN decided that before creating a gang exit strategy, they would first need to consult with the larger community. As a result of these consultations, GAIN released report, *Community Assessment of a Gang Exit Strategy for Winnipeg, Manitoba,* in 2014. Based on that report, GAIN applied for funding for a full time staff person who would be tasked with pulling together a Winnipeg specific gang strategy.

Institutional design

In order to make positive movement on the issue of gangs in Winnipeg, everyone must work together; no single organization or governmental department has the ability to tackle this issue alone. With that in mind, GAIN created a governance structure that would pull on the expertise and guidance of every source available. There is an overarching leadership advisory board, which is populated by community and government leaders, for example, the Chief of Police, Indigenous leaders, individuals with lived experience, youth, city councillors, etc. ... The purpose of this leadership advisory board is to champion the gang strategy and provide overarching guidance. They help to publicize the strategy, pushing for community and funder buy-in. Their role is to publicly support the strategy and network. This is done through attending bi-annual meetings to provide guidance to the strategy's implementation and receive feedback on updates on its progress. In addition, board members' role is to raise awareness of the strategy and the issue of gangs in Winnipeg in their respective fields and communities.

GAIN operates by consensus, with the larger network having the opportunity to provide feedback, advice or recommendations in regards to the work being done. However, this information is brought back to the GAIN executive for final decision and direction. GAIN is currently reviewing this process in order to move towards a more formalized decision-making process.

The strategy was released in June of 2017. At the time of writing, the first Leadership Advisory Board Meeting had not yet occurred. The GAIN executive chair would be responsible for facilitating the meetings. The GAIN coordinator would be responsible for creating agendas, and presenting relevant topics to the Leadership Advisory Board. Additionally, the coordinator would also be responsible for taking minutes and disseminating relevant information both to the GAIN executive and the entire network.

Under the leadership advisory board falls the GAIN executive. They are responsible for overseeing the GAIN coordinator and staff. The executive provide guidance on day-to-day work and guide the implementation of the strategy and network. The GAIN coordinator is responsible for organizing and facilitating all executive meetings. GAIN executive members include:

- **Jamil Mahmood – Chair of GAIN** – The executive director of Spence Neighbourhood Association, a local neighbourhood organization that seeks to activate and engage the people of Spence in building and rebuilding their neighbourhoods in the areas of holistic housing, community connection, community economic development, environment and open spaces, and youth and families.
- **Kate Kehler – Vice Chair of GAIN** – The executive director of Social Planning Council of Winnipeg, a local

organization that strives to create a sustainable community that is caring, just and equitable through leadership that improves social conditions through effective solutions, progressive public policy, community development and partnerships.

- **Tammy Christensen – GAIN Executive Member –** The executive director of Ndinawemaaganag Endaawaad Inc., an Indigenous Winnipeg-based agency that offers integrated services for youth, focusing on shelter, culture, recreation, education, outreach and support.
- **Matt Fast – GAIN Executive Member –** The Youth Mentorship Program Coordinator for the Newcomers Employment and Education Development Services Inc. (NEEDS), a Winnipeg-based organization that enhances the integration of immigrant and refugee youth into Canadian society by providing accessible services and support in the areas of employment, education and social programming.
- **Mandela Kuet – GAIN Executive Member –** Youth Support Worker for Immigrant and Refugee Community Organization of Manitoba Inc. (IRCOM), a local organization that strives to empower newcomer families to integrate into the wider community through affordable transitional housing, programs and services.
- **Karen Beaudin – GAIN Executive Member –** Community Resource Coordinator for the City of Winnipeg. The city's Community Service Department offers a wide range of programs and services for Winnipeggers. Their focus is on providing efficient, responsive and innovative community-based services that promote healthy and safe neighbourhoods that meet the communities' diverse cultural, recreation and information needs.

The GAIN coordinator and staff are responsible for the day-to-day work of GAIN and the gang strategy, and for coordinating the network and the implementation of the gang strategy. The GAIN staff is quite small at one coordinator and one term position of an Inventory Mapping coordinator, who created a youth focused app, *ResourceConnect*.

An important component of the governance structure is the use of working groups. This is where a lot of the work is done and where true collaborative governance takes place. These working groups are created around the various priorities identified through the gang strategy. Here experts in their fields are pulled in to create action around the various priorities, bringing together many necessary individuals. The working groups are time-limited, each area of the GAIN strategy has activities and timelines associated with it. Once activities and timelines are completed, the working group will disband in order to make room for other priorities items. Each working group will be chaired by a GAIN Executive member; the GAIN coordinator will ensure that information regarding the efforts of each working group is disseminated to the larger network and the GAIN executive. The governance structure also identifies the various systems and organizations that a young person involved with gangs encounters, for example police, the justice system, education, community housing, community-based services etc.... By highlighting the multitude of systems that can touch a young person facing the issue of gangs in Winnipeg, one can see that it is imperative to have representatives from each of these areas all working together to enact positive change.

FIGURE 1

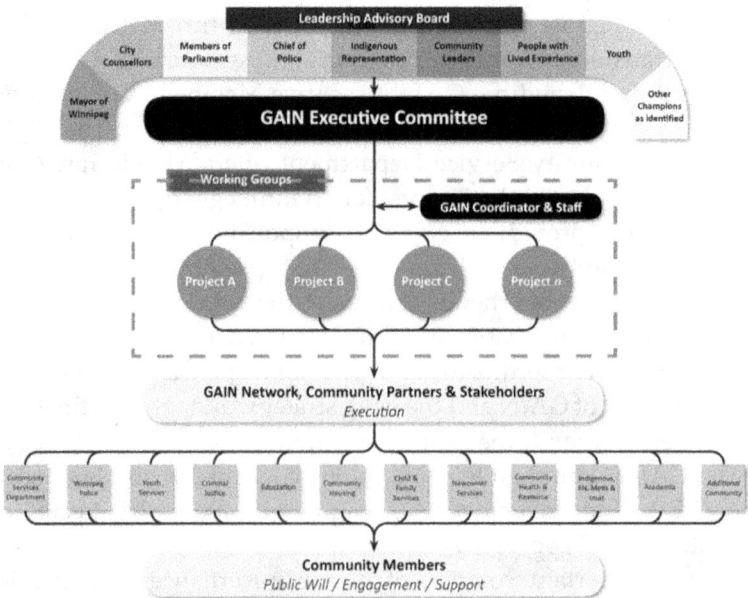

Collaborative process

The Gang Action Interagency Network's collaborative process works for a variety of reasons, including a commitment to mutual respect, understanding and trust, transparent communication and a common purpose.

Over the years, GAIN has fostered a culture of respect, understanding and trust. This has been solidified through the GAIN full network meetings. During each of these gatherings, network members have the opportunity to obtain peer support on issues they are facing in their respective organizations or departments. This sharing of information and sometimes struggles, has allowed for members to develop an understanding of the unique and sometimes similar issues that organizations are facing. It also provides a space for brainstorming on potential solutions or strategies. This sharing of information has helped to foster connection among network members, which in turn has strengthened GAIN.

GAIN believes in open and frequent communication. The transparency that is created by coordinator updates and meeting minutes has helped to solidify a trust in our collaborative process. The network receives updates through regular emails and social media posts. GAIN also solicits feedback from the network through surveys, strategic planning updates and reviews to ensure that the network is working towards a collectively agreed-upon common purpose.

A collective purpose has also allowed for GAIN's collaborative process to thrive. Since its inception, GAIN has heavily consulted with its network members as well as the community at large to determine the need and focus of the organization. Through strategic planning sessions, path planning and consultations, GAIN has developed concrete, attainable goals and objectives that dictate the work the organization focuses on. By widely disseminating GAIN's purpose among the network and larger community, GAIN is held accountable in achieving the goals set out. The network played a large role in determining what those goals and the overarching purpose of the network are, therefore there is a built-in buy-in from the network members in helping to propel the organization forward towards its goals.

Funding agreements do tend play a role in dictating which goals take priority in a given year. However, since the Province of Manitoba cut all of GAIN's funding in 2017, it is able to focus more closely on network identified priorities. With that being said, it is important to note that GAIN is first and foremost accountable to those it serves, gang involved, at risk and affiliated youth in Winnipeg. GAIN reports on its progress to funders if applicable and to the network as a whole.

Facilitative leadership

Leadership for GAIN is both situated in one person (the GAIN Chair) and distributed throughout the wider network. The network coordinator meets with the GAIN Chair every week. These meetings help to guide and oversee the day-to-day operations of GAIN. As a result a lot of leadership exists within the GAIN chair position. However all major decisions are discussed at the network level. In addition leadership also exists at the working group level; this is where a lot of the work is conducted and individuals who sit on the groups provide leadership to that specific work.

Conclusion

A common misconception is that gangs only affect a small amount of people and, therefore, it is their issue to deal with and not the issue of society in general. However gangs are an issue that affects individuals and society in a multitude of ways. Many people view gangs as just a Department of Justice issue or just a Police issue. In reality if a person is involved with gangs they are likely to have other needs and issues that aren't being adequately dealt with. For example, the majority of individuals involved in gangs are also living in poverty; they may or may not have substance abuse or mental health issues; they may or may not be involved with Child and Family services, and the list goes on and on. That is why it is crucial to utilize a Collective Governance model when tackling the overarching issue of gangs in Winnipeg, so that all the other issues associated with gangs can be properly addressed.

As a result of these misconceptions, it requires extra effort on the part of GAIN to highlight the importance of Collective Governance. For example during the consultations phase of creating the gang strategy, *Bridging the Gaps: Solutions to Winnipeg*

Gangs, GAIN reached out to various provincial departments to present on the strategy and receive their feedback, as young people involved in gangs tend to be involved in various systems and departments. There were a couple of departments that redirected GAIN back to the Department of Justice as they were unable to see how the issue of gangs could relate to their respective departments. However after a conversation or two GAIN was able to highlight the connection between gangs and various provincial departments, not just justice. Through dialogue, we were able to strengthen our Collective Governance model by identifying connections that otherwise might not have been seen and most importantly obtaining buy-in from key departments and individuals.

By utilizing a Collective Governance model, GAIN is able to incorporate the knowledge and expertise that all of its members bring to the table. It is also able to achieve greater awareness of the services and programs that member organizations offer through accurate dissemination of information. This is very helpful for the avoidance of service duplication. By working collectively, there is increased collaboration and service alignment across our multi-sectoral members. GAIN's Collective Governance model also allows for members to share issues that their organization is facing and obtain peer support.

Through the use of a Collective Governance model, GAIN is able to build off of the success of other strategies and plans that have similar focuses while simultaneously avoiding duplication. For example the Winnipeg Plan to End Youth Homelessness' put out their strategy, *Here and Now,* a few months before GAIN released the gang strategy. As there is a lot of overlap between these two areas, GAIN was able to align its strategy with key components of Homelessness' strategy. By aligning priorities through a Collective Governance model, both organizations are able to work together to make positive change in their own areas while also understanding the connection and overlap that exists.

A great example of how Collective Governance is especially useful for an organization like GAIN is the Gang Exit Strategy (see Figure 2). Prior to the release of the gang strategy, there were no formalized processes in Winnipeg for dealing with individuals looking to exit a gang. There are a few individuals doing great *ad hoc* work but outside of that there was nothing. Therefore, a large component of the gang strategy is a transition service to help young people looking to exit gang involvement. The process uses the expertise and experience of the GAIN network. When a young person decides to exit a gang, they may contact GAIN directly, or any of our 180 plus members, who then bring the case back to the larger network. The strategy has identified areas that a person looking to exit will typically need help with and has broken them down into two phases. The first is crisis response needs. These include addressing: immediate safety needs, basic needs, housing, mental health and addiction issues. Network members will fill those roles and help to coordinate services in the crisis response phases. Once the individual is settled, they move towards the second phase, which is long-term resources. Here GAIN will focus on helping a young person connect with employment and education, mentorship opportunities, access to recreation, permanent housing options and long-term mental health and addiction support. Currently there are no formalized processes or structures in place to do this type of transition work in Winnipeg.

Without a model of Collective Governance, it would be incredibly difficult and very expensive to mobilize this process. However, the expansive reach of a network like GAIN enables it to make connections with various service providers and other individuals who are willing to "wrap around" an individual in their time of need to help them transition out of gang involvement.

Due to the pervasive nature of gangs, Collective Governance continues to be the most effective way of tackling the issue in Winnipeg. As a result it is embedded in all aspects of the Gang Action Interagency Network. Through this model, GAIN is able to attain better collaboration and alignment among organizations, departments and sectors who all are doing their part in reducing the number of young people involved in gangs. Due to heightened service alignment, GAIN is able to keep track of the work being done across various sectors for the purpose of avoiding duplication of services and highlighting any gaps that may exist.

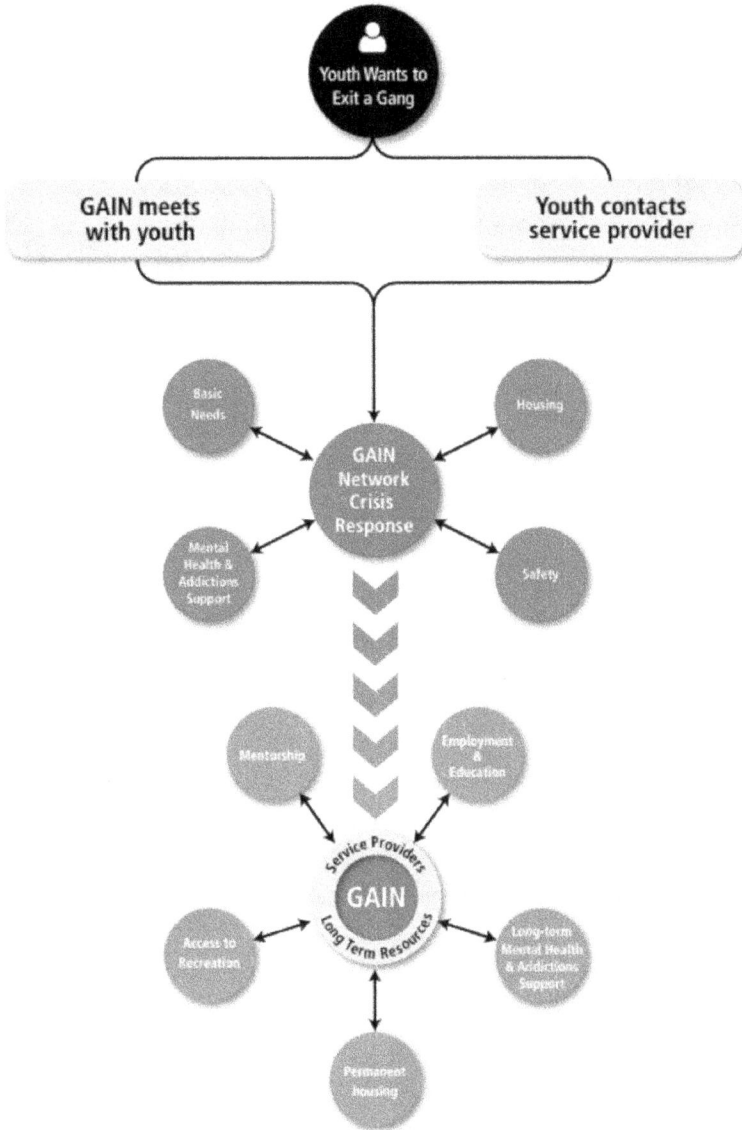

FIGURE 2

Youth Wants to
Exit a Gang

GAIN meets
with youth

Youth contacts
service provider

Basic
Needs

Housing

GAIN
Network
Crisis
Response

Mental
Health &
Addictions
Support

Safety

Mentorship

Employment
&
Education

Service Providers
GAIN
Long Term Resources

Access to
Recreation

Long-term
Mental Health
& Addictions
Support

Permanent
housing

CHAPTER 3

Collaborative Governance for the Development and Implementation of Revitalization Plans to Enhance and Sustain Ecosystem Resilience: The Collingwood Harbour Remedial Action Plan[1]

By Gail Krantzberg

Introduction

In 1972 the governments of Canada and the United States created the Great Lakes Water Quality Agreement to address excessive phosphorus loadings and curb eutrophication. It was signed by the Prime Minister Trudeau and President Nixon on April 15, 1972 (United States and Canada 1972). With the release of Rachel Carson's *Silent Spring* (1962), and the growing environmental movement against the release of toxic chemicals, a revision to the 1972 Agreement in 1978 provided new programs and more stringent goals to eliminate persistent toxic substances from the lakes. The concept of a Great Lakes Basin Ecosystem was also adopted, which recognized that water quality depends on the interplay of air, land, water and living organisms, including humans, within the system.

[1] This paper is modified from a chapter in *The Story of Brownfields & Smart Growth in Kingston Ontario: From Contamination to Revitalization*, 2009, edited by P. Welbourn and reproduced with copyright approval from Classroom Complete Press. ISBN: 155319456X, 9781553194569.

A more comprehensive assessment of the Great Lakes cleanup effort was undertaken by the International Joint Commission (IJC), who were given the role to assess the Parties' progress in meeting the purpose of the Agreement when it was signed in 1972. As a result of this evaluation, in 1987, the governments signed a Protocol to strengthen the programs, practices and technology prescribed in the 1978 Agreement. The governments made the commitment to restore and maintain "beneficial uses" or ecological services in particularly degraded geographic locations, named Areas of Concern. Remedial Action Plans (RAPs) for the Areas of Concern were described in the 1987 amendment of the Agreement under Annex 2. A RAP is a mechanism that directs the federal governments to collaborate with state and provincial agencies, and consult with local citizenry, to develop and then implement the action plan.

These restoration experiments, as suggested by Sproule-Jones, promised a way in which resource users, regulators, and those with an interest in restoring the local ecosystem can collaborate towards a common purpose (Sproule-Jones 2002). They were intended to empower local stakeholders to determine their own solutions for environmental revitalization provide a modern context for collaborative decision-making and inclusive collaboration.

To enable this "consultation with local citizenry," governments tended to go for advisory council/committee with community stakeholders representing for example, Aboriginal government, agriculture, business and industry, citizens-at-large, environment groups, educators, outdoor clubs, the health sector, municipal officials, and tourism and recreation. Samy *et al.* purport that engaging stakeholder groups in the design of an action plan minimizes the risk of future polarization (Samy *et al.* 2003). The RAPs included a central understanding that residents possess local information and knowledge, and can provide informed comments on the social impacts of pending decisions (Harris *et al.* 2003). The importance of involving communities in the management of water resources was one of the strongest and most consistent messages coming forward from an international conference on interjurisdictional water resource programs (Managing Shared Waters 2002). Gurtner-Zimmermann notes that the commitment of individuals who participate in the RAP process, local support for the RAP goals, and the scientific basis and sound analysis of environmental issues contribute to the positive outcomes (Gurtner-Zimmermann 1995).

The importance of collaborative governance, as exemplified in a successful RAP, is elaborated on by Cheng *et al.*, "Collaborative governance of common-pool ecosystems and resources is expanding globally and is widely seen as contributing to the adaptive capacity of social-ecological systems... Empirical research across ecosystem management contexts demonstrates how collaborative approaches can help in managing conflicts, building trust, pooling resources, building capacity, and sustaining action; collaboration is also shown to spark innovation, risk-taking, and more flexible, responsive actions because of the multiple viewpoints and resources that are leveraged through the collaborative process" (Cheng *et al.* 2015).

Emerson *et al.* define collaborative governance as the processes and structures of public policy decision-making and management that engage people constructively across the boundaries of public agencies, levels of government, and/or the public, private and civic spheres, in order to carry out a public purpose that could not otherwise be accomplished (Emerson *et al.* 2011). Indeed, stakeholders have been instrumental in helping governments be more responsive to and responsible for restoring ecological services such as healthy fish and wildlife communities, water that is safe for swimming and drinking, and wetland habitats in areas of concern (AOCs). While the participants in collaborative governance processes designed to address water management challenges can be extremely diverse, and often have vastly different interests and motives (de Loe *et al.* 2016), broad-based partnerships among diverse stakeholders, as described by Hartig and Zarull are a step towards "grassroots ecological democracy" in the Great Lakes Basin (Hartig and Zarull 1992).

This grassroots, collaborative decision making has resulted in considerable progress towards the restoration of ecological and human use of the environment in the AOCs. In approximately the two decades since the inception of the RAP program, hundreds of kilometres of riparian vegetation and thousands of hectares of wetlands have been rehabilitated (Canada-Ontario 2007). Sediment quality is improving (IJC 1997). More fish are edible in more places, and swimming is again possible in parts of our urban centres for the first time in decades (Krantzberg *et al.* 1999).

Research is being advanced basin-wide on the insidious nature of toxic chemicals (IJC 2009). Technologies are emerging to better manage storm water and wastewater and contaminated sediment, and there have been declines in chemical concentrations in Great Lakes fish (SOLEC 2009). Further examples of successes include the removal of over 1.3 million cubic yards (1 million cubic metres) of sediment contaminated with polychlorinated biphenyls (PCBs) from the Kalamazoo River, Manistique River, Maumee River, Rouge River, Saginaw River, Saginaw Bay, and St. Lawrence River. At least CDN$270 million and at least US$3 billion had been invested from 1987-2003 to improve the condition of wastewater infrastructure in various AOCs (IJC 2003). (This is the most recent accounting, and no update has yet been compiled by the governments or the IJC.)

Notwithstanding these strides forward, human health is still being compromised by toxic chemicals, particularly for those consuming fish that are contaminated at unsafe levels, and particularly for children exposed to contaminants *in utero* (Schwartz *et al.* 1983; Davidson *et al.* 1995; Jacobson and Jacobson 1996; Lonky *et al.* 1996). Dioxins and PCBs suppress immune system function (Dallaire *et al.* 2006), disrupt hormonal function (Richthoff *et al.* 2003) and are associated with elevated risk of diabetes (Lee *et al.* 2006; Codru *et al.* 2007) and cardiovascular disease (Goncharov *et al.* 2008). Chlorinated pesticides such as DDT and its metabolite, DDE, are associated with elevated risk of cancer (Cocco *et al.* 2000), impaired neurodevelopment in children (Torres-Sanchez *et al.* 2007) and altered sex hormonal function (Ouyang *et al.* 2005). Pollution control at source continues to be a challenge to Great Lakes ecosystem integrity.

Successful clean-up strategy case study: Collingwood Harbour

It is instructive to explore the elements that fostered successful cooperative and collaborative initiatives and sustain the objectives of a community engaged in place-based action. The RAP process clearly embraces the ecosystem approach. Here, the ecosystem approach is based on the man-in-system concept rather than a system-external-to-man concept (IJC 1978), where the ecosystem is composed of the interacting elements of water, air, land and living organisms including man. While Lee *et al.* (1982) discuss several variants of the ecosystem approach, most share a focus on the responsiveness of ecological systems to natural and human activities, and a readiness to strike a programmatic compromise between detailed understanding and more comprehensive holistic meaning.

This flexible pragmatism was reflected in the manner in which the Collingwood Harbour RAP was developed and implemented. The following analysis of local capacity to achieve consensus and sustain momentum for implementation of the clean-up is based predominantly on the action plan that led to Collingwood Harbour being considered no longer one of the Great Lakes degraded areas, the first location to achieve this milestone (Krantzberg and Houghton 1996).

Collingwood Harbour is situated on the south shore of Nottawasaga Bay, the southern extension of Lake Huron's Georgian Bay (Figure 1). The Town of Collingwood surrounds the harbour with a population of approximately 21,500. During the mid to late 1800s, Collingwood was the railhead of Ontario and its harbour was the trans-shipment point for goods destined to Western Canada. Shipping produced a need for ship repairs, and in 1883, the Collingwood Shipyards, known then as Collingwood Dry Dock Shipbuilding and Foundry Company Limited, opened. The shipyards became one of the principal industries in the town, employing at some periods, until its closure in 1986, as much as 10 percent of the total labour force.

The RAP began with an analysis of "starting conditions," after Rocan (2009, figure 1). Nuisance algal growth plagued the harbour waters up until the mid-1980s as a result of excessive phosphorus inputs to the harbour from the Collingwood sewage treatment plant (STP), which at the time, was a primary treatment facility (Collingwood Harbour RAP 1992). The harbour, as an industrial port for over a century, suffered from habitat and wetland loss, shoreline hardening, and contamination of sediment.

In 1987 the author was assigned by the Ontario Ministry of Environment (MOE) to coordinate the Collingwood Harbour RAP. As the coordinator, my duties involved providing access to government expertise and funding, and collaborating with local experts to provide the broader community with the technical information they would need to develop the RAP. The RAP team had leaders from the Ontario Ministry of Environment, the Ontario Ministry of Natural Resources and Environment Canada, that brought the scientific and engineering expertise to diagnosing the starting conditions and offering options for RAP interventions to address the sources of degradation.

The coordinator served to network among the citizenry, to develop and ensure the monitoring program tracked the response of the environment to actions, and to report on progress regarding the restoration of beneficial uses publicly and to the governments, through funding from the provincial and federal governments. That funding also facilitated the PAC/RAP Team meetings that took place four to five times a year.

FIGURE 1. Location of Collingwood Harbour, Ontario

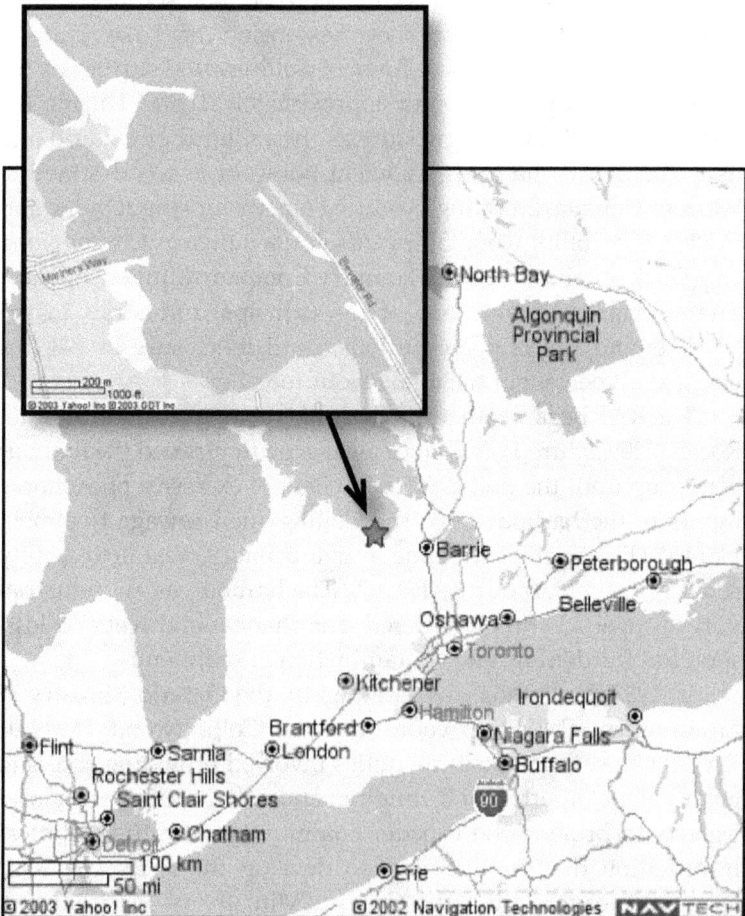

Eutrophication, the clean up program

To address eutrophication, the Collingwood Harbour RAP first determined that in fact the wastewater treatment plant (WWTP) was responsible for more than 95 percent of phosphorus loading to the harbour. The Team worked with the Public Advisory Committee (PAC) to develop a series of options, and to select the preferred option. Some possibilities included extending the WWTP outfall from the nearshore location to the deeper reaches of the harbour, upgrading the plant to tertiary treatment, changing circulation patterns in the harbour to reduce stagnation, and then optimizing the WWTP. Modeling based on circulation and current patterns, loadings, and receiving water characteristics resulted in the calculation of a maximum daily load of phosphorus that could be assimilated within the harbour so as to maintain concentrations of phosphorus in the open waters below 20 ug/l, the guideline used to prevent nuisance algal blooms (MOE 2005). To achieve this, the secondary plant needed to maintain phosphorus concentrations in the effluent at 0.3-0.4 mg/l, whereas typical secondary plants in the early 1990s were discharging at 1.0 mg/l. Expansion to tertiary treatment was estimated at $8 million in capital, not including land appropriation or operating costs. Extending the outfall was rejected by the PAC as simply diluting the pollution, and not addressing the source of phosphorus directly. Changing the circulation patterns by creating openings in the west berm of the harbour (Figure 1) put the adjacent wetland at risk and was also rejected. Optimization was further explored. As noted by ECP Consulting, "[a] well optimized system can consume around 20-30 percent less electrical power, reduce maintenance works by 50 percent, and increase the life-time of the treatment units by around 10-20 percent. Optimization also ensures that the waste water treatment facility always meets environmental compliance (discharge norms), provided a suitable treatment system is already in place" (ECP Consulting 2009).

    In the end, optimization was selected and implemented as a collaboration between the three orders of government. Optimization of the Collingwood Harbour WWTP involved a phosphorus auto-analyzer that controlled dual alum injection based on influent concentrations and concentrations within the plant. By improving the feed rate control and mixing of chemicals at the point of addition, the project reduced chemical use for further savings. The project cost was approximately $100,000; as compared to the $8 million in capital investments that would have been required for plant expansion.

Through a comprehensive performance evaluation, performance limiting factors were identified, resulting in significant improvements in plant performance. This allowed the plant to attain phosphorus limits not considered achievable without major capital expenditures. Similar to the experience at Hamilton Harbour, Ontario, "substantial savings in capital costs for future plant expansion were deferred as a result of the additional capacity realized at the plant" (NRC 2003).

Sediment remediation

A second major undertaking was the remediation of contaminated sediment associated with the shipbuilding industry that had serviced the Town of Collingwood for the better part of a century. Within the shipyard, slips were high concentrations of heavy metals including lead, copper and zinc in particular. Bio-assessment of the harbour sediment included laboratory toxicity testing and field collection of benthos to determine community structure.

Based on multiple lines of evidence provided by laboratory bioassays and field observations of invertebrates and sport fish collected during the late 1980s and early 1990s, it was determined that sediment contamination and impacts were confined to the Canada Steamship Limited (CSL) slips and water lots adjacent to at the shipyard property. Site-specific guidelines for benthos are established from a reference site database (i.e., biological attributes and environmental variables) using multivariate techniques, such as cluster and ordination analysis (Reynoldson and Zarull 1993).

Reynoldson *et al.* describe the statistical treatment of the data (Reynoldson *et al.* 1995). Reference site benthic communities are grouped using cluster analysis. The site environmental variables, which are not affected or minimally affected by anthropogenic activity, are then used as predictors to group the sites into the appropriate biological clusters. The benthic community structure and the same nine environmental variables (depth, NO_3, silt, aluminum, calcium, loss on ignition, alkalinity, sodium, pH) are measured at the test sites. Using the environmental predictors and the discriminant model (derived from the reference site database), each site is assigned to a biological cluster. The benthic invertebrate data are then similarly analyzed. If the site lies outside the reference site cluster, then that site is judged to be impaired.

Evidence indicated that remediation was appropriate. To commence the RAP selected a removal demonstration area, CSL Equity Investments' west slip, which measured approximately 32 m x 150 m. Water depth ranged from 4.1 m to 6.3 m. The west slip sediments were a mixture of sandy silt with some clay (26 percent sand, 64 percent silt and 10 percent clay). Pneuma Pump model #150/30 was tested at the selected area. This technology is owned and operated by Voyageurs Marine Construction Co. Ltd. from Dorion, Quebec (Environment Canada).

The demonstration took place over nine days in November, 1992. The Pneuma Pump was attached to a crane which was loaded on a flat deck barge. The pumping system is based on a principal of using static water head and compressed air inside cylinders. Each of three cylinders is rapidly filled with slurry by counter pressure due to a hydrostatic head and induced vacuum. When one cylinder is filled, compressed air acts as a piston and the slurry is then forced through a check valve to the discharge pipeline. The pump has no rotating parts or mechanisms in contact with the sediment, minimizing sediment resuspension problems. The pump was used on a trailing mode and a cable winch pulled the barge from the beginning of a sweep to the end. The material was transported through a 15 cm diameter pipeline for a distance of 1.2 km, to a confined disposal facility (CDF) located at the mouth of Collingwood Harbour (Figure 2). A silt curtain located at the north end of each slip was used to confine any possible particle resuspension due to unforeseen dredging complications. The silt curtain was constructed of geotextile material, with the top connected to a floating boom which was monitored daily for any indications of damage. Turbidity, suspended solids, and total organic carbon concentrations were minimal. The pumping system was found to be most efficient when semi-submerged in sediment

Using this technology, a full-scale cleanup of contaminated sediment remaining in the harbour was completed. In the end, approximately 8,000 m^3 of sediment from the shipyard slips and adjacent areas in the harbour were removed using the Pneuma airlift pumping system. After cleanup, the Pnuema Pump was used by Transport Canada to supply fill and cap material for the CDF.

The partners involved in the cleanup were Environment Canada (Great Lakes Cleanup Fund), the Town of Collingwood, Transport Canada, the Ontario Ministry of Environment and Energy, Collingwood Terminals, the Aquateers of Base Borden, and CSL (Canada Steamship Lines) Equity.

FIGURE 2. The Pneuma Pump deployed from a barge for sediment remediation in Collingwood Harbour

Making it happen: lessons learned

What follows is a description of a lesson learned in the Collingwood experiment, followed by the Collingwood Harbour manifestation of the lesson. The lessons are part of the framework of Multi-level Collaborative Governance (Rocan 2009), and encompass:

- acquiring an understanding of the starting conditions, and the causes of those conditions;
- an appropriate institutional design and decision-making process;
- establishment of a collaborative process, from individuals to institutions; and,
- ensuring facilitated leadership with an appropriate accountability directive.

Lesson one - Leadership

Engage local leaders who are committed to their community and can affect change. One view, one voice.

The selection of candidates for the Public Advisory Committee (PAC) was based predominantly (but not exclusively) on identifying decision makers who could affect change within the sector or stakeholder group they represented. This is in keeping with the observation that plan effectiveness will be, in part, a function of the inclusiveness of stakeholder and user representation and goal setting. Inclusivity lends legitimacy, stimulates funding, and can galvanize potentially marginalized but important stakeholders through peer pressure. The PAC elected the chair, who served in that capacity for the duration of RAP development, implementation and delisting.

Lesson two – Consensus on goals

Articulate clear and meaningful goals early in the process to unite the team. This gives the group the means to overcome conflicts and obstacles during the development and implementation of the Plan.

The leaders constituted the PAC (Figure 3) which, in consultation with the community at large, reached consensus on the vision for the future of their harbour. To gain support for a restoration and rehabilitation strategy, the common vision for the future of the harbour and its watershed was of paramount importance. To reach this vision, blue-sky thinking opened the process with an array of options. Then a priority-setting session resulted in criteria surrounding pragmatic realism, rather than unachievable targets. The PAC decided upon balanced goals and uses, which were critiqued during poster-session open houses with background materials and rationale offered along with citizen platforms for comments. The vision met with inclusive public favour early in the RAP process (Collingwood Harbour RAP 1992).

When there were conflicting opinions on aspects of the restoration plan that threatened progress, returning to the fundamental purpose of the RAP enabled the group to re-establish consensus-based decision making. Professional facilitation was used rarely, since consensus was the norm. However, when there were differences of opinion, seeking a common understanding through facilitated dialogue and debate resolved the conflict, with the understanding that any dissenting opinion would be documented and made public record.

FIGURE 3. Composition of the Collingwood
Harbour Public Advisory Committee
The equity of the pies is intended to represent "one view, one voice."

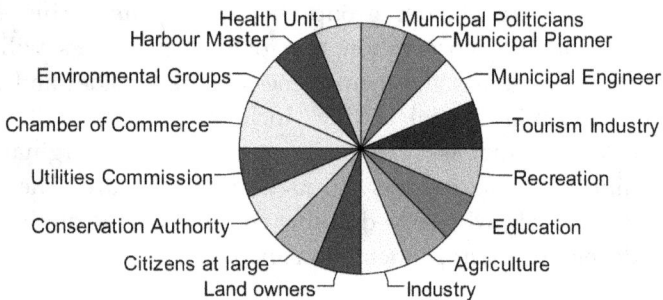

Lesson three - Quantifiable endpoints

Specifying, to the extent possible, quantifiable endpoints or delisting targets that signify success and the achievement of the goals allows the group to recognize progress, prioritize actions and reach consensus on delisting.

To evaluate when or whether the Harbour could support the goals and uses formulated by the community, the RAP Team and PAC jointly delineated rehabilitation targets (or delisting criteria) that were, to the extent possible, quantitative and science based.

The ultimate goal of RAPs as described in Annex 2 of the Agreement is to confirm that the beneficial uses have been restored. Since our knowledge regarding the threats posed by degraded environmental conditions contains uncertainty, the restoration targets need to be reviewed and updated systematically. The absence of suitable restoration targets and lack of understanding of the current status of beneficial uses represent a real challenge to progress. Tracking the resultant incremental improvement in the restoration of the ecosystem helps identify shortfalls, guide future actions and work plan development, and allows for the prioritization of the most effective activities (Sustainability Network and Ontario Ministry of the Environment 2000; IJC 1998).

Lesson four - Ownership

The formulators of the plan are the owners of the plan. Ownership results in pride in delivery, which sustains the process.

In the Collingwood Harbour RAP model, the government RAP Team was not the decision-making body, but was a resource offered to the community. The provincial and federal government representatives did not weigh in on the preferred plan. They served, instead as technical advisors, informing the PAC of the feasibility, scientific merit, and policy implications of their recommended plans. The PAC and RAP Team met together at the call of the PAC chair, and the meetings were shared in all instances. Through this process, the PAC was advised that the governments might reject any plans that were inconsistent with government policy and the goals of the GLWQA. At such junctures, the PAC often reconsidered their recommendations in light of new information and adjusted their approach.

Lesson five - Respect

Trust and respect derived from a common purpose and reliability, strengthened the group's credibility and ability to solve challenges as a team.

Sharing a common vision and set of goals for the future of the Harbour was unifying, with trust, respect and honesty emerging from the participants. An important point was to be able to return to the crux of agreement, that the ecosystem needed to be restored, and that there was a shared vision regardless of individual motives. This allowed the participants to appeal directly to the interests of a diverse cross section of citizens and opinion leaders in ways that compelled others to take action (Bonk *et al.* 1998).

Credibility, and therefore respect, was also gained by making achievable commitments and being accountable to the community and local governments. Municipalities make decisions that can protect environmental quality and preserve sensitive and valuable natural features. Land use planning, investments in infrastructure, water and energy conservation, sewer use bylaws and other tools and practices offer appreciable opportunities to advance the mission of the RAP. "Mayors understand that actions taken in our cities have a positive impact across the Great Lakes Basin," said Chicago Mayor Richard M. Daley, founding United States Chair of the Great Lakes and St. Lawrence Cities Initiative (GLSLCI) at a meeting in 2010. "Today, cities are committing to expand and accelerate the implementation of innovative municipal projects and programs so that we can continue to lead the way on the protection and restoration of the Great Lakes and St. Lawrence River" (GLSLCI 2010).

Conclusions

The International Joint Commission's Water Quality Board asserted that RAPs are on the cutting edge of community-based and ecosystem-based management processes (IJC 1996). This holds true only when participation involves the appropriate community leaders, there is a distributed decision-making process, a common vision and purpose coalesces the group, political support is garnered and public participation and funding are present. These were are all central prerequisites to achieving the success of the Collingwood Harbour RAP and as noted by Mackenzie (1996) successfully operationalizing the ecosystem approach. Such a process builds community capacity for sustaining the gains achieved as future uncertainties in pressures, growth, and new emerging environmental threats emerge.

Capacity-building means enhancing the ability, in this case of a community, to recognize and achieve consensus on problem statements, collectively define policies and appropriate programs to address them, and as pointed out by Hartig et al., to mobilize appropriate resources to fulfil the policies and programs (Hartig et al. 1995). The Collingwood Harbour RAP can be characterized as an experiment that used a blend of human, scientific, technical, and institutional characteristics that enabled the capacity for necessary changes required to resolve the Harbour's environmental constraints.

Hartig and Law concluded that RAPs (and here one could substitute any place-based approach to ecosystem restoration) require cooperative learning that involves stakeholders working in teams to accomplish a common goal under conditions that involve positive interdependence (all stakeholders cooperate to complete a task) and individual and group accountability (each stakeholder is accountable for the final outcome) (Hartig and Law 1994). Place-based types of restoration initiatives like RAPs are an unprecedented collaboration of international significance (Krantzberg 1997).

Creative, distributed governance mechanisms and new institutional arrangements are needed to stimulate and sustain advances in the clean up of local waterways, raise public awareness of individuals' responsibilities, unite a community around a shared purpose and need, and make the Lakes great.

Acknowledgements

I thank my revered colleague Douglas N. Markoff for his unwavering support for Great Lakes excellence. Ed Houghton, as the PAC Chairman, provided community leadership and mentoring. The mayors of the Town of Collingwood recognized the importance of this initiative to their economic, environmental and cultural future. Ontario Ministry of Environment, Ministry of Natural Resource, and Environment Canada provided expertise to the RAP team and were indispensable to me as RAP Coordinator.

References

Bonk, K, H. Griggs and E. Tynes. 1998. *Strategic Communications for Nonprofits*. San Francisco, CA: Jossey Bass.

Canada-Ontario. 2007. *Progress under the Canada-Ontario Agreement Respecting the Great Lakes Basin Ecosystem 2002-2007.* Unpublished report.

Carson, R. 1962. *Silent Spring*. Boston, MA: Houghton-Mifflin.

Cheng, A.S., A.K. Gerlak, L. Dale, and K. Mattor. 2015. "Examining the adaptability of collaborative governance associated with publicly managed ecosystems over time: insights from the Front Range Roundtable, Colorado, USA," *Ecology and Society*, 20(1): 35.

Cocco, P., N. Kazerouni and S.H. Zahm. 2000. "Cancer mortality and environmental exposure to DDE in the United States," *Environmental Health Perspectives*, 108: 1-4.

Collingwood Harbour RAP. 1992. *Stage 2 Document*. Prepared by the Ontario Ministry of Environment and Energy, Toronto, Ontario; Environment Canada, Ministry of Natural Resources, and the Collingwood Harbour Public Advisory Committee. ISBN # 0-7778-0162-0.

Collingwood Harbour RAP. 1994. *Stage 3 Document. Right on Target*. Prepared by the Ontario Ministry of Environment and Energy, Toronto, Ontario; Environment Canada, Ministry of Natural Resources, and the Collingwood Harbour Public Advisory Committee.

Codru, N., M.J. Schymura, S. Negoita, The Akwesasne Task Force on the Environment, R. Rej and D.O. Carpenter. 2007. "Diabetes in relation to serum levels of polychlorinated biphenyls and chlorinated pesticides in adult Native Americans," *Environmental Health Perspectives*, 115: 1442-1447.

Dallaire, F., E. Dewailly, C. Vezina, G. Muckle, J-P Weber, S. Bruneau and P. Ayotte. 2006. "Effect of prenatal exposure to polychlorinated biphenyls on incidence of acute respiratory infections in preschool Inuit children," *Environmental Health Perspectives*, 114: 1301-1305.

Davidson, P.W., G.J. Myers, C. Cox, C.F. Shamlaye, D.O. Marsh, M.A. Tanners, M. Berlin, J. Sloane-Reeves, E. Cernichiari and O. Chloisy. 1995. "Longitudinal neurodevelopmental study of Seychellois children following in utero exposure to methylmercury from maternal fish ingestion: outcomes at 19 and 29 months," *Neurotoxicology*, 16: 677-688.

de Loe, R.C., D. Murray, and M.C. Brisbois. 2016. "Perspectives of natural resource sector firms on collaborative approaches to governance for water," *Journal of Cleaner Production*, 135: 1117-1128.

ECP Consulting. 2009. *Performance Optimization of Wastewater Treatment Plants*. http://www.scribd.com/doc/10209693/Performance-Optimization-of-Waste-Water-Treatment-Plants [Accessed May 10, 2018].

Emerson, K., T. Nabatch, and S. Balogh. 2011. "An Integrative Framework for Collaborative Governance," *Journal of Public Administration Research*, 22: 1-29.

Environment Canada. 1997. *Great Lakes 2000 Cleanup Fund Project Summaries Report*. ISBN 0B662-26232-8.

Environment Canada. (no date). Unpublished report.

GLSLCI. 2010. *Green Cities Chart Sustainable Future for Great Lakes and St. Lawrence*. Unpublished report.

Goncharov, A., R.F. Haase, A. Santiago-Rivera, G. Morse, The Akwesasne Task Force on the Environment, R.J. McCaffrey, R. Rej, and D.O. Carpenter. 2008. "High serum PCBs are associated with elevation of serum lipids and cardiovascular disease in a Native American population," *Environmental Research*, 106: 226-239.

Gurtner-Zimmermann, A. 1995. "A mid-term review of Remedial Action Plans: Difficulties with translating comprehensive planning into comprehensive actions," *Journal of Great Lakes Research*, 21: 234-247.

Gurtner-Zimmermann, A. 1996. "Analysis of Lower Green Bay and Fox River, Collingwood Harbour, Spanish Harbour, and the Metro Toronto and Region Remedial Action Plan (RAP) Processes," *Environmental Management*, 20: 449-459.

Harris, C.C., E.A. Nielsen, W.J. McLaughlin and D.R. Becker. 2003. "Community-based social impact assessment: the case of salmon-recovery on the lower Snake River," *Impact Assessment and Project Appraisal*, 21: 109-118.

Hartig, J.H. and N.L. Law. 1994. "Institutional frameworks to direct the development and implementation of Great Lakes remedial action plans," *Environmental Management*, 18: 855-864.

Hartig, J.H., N.L. Law, D. Epstein, K. Fuller, J. Letterhous and G. Krantzberg. 1995. "Capacity-building for restoring degraded areas in the Great lakes," *International Journal of Sustainable Development & World Ecology*, 2: 1-10.

Hartig, J.H. and M.A. Zarull (eds.). 1992. *Under RAPs. Toward Grassroots Ecological Democracy in the Great Lakes Basin*. Ann Arbor, MI: University of Michigan Press.

International Joint Commission (IJC). 1978. *The Ecosystem Approach. Special Report to the International Joint Commission.* Windsor, ON: Great Lakes Research Advisory Board.

International Joint Commission (IJC). 1996. *Position Statement on the Future of Great Lake Remedial Action Plans.* Windsor, ON: Report of the Great Lakes Water Quality Board.

International Joint Commission (IJC). 1997. *Overcoming Obstacles to Sediment Remediation.* Report of the Sediment Priority Advisory Committee (SedPAC) to the Great Lakes Water Quality Board. Unpublished report.

International Joint Commission (IJC). 1998. *If You Don't Measure It, You Won't Manage It! Measuring and Celebrating Incremental Progress in Restoring and Maintaining the Great Lakes.* Windsor, ON: Report of the Great Lakes Water Quality Board.

International Joint Commission (IJC). 2002. *Eleventh Biennial Report on Great Lakes Water Quality.* Ottawa, ON; Washington, DC; Windsor, ON.

International Joint Commission (IJC). 2003. *The Great Lakes Areas of Concern Report.* Ottawa, ON; Washington, DC; Windsor, ON.

International Joint Commission IJC). 2009. *The Challenge of Substances of Emerging Concern in the Great Lakes Basin: A review of chemicals policies and programs in Canada and the United States.* A report prepared for the International Joint Commission Multi-Board Work Group on Chemicals of Emerging Concern in the Great Lakes Basin, http://www.chemicalspolicy.org/downloads/ IJC_FINAL92009ES.pdf [Accessed May 10, 2018].

Jacobson J.L. and S.W. Jacobson. 1996. "Intellectual impairment in children exposed to polychlorinated biphenyls in utero," *New England Journal of Medicine*, 335: 783-789.

Krantzberg, G. 1997. "International Association for Great Lakes Research Position Statement on Remedial Action Plans," *Journal of Great Lakes Research*, 23: 221- 224.

Krantzberg G., H. Ali, and J. Barnes. 1999. "What progress has been made in the RAP program after ten years of effort?" in T. Murphy and M. Munawar, (eds.). *Aquatic Restoration in Canada.* Ecovision World Monograph Series Leiden, Netherlands: Backhuys Publishers, p. 1-13.

Krantzberg, G., and E. Houghton. 1996. "The Remedial Action Plan that lead to the cleanup and delisting of Collingwood Harbour as an Area of Concern," *Journal of Great Lakes Research*, 22: 469-483.

Lee, B.J., H.A. Regier and D.J. Rapport. 1982. "Ten ecosystem approaches to the planning and management of the Great Lakes," *Journal of Great Lakes Research*, 8: 505-519.

Lee, D-H., I-K. Lee, K. Song, M. Steffes, W. Toscano, B.A. Baker and D.R. Jacobs. 2006. "A strong dose-response relation between serum concentrations of persistent organics pollutants and diabetes," *Diabetes Care*, 29: 1638-1644.

Lonky, E., J. Reihman, T. Darvill, J. Mather, Sr. and H. Daly. 1996. "Neonatal behavioral assessment scale performance in humans influenced by maternal consumption of environmentally contaminated Lake Ontario fish," *Journal of Great Lakes Research*, 22: 198-212.

Mackenzie, S.H. 1996. *Integrated resource planning and management: the ecosystem approach in the Great Lakes basin.* Washington, DC: Island Press.

Managing Shared Waters. 2002. Unpublished report.

MOE. 2005. *Ontario Ministry of Environment Water Management Policies, Guidelines, Provincial Water Quality Objectives of the MOE.* Toronto, ON: Queens Press.

NRC. 2003. *Wastewater Treatment Plant Optimization* – November 2003. Unpublished report.

Ouyang, F., M.J. Perry, S.A. Venners, C. Chen, B. Wang, *et al.* 2005. "Serum DDT, age at menarche, and abnormal menstrual cycle length," *Occupational and Environmental Medicine*, 62: 878-884.

Reynoldson, T.B. and M.A. Zarull. 1993. "An approach to the development of biological sediment guidelines," in G. Francis, J. Kay, and S. Woodley (eds.). *Ecological Integrity and the Management of Ecosystems.* Boca Raton, FL: St. Lucie Press.

Reynoldson, T.B., R.C. Bailey, K.E. Day, and R.H. Norris. 1995. "Biological guidelines for freshwater sediment based on BEnthic Assessment of SedimenT (the BEAST) using a multivariate approach for predicting biological state." *Australian Journal of Ecology*, 20: 198-219.

Richtoff, J., L. Rylander, B.A.G. Jonsson, H. Akesson, L. Hagmar, P. Ehle-Nilsson, M. Stridsberg and A. Giwercman. 2003. "Serum levels of 2,2',4,4',5,5'- hexachlorobiphenyl (CB-153) in relation to markers of reproductive function in young males from the general Swedish population," *Environmental Health Perspectives*, 111: 409-413.

Rocan, Claude. 2009. "Multi-Level Collaborative Governance: The Canadian Heart Health Initiative," *Optimum Online*, 39(4): 1-10.

Samy, M., H. Snow and H. Bryan. 2003. "Integrating social impact assessment with research: the case of methylmercury in fish in the Mobile-Alabama River Basin," *Impact Assessment and Project Appraisal*, 21: 133-140.

Schwartz, P.M., S.W. Jacobson, G. Fein, J.L. Jacobson and H.A. Price. 1983. "Lake Michigan fish consumption as a source of polychlorinated biphenyls in human cord serum, maternal serum, and milk," *American Journal of Public Health*, 73: 293-296.

SOLEC. 2009. State of the Lakes Ecosystem Conference report. Unpublished report.

Sproule-Jones, M. 2002. *The Restoration of the Great Lakes*. Vancouver, BC: University of British Columbia Press.

Sustainability Network and Ministry of the Environment. 2000. *The Road to Delisting: Addressing RAP Challenges*. Unpublished report.

Torres-Sanchez, L., S.J. Rothenberg, L. Schnaas, M.E. Cebrian, E. Osorio, M. del Carmen Hernandez, R.M. Garcia-Hernandez, C. del Rio-Garcia, M.S. Wolff and L. Lopez-Carrillo. 2007. "*In Utero* p,p' - DDE Exposure and Infant Neurodevelopment: a Perinatal Cohort in Mexico," *Environmental Health Perspectives*, 115: 435-439.

Town of Collingwood. 2001. Unpublished report.

United States and Canada. 1972. *Great Lakes Water Quality Agreement* (GLWQA), http://www.ijc.org/en_/Great_Lakes_Quality [Accessed May 10, 2018].

United States and Canada. 1987. Revised *Great Lakes Water Quality Agreement* of 1978, as Amended by Protocol, Signed November 18, 1987. Consolidated by the International Joint Commission, http://ijc.org/en_/1987_Agreement [Accessed May 10, 2018].

CHAPTER 4

Collaborative Governance to Meet
the Challenge of Aging:
The Case of Age-Friendly Cities and Communities

By Mario Paris and Suzanne Garon

Introduction

The aging of the population is a real challenge facing most countries, but most particularly western nations such as Canada. To be more specific, in 2016 Statistics Canada established the proportion of persons aged 65 or older at 16.9 percent (Statistics Canada 2107), which is greater than that of children under 14 (16.6 percent). This proportion has not stopped growing throughout the 20th century and is expected to continue to rise until the middle of the 21st century (*Ibid.*). Canada's provinces and territories have different rates of population aging. The eastern part of the country has on average higher populations of older people, while the west and the north are younger.

Quebec exhibits a portrait unique in the country. The province is experiencing rapid growth of its older population. As a matter of fact, in 1970 the proportion of older persons in the province was among the lowest in Canada, whereas since 2010, it has reached the average for the country (Azeredo & Payeur 2015). In 2016, the proportion of persons aged 65 or more in Quebec stood at 18.3 percent, higher than the national average (16.9 percent) (Statistics Canada 2017). This proportion will continue to grow right up until 2061 when the proportion of older adults is estimated to reach 28.5 percent. Then again, it is the increase in persons aged

75 or more that is gaining the attention of local, regional and provincial decision makers. Thus, the number of Quebecers aged 75 or more will double between 2006 and 2031, and then double again between 2031 and 2046 (Payeur 2012). We estimate that there will be more than a million persons aged 75 or more in Quebec in 2056.

The aging of the population is a phenomenon that political and public officials can respond to adequately without falling into the alarmism of "demographic shock" (Fortier & Hébert 2015). In fact, the aging of the population and the amplitude of the changes it implies can lead to questioning our ways of doing things and can even become an opportunity, in much the same way as climate change has allowed the development of new sources of renewable energy. Social innovation finds its leverage in the community rather than in new technologies. It therefore seems opportune to consider innovation from the viewpoint of Klein *et al.*, that is to create "[...] new social arrangements, new ways to mobilize resources and new responses to problems whose known solutions are inadequate *[our translation]*" (Klein *et al.* 2009: 3). Thus, as we will see later on, there is no social innovation without collaboration between diverse actors leading to a more complete comprehension of the problems which affect the elderly, to developing solutions and to investing the expertise and resources necessary to effect change (Garon, Paris, Beaulieu, Veil & Laliberté 2014).

The goal of our text is to throw light on a program, initiated by the World Health Organization, but improved by the Government of Quebec in 2008. The Age-Friendly Cities and Communities Program of the Quebec government has the goal of assisting municipalities to adapt to the aging of their population (Gouvernement du Québec 2012). To do this, we will examine it in the light of research results on the concept of governance in general. We will first describe the Quebec Age-Friendly Cities Program and its founding principles. We will then present data from various research projects that we have carried out in cities in Quebec. Finally, using the Ansell and Gash model, we will analyze the research results, based on a case-study approach of four very different municipalities within the Age-Friendly Cities Program.

The AFCC Program in Quebec: a brief overview

An age-friendly city "[...] encourages active ageing by optimizing opportunities for health, participation and security in order to enhance quality of life as people age. In practical terms, an age-friendly city adapts its structures and services to be accessible and inclusive of older people with varying needs and capacities" (WHO 2007: 1). In the last almost 10 years there have appeared a multitude of initiatives related to age-friendly cities around the world (Moulaert & Garon 2016). The WHO Global Network of Age-Friendly Cities and Communities reaches 500 initiatives as well as 13 affiliated programs in 37 countries, reaching more than 155 million people around the world (WHO 2017).

The Canadian government, through its Public Health Agency, was an important contributor to the work of the WHO (*Ibid.*). While Canada has made important progress in deploying the Age-Friendly Cities Program, it is in Quebec that most of these initiatives are found. This can be explained by the engagement of the provincial government, through its Seniors' Secretariat (*Secrétariat aux aînés*). Today, Quebec has 862 age-friendly cities, such that 90 percent of the Quebec population live in a municipality that has undertaken the process to become 'age-friendly.' This can be explained by the fact that two researchers from the Research Centre on Aging (RCA) of the University of Sherbrooke participated in the research carried out by the WHO in 2005-07. In 2007, these researchers were able to present the WHO experience to a public consultation on the living conditions of older adults (Ministère de la Famille et des Aînés 2008) organized by the Seniors' Secretariat. The secretariat then decided to develop a Quebec model, inspired by the community development approach which had been conceived primarily by the research team at the RCA (http://madaquebec.com/fr/).

The age-friendly cities experience in Quebec wishes to improve on the orientations put forward by the WHO, in the sense that it foresees setting up a steering committee which includes all stakeholders, particularly older adults and their organizations, in order to favour a three-step process: a social diagnosis, the development of an action plan and the implementation of this plan.

FIGURE 1. Steps in the Age-Friendly Cities Process

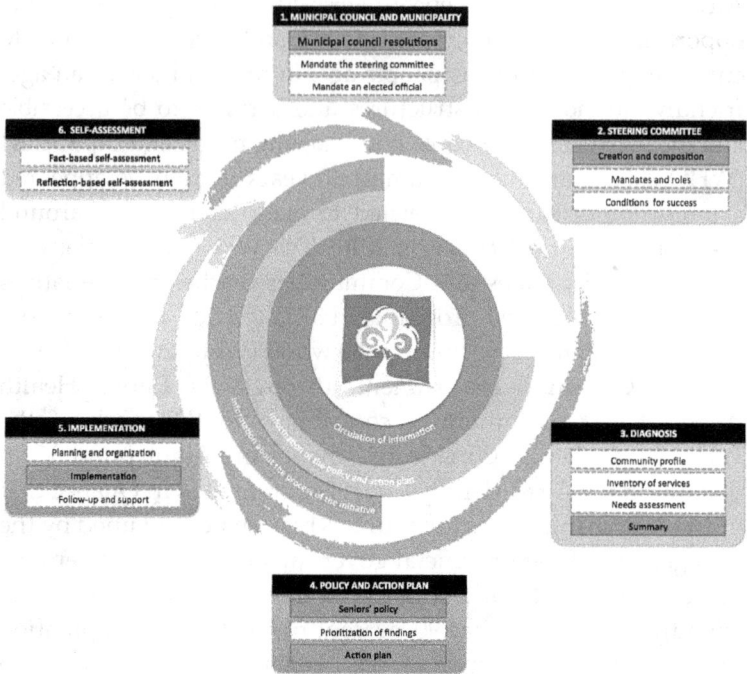

These steps, which echo those used in strategic planning (Mintzberg 1994), have one important addition in Quebec, namely permitting the participation of various actors over the course of the process. It is clear that:

"For those municipalities and regional county municipalities using the support offered by the Ministry in the context of this programme, the process leading to the elaboration of a municipal policy for its older population and its action plan must necessarily solicit the engagement of its elected officials, its municipal services, other partners in the milieu, older adults and those organizations which represent them, and lead to the implementation of concrete actions for the elderly in their respective territories [our translation]" (Gouvernement du Québec 2012: 4).

These actors must be the true masters of the age-friendly city initiatives. The process may be spread out for as long as five years: the first 18 months are consecrated essentially to carrying out a diagnosis and developing an action plan prior to the implementation step. After this period, it is possible for the municipalities to update their process and their age-friendly cities action plan.

Steering Committee

This is a central component of the age-friendly cities process, and is where collaborative governance occurs. The constitution of a multi-sectoral steering committee in the municipalities puts a structure in place that is favourable to the concerted mobilization of the actors of the milieu, seen from the beginning as desirable for the inception of projects having a mobilizing perspective for the development of the community. The municipalities are free to choose the members, although the presence of individuals from seniors' organizations, the health and social services sector, the municipal administration and finally an elected municipal official, are heavily solicited by the Seniors' Secretariat. The role of this committee consists of following and facilitating each of the three steps, collaborating in the implementation of the actions, circulating information, as well as participating in mobilizing the actors and decision makers of the milieu. Once the action plan is published, the steering committee gives way to an implementation follow-up committee.

Diagnosis

A social diagnosis is essential to the success of all subsequent steps of the age-friendly cities process. This step permits the emergence of a vision shared by all of the actors with respect to the reality of aging in their community. In the Quebec experience, three sources of data gathering ensure the rigour of this social diagnosis.

The socio-demographic portrait of the milieu. This data collection aims to describe the milieu based on population statistics, available to the public, among others with the help of specialized organizations, public and municipal services, or through the Internet. It includes the proportion of persons aged 65 or older, the evolution of aging, the social, ethnic and economic characteristics of different areas of the municipality, as well as housing types. Its pertinence exceeds that of a simple technical operation as it may raise awareness among the members of the steering committee and the municipal administration as to the scale of the challenge they have before them.

The consultation on the needs of older adults. The goal of this process is to arrive at a good understanding of the perspectives which older adults have of their needs, and at the same time the solutions which they themselves propose so that they can better live and evolve in their community (be it urban or rural), according to the eight areas identified by the WHO (2007). In order to do this, various means are available to municipalities, but the Seniors' Secretariat strongly encourages the use of discussion groups or of a community forum.

The services grid. This information gathering is necessary in order to measure the services actually offered in a given milieu and their geographic accessibility. Combined with information collected from the discussion groups, the grid makes it possible to gauge the degree of knowledge about the services offered to older adults. This perception of the availability of services is as important as the actual services offered, as many services are not well known by older adults.

Action Plan

After it has appropriated the portrait of its milieu and the needs expressed by the older adults of the community, the steering committee constructs its vision of the entire situation, elaborates ideas for intervention, and shares its preoccupations with the group. Starting with the evidence of the situation in their community as well as their knowledge of the local culture, the practices and the conditions, they must set priorities among the projects destined to improve the conditions of life for older adults. From this, they choose the scenario or scenarios envisaged for the duration of the age-friendly cities project. This process is carried out within the group and allows its members to arrive at a common vision, even at times a strategic vision, which takes local contingencies into consideration. By doing this, the steering committee builds a vision of the results it wishes to attain, which is evidenced during the implementation period.

The action plan is a logical framework where the members of the steering committee determine the goal, the objectives, the inputs, the resources, the activities and the outcome. The process of elaborating the plan serves to reinforce the capabilities of the group which profits from this exercise to share their values, to better recognize the complementary expertise of its members, to transpose into the action plan projects which are attractive for the elderly. This also presents an occasion to see whether new partnerships can be created and whether old partnerships can be renewed.

Implementation

The final step consists of planning and organizing the resources necessary to implement the actions and to carry out a follow-up. In fact, the implementation must produce the results anticipated by the action plan and contribute to reaching the objectives set by the steering committee. It is important to mention that the financing offered by the Quebec government to municipalities participating in the Age-Friendly Cities Program contributes only to the elaboration of the action plan and not to the financing of projects. In order to make up for these financial issues, although there is no obligation for the follow-up committee to do it; frequently it assumes a proactive stance by quickly searching for new subsidies. Conscious of this limitation from the program, the Seniors' Secretariat has prepared, with the collaboration of the Ministry of Municipal Affairs and of the Occupation of the Territory (*Ministre des Affaires municipales et de l'Occupation du territoire*) a specific program to finance light infrastructure (e.g., light exercise equipment, exterior dance floors).

Four different research projects and the importance of governance

Our research team on age-friendly cities have participated in the conceptualization of the Quebec program, as well as in the training of the staff in the non-profit organization responsible for implanting it within the municipalities (Moulaert & Garon 2015). This organization, the *Carrefour action municipale et famille* (CAMF) has extended experience working with municipalities on the elaboration of family policy. The first mandate that the RCA research team obtained was to evaluate the implantation of pilot projects and to translate the results through knowledge transfer activities addressed to various actors (municipalities, CAMF staff, associations of older adults, etc.). Subsequently, the research team undertook different research projects with a case studies methodology (MADA-Innov and IRSC-MADA) and developed a questionnaire for participating municipalities. We propose painting a general portrait of these research projects, with a particular accent on the IRSC-MADA study as it serves as an empirical example of collaborative governance.

Pilot projects (2008-13)

This research project aimed to evaluate the implantation of seven pilot projects, as well as to conduct knowledge transfer to actors within the milieu. This project centred on five municipalities to which were added a district of a large city and a regional county municipality (MRC) of 22 municipalities. These very different milieu ranged from urban areas offering a panoply of organized services (including public transport, for example), to mid-size cities with fewer services, and finally to a rural area where the organization of services are scarce.

With regard to the theme which interests us, governance, the results of this research (Garon *et al.* 2014; Garon, Veil, Paris & Rémillard-Boilard 2016; Garon, Paris, Laliberté & Veil, 2016) demonstrated the importance of collaborative partnership as a condition of success. Follow-up with the steering committees and exchanges among the members over a five-year period allow us to come to the following conclusions:

- While the presence of the elderly is essential to the realization of a social diagnosis, responsibility for the program cannot be transferred to an organization which represents them. The participation of all concerned parties is necessary, including the actors from various municipal services.
- A municipality is not a homogenous entity. It is composed of various actors from the political sphere (mayor, municipal councillors) and the administration (directors of various services such as roads and leisure). Each of these groups must have a common vision in order to adapt municipal services to the reality of their aging population. In certain cases, it was observed that resistance at the administrative level was responsible for maintaining the *status quo*.

- The implementation of concerted actions frequently happens because of informal relationships. If restrained to their job descriptions, the various actors could not have implemented many important projects which contributed to change.

MADA-Innov (2013-17)

This project consisted of multiple case studies of 19 age-friendly city projects in Quebec. It attempted to bring to light the evolution of age-friendly cities with respect to social innovations (Klein *et al.* 2009) which play a role in the social inclusion of older adults. Thus, a convenient sample of 15 municipalities and regional county municipalities (MRC) of different sizes was selected on the basis of social innovations, while a sample of four rural municipalities allowed experimentation with a co-construction approach destined to remediate the difficulties experienced.

Among the results of this study of multiple cases, those which concern collaborative governance were associated with the governance practices of MRCs, which are akin to territorial governance (Rey-Valette *et al.* 2011). Both through the age-friendly cities process and in the deployment of projects in the action plans, it became clear that depending on the approach advocated, distinctive in each case, conditions were created which were either favourable or not to social innovation. We found many initiatives which led to the implementation of community revitalization projects, and this, starting from the social diagnosis step.

As previously, seen, regional governance of the age-friendly cities requires the collaboration of numerous networks from different levels of government which intersect with models of local powers. Interdependence between administrative and political actors with respect to resources (material, financial, social, expertise) can translate into participative governance where top-down forces encounter those from mobilizing communities, or bottom-up forces, particularly older adults themselves and civil society participating in the reinforcement of social capital, and this, even in devitalized communities. In one case, the political actor played the role of a facilitator. In another case, the influence of the central city did not seem to allow local actors from small municipalities to join their efforts to those of the MRC. We observed a de-federalizing dynamic, while the efforts of the central city turned principally around the lack of manpower associated with the aging of the population, its principal preoccupation. Finally, we look at the MRC in a remote region where the integrity of its networks was weakened in the context of major governmental reforms in the local and regional development. This case attempted to lean on regional actors in health and social services, themselves affected by government reforms, to develop age-friendly city projects anchored in the community. This strategy neutralized local political powers and centred the Age-Friendly Cities program on the MRC.

Questionnaire for municipalities (2015-16)

A questionnaire was distributed to the municipalities' personnel who were or currently are responsible for the Age-Friendly Cities Program in Quebec. This questionnaire was sent to all municipalities enrolled in the program. In 2015, this amounted to 759 municipalities and MRCs. Of these, 361 replied to the questionnaire, a response rate of 48 percent. The municipalities that responded represented a total population of 4,134,531 inhabitants, or 50 percent of the Quebec population. This survey allowed us to obtain much information about the process of the Age-Friendly Cities Program: the number of cities which had completed the different steps of the program (social diagnosis, action plan and implantation), according to size and to the type of program (e.g., Age-Friendly Cities Program, or integration with municipal family policy), as well as the level of governance (municipality or MRC). Also, the survey included other items: the composition of steering committees, the action fields considered during different stages, the projects they were proud of, etc. We were surprised to realize that the process allowed municipalities to create new ways of working within their municipal structure. In fact, our data shows that 67 percent of municipalities said they "strongly agree" or "agree" with the fact that the Age-Friendly Cities Program had allowed them to establish new ways of doing things within the municipal apparatus. With regards to new ways of doing things with their partners, the response rate was 68 percent.

CIHR-AFCC (2014-17)

A multiple case study of Age-Friendly Cities Program in Quebec was financed by the Canadian Institutes of Health Research (project No. 322702). Its objective was to understand the impact of age-friendly cities on the social determinants of health. The social determinants of health are "socially produced conditions which influence the health of populations. A non-exhaustive list would include: employment policies, types of employment, education, transportation infrastructure, revenue, the built environment such as dwellings and other buildings *[our translation]*" (Potvin, Moquet & Jones 2010: 30). In other words, these are the circumstances in which people are born, grow up, live, work and grow old (WHO 2011).

Research specifications and objectives

Three research objectives allowed us to examine the case studies, as well as to accompany them in the deployment of their Age-Friendly Cities Program:

1. To describe the different community building factors within the Age-Friendly Cities process.
2. To understand how the conditions and the long-term effects of the Age-Friendly Cities program contributed to interventions promoting the health of older adults in terms of their living conditions and their lifestyles.
3. To consolidate the actions through the development of collective intervention and evaluation tools for the Age-Friendly Cities process and for effects on the social determinants of health.

Two evaluation models were used during this research, realistic evaluation (Pawson & Tilley 1997) and developmental evaluation (Patton 2011). Realistic evaluation helps us understand the Age-Friendly Cities Program through the different contexts studied, as well as the mechanisms and the results. The realistic evaluation of a program such as Age-Friendly Cities seeks an answer to the question "what works, for whom and under what circumstances" (Pawson & Tilley 1997). This evaluation model postulates that all programs are based on "theories" of functioning. It is necessary to question them as the realities encountered in the deployment of a program are not the same from one case to another. Developmental evaluation permits accompanying and supporting the cases being studied in order to facilitate adaptation to the complexity of social innovation. In the municipal and regional context, the Age-Friendly Cities Program exists within complex dynamics with a high level of interdependence between actors, the actions and the program.

Research sample

The study of multiple cases (Yin 2009) considers four contrasting initiatives of the age-friendly cities experience in Quebec:

	Case A	Case B	Case C	Case D
Geographic Description	Seven rural villages surrounding a central city	A dense urban milieu	A suburb of a metropolis	A rural municipality
Superficies Area	340.2 km²	122.9 km²	48.9 km²	24.9 km²
Population in 2013	7,550 persons	238,935 persons	30,280 persons	7,400 persons
Proportion older adults in 2013	20%	15.5%[1]	12.6%	12.9%
Date of the process[2]	spring 2013 to autumn 2016	autumn 2012 to autumn 2016	autumn 2012 to autumn 2016	autumn 2012 to autumn 2016

[1] Data from 2012
[2] From social diagnostic to the implantation of the action plan

These cases under study are complex (Patton 2011) as they are situated in particular local and regional contexts, with variable resources and different types of actors. The participants under study are local and regional actors, participating in steering committees, including those elected municipal officials involved as well as municipal employees, project managers, community organizers and older citizens.

Data collection and analysis strategy

Data collection was the result of an iterative process done around seven strategies, as illustrated in the following:

Data Collection Strategy by Case

	Case A	Case B	Case C	Case D	Total
Group interviews	3 (N 32)	3 (N 16)	5 (N 27)	2 (N 16)	13 (N 91)
Individual interviews	4	3	8	5	20
Direct observation	6	3	2	1	12
Collaboration questionnaire[1]	12	8	9	9	38
Network questionnaire[2]	12	7	9	9	27
Documentation	30	12	12	5	59

[1] Mattessich, Murray-Close, Monsey, & Wilder Research Center, 2001
[2] Provan, Veazie, Staten et Teufel-Shone, 2005

In order to seize the complexity of the cases studied, the analysis strategies used are organized in an iterative process between data collection and analysis. For example, three aspects of community building (Leroux & Ninacs 2002) were taken into consideration to discern the role of age-friendly cities on the social determinants of health: 1) mobilization and participation; 2) collaboration, concertation and partnership; and 3) inter-sectorality.

AFCC Examples of Collaborative Governance

As one can see, governance was revealed as an important dimension in our research on the Age-Friendly Cities process. In this text, we look at governance using the large conceptual categories proposed by Ansell and Gash. They defined collaborative governance as:

"A governing arrangement where one or more public agencies directly engage non-state stakeholders in a collective decision-making process that is formal, consensus-oriented, and deliberative and that aims to make or implement public policy or manage public programs or assets" (Ansell and Gash 2008: 544).

Within the Age-Friendly Cities context, this manner of conceiving of governance takes place on the steering committee. This exercise puts Ansell and Gash's model to empirical proof.

Starting Conditions

Ansell and Gash showed that the initial conditions surrounding governance could either facilitate or discourage the collaborative process. In this regard, they defined three variables: power/resource imbalances, incentives to participate, and prehistory of antagonism and cooperation (*Ibid.*). These variables constitute, in the opinion of the authors, the bases recognized in the scientific literature for good collaboration among actors. Our previous studies are entirely of this opinion and demonstrate the importance of these variables for the Age-Friendly Cities process (Garon *et al.* 2014; Garon, Paris, Veil, Beaulieu & Laliberté 2015).

Before we look to these variables, we must recognize the impact of context on the development of the Age-Friendly Cities process. During our research, a new provincial government was elected in the spring of 2014. It coincided with the beginning of the Age-Friendly Cities process for these cases. This election, as we have already mentioned, led to changes in many public policies. The pursuit of budget equilibrium, more specifically of a zero deficit, was a priority for the new government (Vaillancourt 2017). This priority translated into a series of major legislative reforms whose effects were felt on local and regional development, urban and rural planning, as well as the centralization of the health and social services network. These reforms include the:

- abolition of the Regional Conferences of Elected Representatives;
- abandonment of the National Policy on Rurality;
- partial dismantling of Local Development Centres;
- creation of *Centres intégrés de santé et de services sociaux*; and the
- abolition of regional health and social services agencies

These reforms had consequences for the Age-Friendly Cities process and on the functioning of collaborative governance: reorganization of local and regional actors, disappearance of financial programmes, reorientation of the priorities of the milieu, etc.

In addition to this context, which is very important in understanding the way collaboration unfolded, three variables influenced the prerequisite conditions of governance: 1) the capacity of individuals and organizations to commit their resources and to assume their authority in governance; 2) motivation within the collaborative process; and 3) antecedents of cooperation or conflict among the actors (Ansell & Gash 2008).

Power/Resource imbalances

This variable relates to the issue of ensuring equalitarian relationships between the parties involved in the collaborative process. In our case study, this equality is the result of the composition of the steering committees of the Age-Friendly Cities Program.

FIGURE 2. Comparison between steering committees by the organizational affiliation of their members, 2014

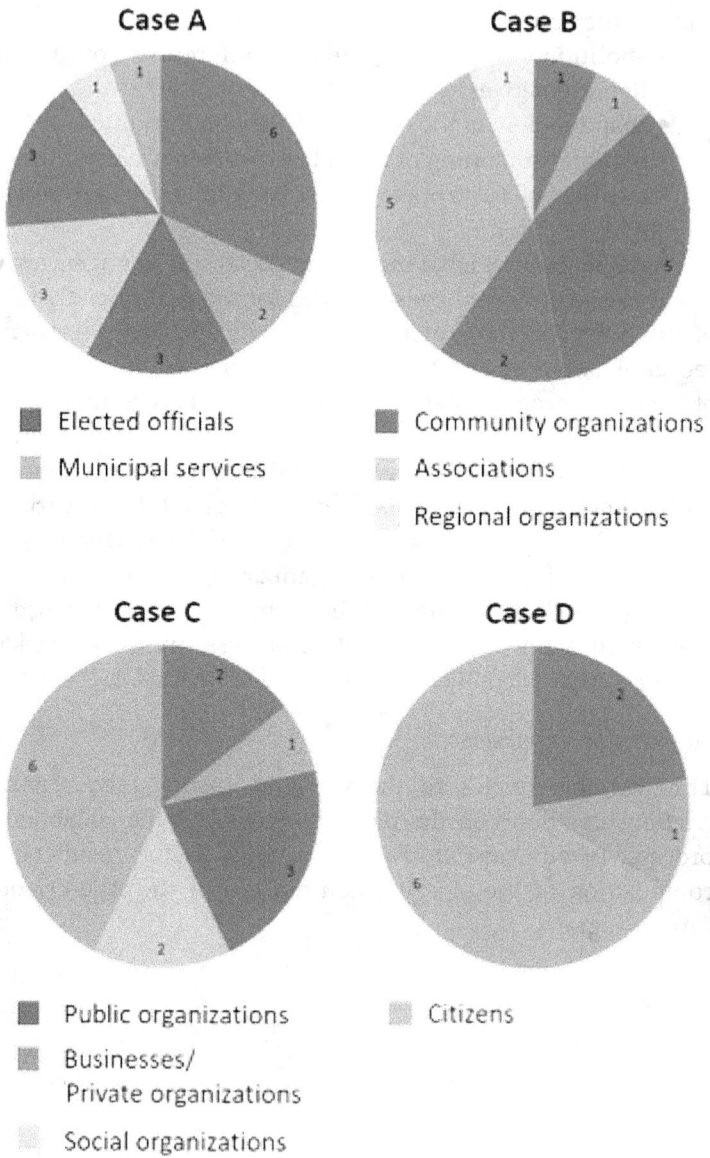

Case A

Case B

Elected officials

Municipal services

Community organizations

Associations

Regional organizations

Case C

Case D

Public organizations

Businesses/
Private organizations

Social organizations

Citizens

We see at a glance that the composition of steering committees varies from one case to another, reflecting the diversity of local collaboration dynamics. As the space available does not allow us to go into detail in all cases, we will concentrate our analysis on cases C and A. The first shows inequalities among the resources belonging to different groups of actors on the steering committee, while the second shows these inequalities between members of the same group.

In Case C, municipal representatives hold the human and economic resources in large part, that is, two elected officials and the Director of Leisure Services. This illustrates the power they exercise on the steering committee of the Age-Friendly Cities process. Within this committee, we can see that older citizens constitute an important group in terms of numbers. They represent six out of 14 people. Municipal officials invited these citizens to the steering committee. They recognized that older citizens, even though they have few resources, were able to bring an "inside view" reflecting the daily reality of older adults. As well, the other group in the steering committee consists of community organizations and associations. Within this group, only one actor out of five people was an executive director who had access to the resources of his organization. The other persons were present as members or volunteers. This portrait allows us to measure the gaps in resources available to members of the steering committee. The municipal representatives were certainly listening to the needs of older adults, but the implantation of the actions of the Age-Friendly Cities Program were essentially their responsibility. In other words, they were magnanimous, but it would be an exaggeration here to talk of participation.

As for Case A, the role of elected municipal officials is different even though they constitute the largest groups in the steering committee. Their six members represent the clear engagement of the eight municipalities mobilized in this regional age-friendly city process. However, the number of elected officials cannot be taken for granted, as it can fluctuate over the course of the process; it does not in itself reflect a dynamic governance process. From the beginning of the age-friendly cities process, it is clear in Case A that uniting "the elected officials from eight municipalities was a challenge *[our translation]*" (Case A, group interview, steering committee). In addition, during observations of the meetings of this committee, only one or two elected officials attended on average, far from the "image" of 2014. In fact, in all cases there was variability in the participation of members of the steering committees. This variability may, however, be partially explained by the inequalities of human resources within the municipalities or, as Ansell and Gash said so eloquently, "[...] some stakeholders do not have the time, energy, or liberty to engage in time-intensive collaborative process" (Ansell and Gash 2008: 551). Practically speaking we must say that small municipalities must cope with very limited human and financial resources. As a result, the task of elected municipal officials involved in local development is much more arduous. In Case A, which groups together several small villages, this reality raised important issues, as some of the municipalities participating in the Age-Friendly Cities Program could only count on a part-time director, while others had no administrative personnel in the municipality. Thus, this disparity created obstacles for the engagement of elected officials and for the proper functioning of collaborative governance. According to a member of the steering committee in Case A, "In general, the municipalities have difficulty following the process *[our translation]*" (Case A, group interview, steering committee). In fact, elected municipal officials in the case study had little time available to commit to the Age-Friendly Cities process.

In summary, inequalities in resources, as well as in power relationships, exist between different actors on the steering committee, but also within the same group of actors.

Incentives to participate

Motivation is a central condition for success in a collaborative process (Butterfoss 2007) and the Ansell and Gash model reiterates this importance. In our research, it is evident that the motivation to "work together" on the steering committee for age-friendly cities varied throughout the process. First, regardless of the case in question, they all demonstrate the contribution of the Age-Friendly Cities Program in bringing actors of the milieu together to take action on the aging of the population. For example, again in Case A, the project manager realized that "the age-friendly cities process served as a space in which to bring together the partners who have interest in older adults *[our translation]*" (Case A, interview, project manager). How was it possible to assemble these actors around the same table? The response is two-fold.

First, the age-friendly cities process, through its social diagnosis step, makes possible the identification of the elements crucial to collaboration: shared analyses and a common goal. The clear portrait of the municipality or of the region, the services offered to the population, as well as the needs expressed by the older adults of the milieu, all components of the social diagnosis step, are known to reinforce the relationship among the actors (Garon *et al.* 2014). In addition, the motivation to collaborate between members of the steering committee depends in particular on the needs of older adults, as they are able to put into words the difficulties older adults experience and to reinforce the compassion felt by members of the committee. "We started with us, the elderly, and we did something. That contributes a lot to our motivation, as it was not a summary provided by others *[our translation]*" (Case A, group interview, steering committee). The following table demonstrates different strategies for identifying the needs of older adults according to each case:

Strategies in Place during the Social Diagnosis and the Themes Considered

	Case A	Case B	Case C	Case D
Strategies	5 public consultations that reached 88 older adults in total	Survey replied to by 1,000 older adults. 14 discussion groups which reached a total of 117 older adults	5 discussion groups which reached 55 older adults in total	1 survey replied to by 51 older adults. 1 public consultation which reached 12 older adults
Themes	1) housing; 2) transportation; 3) urban planning; 4) social participation; 5) leisure; 6) communications and information; and 7) health	1) living in the city; 2) security; 3) exterior spaces and municipal buildings; 4) transportation; 5) housing; 6) leisure and healthy lifestyles; 7) valorization, social participation and volunteering; and 8) communications	1) leisure and culture; 2) security; 3) housing; 4) urban planning; 5) community development; 6) public administration; 7) information; 8) implication as citizens; 9) health; and 10) transportation	1) leisure, sports, culture and life in the community; 2) security; 3) transportation; 4) municipal organization; and 5) the environment

The differences between these cases illustrate their capacity to reach the older adults in their milieu. Thus, Case B, with its major financial and human resources, obtained the information necessary to develop an action plan to unite the members of the steering committee. At the opposite end of the spectrum, Case D had neither the financial nor the human resources necessary to develop a social diagnosis, and for the same reason, an action plan, which did not have much value in the eyes of local actors. Starting from the tenor of the information gathered, members of steering committees set priorities among various needs in accordance with the importance given to them by older adults as well as their capacities to respond adequately. The Age-Friendly Cities process favours solidifying the commitment of the members of a steering committee around an action plan.

Secondly, the action plan of Age-Friendly Cities constitutes another significant step in the motivation of the actors to intervene in their milieu. On the one hand, the action plan is supposed to confirm the responsibilities, the commitments and the obligations of members of the steering committee (Garon *et al.* 2015). On the other, the process of implementing the action plan often stimulates a realization among the members of the steering committees of the importance of "working together" within their municipality or their region if they hope to respond to the challenge of an aging population. At the same time, a reduction in motivation among the members of steering committees was observed from the moment that age-friendly city began to deviate from the objectives chosen in the action plan. Case C is particular because at the implantation stage, municipal authorities decided to dissolve the steering committee of the Age-Friendly Cities Program in order to replace it with a healthy lifestyle committee. In total, aside from the elected officials and the Director of Leisure Services, only two members of the steering committee found themselves on this new committee of collaborative governance. These members were older citizens with no attachment to an organization or association. They expressed preoccupations both with regard to the implantation of the Age-Friendly Cities action plan and with regard to the commitment of the municipality to respond to the needs of older adults. In the absence of a goal and of clear objectives described in the action plan, the motivation of these members in fact declined.

As we have just seen, the Age-Friendly Cities process, through its program stages, offers the conditions to incite actors to engage in improving the quality of life of older adults. Nevertheless, this commitment is not guaranteed from the moment when the goals or conditions supporting collaborative governance change or abandon the actions around which they are mobilized.

Prehistory of antagonism and cooperation

Ansell and Gash note that the degree of interdependence among actors, in terms of cooperation and conflicts, influences collaborative governance (Ansell and Gash 2008). It therefore seems evident that a positive culture of collaboration, based on trust and openness between the actors, is a condition for governance to succeed. In this regard, the case study illustrates on many occasions this positive culture within steering committees, but also shows that this culture is not always shared by all members of the committee according to the group to which they belong. Case A offers a good example of tensions between different groups. The elected municipal officials have little experience in collaboration and are even distrustful of it. However, in the framework of this Age-Friendly Cities Program, the subsidy received implied developing inter-municipal collaboration, changing the territorial framework to which they were answerable. According to some members of the Case A steering committee, uniting all of the municipalities in a unique regional action plan was difficult because of the "parochial spirit" of many elected officials.

At the other extreme, the association and community actors in Case A as well as the actors of the health and social services network had a long history of collaboration and partnership, which was evident in the observation of their interactions during meetings of the steering committee: trust, reciprocity, friendship, camaraderie, etc. This finding is, moreover, central in the observation of the age-friendly cities process. Steering committees constitute a discussion and decision space for their members, but also a place for conviviality.

- "The committee was very agreeable, with a good atmosphere, good collaboration, the municipality listened [our translation]" (Case C, individual interview, older adult, May 20, 2016).
- "A good atmosphere, the members joked, many teased each other. The committee is convivial [our translation]" (Case D, field notes, observation, October 20, 2014).

This dimension based on sociability and the social relationships among the members of the committee, unlike hierarchical relationships based on power, demonstrate the importance of illustrating conviviality in collaborative governance, among other things, when the actors involved do not all come from organizations or formal bodies but also from civil society.

Facilitative Leadership

Ansel and Gash identified leadership as a central category in collaborative governance (Ansel and Gash 2008). Through our case study, variations of this leadership were apparent depending on the type of actor present.

Actors demonstrating leadership in the steering committees

Case A	Case B	Case C	Case D
1) Elected official of the central city 2) Community organizer 3) Coordinator of Leisure Services and of the steering committee	1) Elected official responsible for age-friendly cities 2) Manager and Coordinator of the steering committee	1) Elected officials responsible for Age-Friendly Cities 2) Director of Leisure Services 3) Older citizens	1) Director of Leisure Services and Coordinator of the steering committee

Our research on age-friendly cities demonstrated the preponderant role of the elected municipal official in the success of the process (Garon *et al.* 2014). This person, because of his authority, permits the commitment of municipal resources to the project. All case studies confirm the central role of the elected official. At the same time, as shown in our table above, leadership also comes from other actors on steering committees. Case A benefited from the competence and the leadership of the community organizer and of the coordinator of leisure services of the central city. These persons did not exercise power on the members of the steering committee. On the contrary, the relationship was based on the trust and the respect which members of the committee had for the devotion of these two people.

The leadership of the community organizer from the health and social services network was an important component in setting up the Age-Friendly Cities process in Case A. She had worked in the milieu for more than 20 years and all members of the steering committee had worked with her on different committees in the region. In the interview with her, the community organizer described her roles as follows:

"At the planning stage, my role was to 'sell' the idea of age-friendly cities in my region. To look for a resource person to be able to do it. To ensure that people participate, to mobilize [...]. At the implantation stage, my role was that of a watchdog, complementary... To notice if something wasn't working or would not work [*our translation*]" (Case A, interview, Community organizer).

She thus assumed leadership in different roles over the course of the stages of the Age-Friendly Cities process. She sensitized and raised the awareness of people about the importance of a regional approach to age-friendly cities. She also helped support existing resources: support for the meetings of the steering committee and in the development of the action plan of Age-Friendly Cities, as well as technical assistance in the implantation of various actions.

The leadership assumed by the coordinator of leisure services of the central city also deserves attention. During implementation, she ensured that the steering committee functioned well by coordinating its activities: emails and invitations to meetings, preparing the agenda, writing the minutes, etc. In addition, the central city housed all the meetings of the steering committee in its offices. The Coordinator of Leisure Activities, Culture and Community Life also made efforts to maintain the motivation of the members of the committee and to create new financing opportunities for the action plan.

In summary, leadership, that is the capacity to influence and to be followed by the members of the steering committee, is expressed by the hierarchical position and the authority of an actor on the other actors, but also by the respect and the trust which one actor inspires in the others.

Institutional Design

This category of Ansell and Gash's model discusses the rules and protocols employed in the process of collaboration (Ansell and Gash 2008). Our study of age-friendly cities demonstrates to what extent this category varies in its empirical application.

Above all, the Age-Friendly Cities program initiated by the Quebec government imposes a clear and structured process of collaborative governance. Participating municipalities know the possibilities and the limitations of the program in the creation of the steering committee and the elaboration of an action plan, as well as in its implantation. The steps of the process are well explained in a practical guide (*Guide d'accompagnement pour la réalisation de la démarche ville-amie des aînés au Quebec* (Équipe VADA Quebec, CSSS-IUGS & Carrefour action municipale et famille 2013).

This institutionalization attached to the Age-Friendly Cities program also can be contained within the rules and procedures of the municipality. Case B, because of its size, is a very good example. The municipality has, in addition to its council and executive committee, 16 directors of services and many committees. The manager of the municipality, who was responsible for the coordination of the Age-Friendly Cities process, is formally charged with the elaboration and the follow-up to many of the municipality's policies: healthy life habits policy, family policy, urban art policy, housing and social housing policy, universal access policy, and many others. Given this portrait which was incomparable with the other cases in the study, Case B was bureaucratized. The public documents about age-friendly cities are accessible: report on the public consultations with older adults, action plan, and even the annual review of the implantation of the action plan. This institutionalization of the process facilitates the observation of how the process evolved and of its collaborative governance. Nevertheless, bureaucratization clearly has its limits. The most frequently recurring examples in Case B were the obstacles encountered by the steering committee with the director of communications. Standardization of the public documents produced by the municipality required time and effort for the steering committee.

In contrast, it is possible to observe the creation of new formal procedures in order to harmonize the implementation of the action plan and also of collaborative governance. Thus, this stage of Age-Friendly Cities in Case A took place in the context of inter-municipal collaboration. This was not easy. Yet some obstacles in inter-municipal collaboration were observed, which were as much the result of lack of resources as they were of communication difficulties.

- In organizing leisure activities, the people responsible were unable to contact the municipality on the day of an activity in order to obtain access to the appointed space ("who has the keys to unlock the door [our translation]"), as well as to the material essential for the activity to function properly ("for a chair-based yoga activity, a municipality does not have chairs adapted to the activity [our translation]").
- In the case of a page reserved for older citizens in a regional journal, few municipalities transmitted texts to the journal because of poor communications ("no email address in the municipality [our translation]").
- In the case of a grant request, the coordinator of leisure services of the central city did not receive all the resolutions from the councils required for the request, and this despite the fact she had furnished a model of the letter needed.

During our study, members of the steering committee frequently expressed the need to better understand local ways of doing things, that is to say the procedures and functioning of each municipality, in order to implement common actions. In order to do this, a new functioning protocol between the municipalities and an up-to-date telephone register of resource persons and municipal officers were put in place by the steering committee. These protocols aimed at improving the efficacy of the implantation of actions foreseen by the age-friendly cities action plan, but they were, for the most part, unknown to or unrecognized by certain municipal officials, including elected representatives.

In summary, the institutionalization of the rules attached to the age-friendly city processes can increase the degree of municipal bureaucratization and of new formal and informal procedures created to improve the functioning of collaborative governance.

Collaborative Process and Conclusion

We conclude our text with the final category presented in the Ansell and Gash model. This category emphasizes the circular process inherent in collaborative governance. In fact, governance is viewed as a process which is not linear, but iterative (Ansell and Gash 2008). In this regard, the Age-Friendly Cities process is organized as a circular process (see figure 1) where ultimately, the municipalities can update their action plans (Équipe VADA Quebec, CSSS-IUGS & Carrefour action municipale et famille 2013).

According to Ansell and Gash, the collaborative process is composed of five variables: 1) face-to-face dialogue; 2) trust building; 3) commitment to the process; 4) share understanding; and 5) the intermediate outcomes (*Ibid.*). As we observed, many of these variables are found throughout the Age-Friendly Cities process in Quebec. Regular meetings of the steering committees permit both formal (e.g., working meetings) and informal (e.g., chatting during breaks) relationships to develop among the members. Shared understanding is reflected in the social diagnosis process, where its components offer an occasion to establish a portrait of the milieu and to seize the highest priority needs of older adults. In fact, it is not astonishing to see so many similarities between the Ansell and Gash model and the Age-Friendly Cities Program in Quebec. It is possible to trace a parallel between this model and the community building approach promoted by the Age-Friendly Cities Program (Garon *et al.* 2015). This approach refers, among other things, to the capacity to act on a collective basis, or, in the words of Leroux and Ninacs, community empowerment (Leroux and Ninacs 2002). It calls on the participation and mobilization of actors, on effective communication, on the competence of each actor and on the diversity of engagement. The last variable in the collaborative process, that is to say the intermediate outcomes, was little discussed in the present text. This is not to minimize its importance, for throughout the Age-Friendly Cities process it was possible to observe the perceptions of the members of steering committees with respect to short-term results as well as intermediate outcomes. From all evidence, obtaining a grant permitting the implantation of a specific project gave a major boost to the sentiment of success of the members of steering committees, but small successes and modest gains also feed the commitment and the motivation of actors. There are numerous examples: the printing of the action plan, more participants present than expected for the official launching of the action plan, positive feedback from the implantation of leisure activities, etc.

We can affirm, from our numerous examples and explanations, that the Ansell and Gash model constitutes a conceptual framework appropriate to understanding the complexity of the Age-Friendly Cities Program of the Government of Quebec. Our study, based on four cases of age-friendly cities, allows us to observe that collaborative governance is not only limited to the exigencies of the governmental Age-Friendly Cities Program. In effect, we were able to observe *ad hoc* collaborative interventions among members of steering committees in order to assist in the organization and lend support to activities outside the age-friendly cities plan, as well as to militate to conserve services judged essential for their milieu. For example, the announced transfer of the day centre of the Health and Social Services Centre in Case A, from the central city to a distant regional municipality, led to resistance by many members of the Age-Friendly Cities steering committee.

"The person responsible for the FADOQ explains that the mobilization (that is to say a petition of 1,750 names, pressure on the CSSS and on the MRC, as well as a meeting with the provincial member of the legislative assembly) had its effect. The CSSS accepted to lend the original location and the human resources for a so-called 'community' day centre. In fact, new partners were implicated, such as the Alzheimer Society. The mobilization resulted in saving the services of the day centre, for they will be carried out by community organizations [*our translation*]" (Case A, field notes, observation).

This example demonstrates the extent to which the steering committee of Age-Friendly Cities constitutes a form of collaborative governance intended for municipalities. It also creates occasions to reinforce the collective power of the milieu. To paraphrase Leroux and Ninacs, most of the case studies demonstrated "the capacity to link local resources together, to see them collaborate and to profit from the synergies this created [...] [*our translation*]" (Leroux and Ninacs 2002: 25), while allowing them to circulate information in their milieu and to reinforce the sense of belonging of members of the steering committee to their community.

References

Ansell, C. & A. Gash. 2008. "Collaborative Governance in Theory and Practice," *Journal of Public Administration Research and Theory*, *18*(4): 543-571.

Azeredo, A.C. & F.F. Payeur. 2015. *Vieillissement démographique au Quebec: Comparaison avec les pays de l'OCDE*. Quebec, QC: Institut de la statistique du Québec.

Butterfoss, F.D. 2007. *Coalitions and Partnerships in Community Health*. San Francisco, CA: John Wiley & Sons.

Équipe VADA Québec, CSSS-IUGS, & Carrefour action municipale et famille. 2013. *Guide d'accompagnement pour la réalisation de la démarche Municipalité amie des aînés*. Quebec, QC: Ministère de la Santé et des Services sociaux.

Fortier, F. & G. Hébert. 2015. *Quels seront les impacts du vieillissement de la population*. Montréal, QC: Institut de recherche et d'informations socio-économiques (IRIS).

Garon, S., M. Paris, M. Beaulieu, A. Veil, & A. Laliberté. 2014. "Collaborative Partnership in Age-Friendly Cities: Two Case Studies from Quebec, Canada," *Journal of Aging & Social Policy*, 26(1-2): 73-87.

Garon, S., M. Paris, A. Veil, M. Beaulieu, & A. Laliberté. 2015. "Villes amies des aînés au Quebec," in J.-P. Viriot Durandal, É. Raymond, T. Moulaert, & M. Charpentier (eds.). *Droits de vieillir et citoyenneté des aînés*. Quebec, QC: Presses de l'Université du Québec, p. 183-205.

Garon, S., M. Paris, A. Laliberté, & A. Veil. 2016. "Age-Friendly City in Quebec (Canada), or 'Alone it goes faster, together it goes further'," in F.G. Caro & K.G. Fitzgerald (eds.). *International Perspectives on Age-Friendly Cities*. New York, NY: Routledge, p. 119-133.

Garon, S., A. Veil, M. Paris, & S. Rémillard-Boilard. 2016. "How can a research program enhance a policy? AFC-Quebec governance and evaluation opportunities," in T. Moulaert, S. Garon, (eds.). *Age-Friendly Cities in Comparative Perspective: Political Lessons, Scientific Avenues, and Democratic Issues*. New York, NY: Springer, p. 99-120.

Gouvernement du Québec. 2012. *Programme de soutien à la démarche MADA*. Quebec, QC: Secrétariat de la famille et des aînés.

ISQ. 2016. *Le bilan démographique du Québec*. Quebec, QC: Institut de la statistique du Québec.

Klein, J.-L., J.-M. Fontan, D. Harrison, & B. Lévesque. 2009. "L'innovation sociale au Quebec : Un système d'innovation fondé sur la concertation," *Les Cahiers du CRISES*, (ET0907).

Leroux, R., & W.A. Ninacs. 2002. *La santé des communautés : perspectives pour la contribution de la santé publique au développement social et au développement des communautés.* Quebec, QC: Institut national de la santé publique du Québec.

Mattessich, P.W., M. Murray-Close, B.R. Monsey, & Wilder Research Center. 2001. *Collaboration: What Makes it Work.* Saint Paul, MN: Amherst H. Wilder Foundation.

Ministère de la Famille et des Aînés. 2008. *Rapport de la consultation publique sur les conditions de vie des aînés : Préparons l'avenir avec nos aînés.* Quebec, QC: Gouvernement du Québec, http://www.mfa. gouv.qc.ca/fr/publication/Documents/rapport_consultation_ aines.pdf [Accessed May 10, 2018].

Mintzberg, H. 1994. *Rise and Fall of Strategic Planning.* New York, NY: Free Press.

Moulaert, T. & S. Garon. 2015. "Researchers Behind Policy Development: Comparing 'Age-Friendly Cities' Models in Quebec and Wallonia," *Journal of Social Work Practice,* 29(1): 23-35.

Moulaert, T. & S. Garon. 2016. *Age-Friendly Cities and Communities in International Comparison.* New York, NY: Springer.

Paris, M., S. Garon & M. Beaulieu. 2012. "Le projet 'Villes-amies des aînés au Quebec'," *Politiques sociales,* 71(1 & 2): 91-100.

Patton, M.Q. 2011. *Developmental Evaluation: Applying Complexity Concepts to Enhance Innovation and Use.* New York, NY: Guilford Press.

Pawson, R. & N. Tilley. 1997. *Realistic Evaluation.* Thousand Oaks, CA: Sage.

Payeur, F.F. 2012. "Espérance de vie et vieillissement démographique au Quebec : Quels scénarios possible?" *Données sociodémographiques en bref,* 17(1): 1-4.

Potvin, L., M.-J. Moquet, & C.M. Jones (eds.). 2010. *Réduire les inégalités sociales en santé*. Saint-Denis, FR: INPES.

Provan, K.G., M.A. Veazie, L.K. Staten, & N.I. Teufel-Shone. 2005. "The use of network analysis to strengthen community partnerships," *Public Administration Review*, 65(5): 603-613.

Rey-Valette, H., M. Pinto, P. Maurel, E. Chia, P-Y. Guihéneuf, L. Michel, B. Nougarèdes, C. Soulard, *et al.* 2011. *Guide pour la mise en oeuvre de la gouvernance en appui au développement durable des territoires*. Montpellier, FR: Cemagref, CNRS, Geyser, Inra, Supagro, Université Montpellier.

Statistics Canada. 2017. *Chiffres selon l'âge et le sexe, et selon le type de logement : Faits saillants du Recensement de 2016* (Le Quotidien). Ottawa, ON: Statistics Canada.

UN. 2002. *Madrid International Plan of Action on Ageing*. New York, NY: United Nations, www.monitoringris.org/documents/norm_glob/mipaa_french.pdf [Accessed May 10, 2018].

Vaillancourt, Y. 2017. *Marges de manoeuvre des acteurs locaux de développement social en contexte d'austérité*. Gatineau, QC: Chaire de recherche du Canada en organisation communautaire.

WHO. 2007. *Global Age-friendly Cities: A Guide*. Geneva, CH: World Health Organization. [Accessed May 2018].

WHO. 2011. *Closing the Gap: Policy Practice on Social Determinants of Health*. Rio de Janeiro: World Health Organization. [Accessed on May 2018]. http://www.who.int/sdhconference/Discussion-paper-EN.pdf

WHO. 2017. WHO Global Network for Age-friendly Cities and Communities, https://extranet.who.int/agefriendlyworld/ [Accessed May 10, 2018].

Yin, R.K. 2009. *Case Study Research: Design and Methods*. Thousand Oaks, CA: Sage.

CHAPTER 5

Stronger Together:
First Nations Community/Municipality Collaborations

By Wanda Wuttunee

"My experience is that it takes time, patience and resilience to build successful partnerships; as municipalities we have a lot to offer and more to receive."
– Vicki Blanchard, Economic Development Manager,
Municipality of Sioux Lookout, ON[1]

Introduction

Partnerships work well when each partner brings something to the table and is committed to the success of the project. Sometimes history, distance, or other obstacles effectively remove any thought of working together and achieving mutual benefits. First Nations communities are struggling for the most part, in the areas that promote well-being and form the basis for a vigorous economic profile. Physical, mental, emotional and spiritual health are often taxed to the limit. Individuals are often not healthy, which impacts family, community and ultimately the ability to engage in work successfully. The *Indian Act*, residential schools, poverty and corollaries of suicide, drugs and gangs have a long legacy that continues to negatively impact communities today. To be accurate, there are some First Nations communities that are bright economic lights across the country for supporting

[1] FCM. *Building First Nations-Municipal Community Economic Development Partnerships*, www.fcm.ca/Documents/reports/CEDI/cedi-tkag-en-screen.pdf [Accessed May 11, 2018].

their citizens and benefiting surrounding communities.[2] Examples include Westbank First Nation, BC; Osoyoos Indian Band, BC; Membertou First Nation, NS and Lac La Ronge Indian Band, SK.

The recent National Truth and Reconciliation Commission's Calls to Action recognize municipalities specifically as essential to successful reconciliation with Indigenous peoples. Eight recommendations focus on "all levels of government," and five refer to municipal governments. "The context for working together is positive and encouraging with a means to set the stage for collaboration discussions. Most of the Calls to Action require federal, provincial and territorial government leadership, and municipal governments to roll up their sleeves to support reconciliation as a national challenge that is felt deeply at the local level."[3]

Communities have been reaching out to their neighbours to explore potential partnerships when doors are open and attitudes are positive. The Federation of Canadian Municipalities (FCM) built on their own history to develop a program that supports First Nations communities and neighboring municipalities in developing collaborations. They partnered with the Council for the Advancement of Native Development Officers (Cando) in the Community Economic Development Initiative (CEDI). FCM has a 2000 municipality membership base while Cando has a broad membership of more than 500 Indigenous economic development officers, economic organizations and academics interested in all aspects of Indigenous community economic development.

In reflecting on FCM's history, FCM's CEDI Program Manager Helen Patterson, identified a long history of interest in First Nations government with their neighbours. A joint workshop in 2004 with Indigenous organizations and FCM members on Indigenous land management sparked interest in other topics such as identifying points of collaboration in service agreements with Indigenous participants, and provincial and federal governments. In 2012, CEDI was developed as a result of an FCM/Cando survey that prioritized joint economic development

[2] Assembly of First Nations Make Poverty History Expert Advisory Committee. 2009. *The state of the First Nation economy and the struggle to make poverty history.* Ottawa, ON: Assembly of Manitoba Chiefs, p. 6.

[3] FCM. 2016. Pathways to reconciliation: Cities respond to the Truth and Reconciliation Commission Calls to Action: p. 3, www.fcm.ca/Documents/tools/BCMC/Pathways_to_reconciliation_EN.pdf [Accessed May 11, 2018].

initiatives. A foundational precept for success is the FCM/Cando approach through CEDI that "acknowledges the importance of history, culture and relationship building before anyone can start doing business transactions," according to Patterson.[4]

CEDI offers an opportunity to bridge the divide that often exists between a First Nations community and a neighbouring municipality. A venue is offered where the two groups come together, lines of communication are open and a partnership can be nurtured. Patterson described a situation where the City of North Battleford, SK, and Battleford's Agency Tribal Chiefs had to deal with the impact of a tragic death of a local young man as they tried to build a partnership. Despite the situation, Chief Lori Whitecalf, Sweet Grass Reserve, SK, brought forward the idea to do a 'blanket exercise' to bring the two councils closer together. It involved members of the First Nations sharing their history and painful personal stories in a circle with both groups. With the assistance of an elder and two Indigenous youth facilitators from Canadian Roots Exchange, meaningful conversation and educating occurred that is setting the basis for a solid relationship and partnership.[5]

The six partner collaborations for CEDI Phase One were geographically diverse and demonstrated a likelihood that they would have a successful collaboration. They are enumerated below. Two collaborations will be explored more thoroughly in the next sections of this paper from the perspectives of two project champions per collaboration. An evaluation report on CEDI Phase One offers useful insights into all the experiences and will inform the summary for this paper.

Phase one – CEDI collaborations

Seabird Island Band and District of Kent, BC

Ten minutes separate these two communities in BC's Fraser Valley that came together in 2009 at a Union of BC Municipalities meeting. The result was a Memorandum of Understanding that acknowledged a willingness to work together. CEDI was the next step in developing this relationship. Top priorities for this partnership include a river management strategy, a new salmon hatchery, regional strategy to bring new investors and

---

[4] Patterson, Helen. 2017, personal communication, May 18.
[5] *Ibid.*

build tourism and improve emergency access for those using logging roads.

"We are collectively the largest landowners in the Fraser Valley and our lands are well situated near critical infrastructure required for development and transport. Now more than ever in history is an opportune time for partnerships between First Nations and the business community to flourish. Business relationships built on honesty, trust and respect will enrich our community and your organization," Chief Clem Seymour, Seabird Island band.[6]

Sawridge First Nation, Town of Slave Lake and
Municipal District of Lesser Slave River, AB

After a 2011 forest fire ravaged the Town of Slave Lake, these three partners came together to rebuild what had been lost. A Tri-Council was formed and a Friendship Accord signed to mark the important relationship. Planning meetings[7] determined that priorities were housing, joint land development, business development, including improved employment and labour opportunities with a focus on tourism development. Relationship-building workshops took place, a regional growth strategy was developed, a joint tourism officer was hired, followed by a family canoe trip with the leaders and their families to shape stronger relationships.[8]

Kebaowek (formerly Eagle Village) First Nation, Town of Témiscaming,
and Municipality of Kipawa, QC

The over-riding priority for these communities is tourism development, highlighting the natural beauty of the region. It

[6] FCM. 2016. *Seabird Island Band and District of Kent, First Nations-Municipal Community Economic Development Initiative*, www.fcm.ca/home/programs/community-economic-development-initiative/participating-communities/british-columbia.htm [Accessed May 15, 2018].

[7] Town of Slave Lake, Sawridge and Lesser Slave River. 2012. *Slave Lake Regional Tri-Council Economic Development Strategic Plan: 2012-2015*, www.fcm.ca/Documents/reports/CEDI/Tri_council_economic_development_strategic_plan_EN.pdf [Accessed May 14, 2018].

[8] FCM. 2016. *First Nations-Municipal Community Economic Development Initiative*. Sawridge First Nation, Town of Slave Lake and Municipal District of Lesser Slave River, AB: https://fcm.ca/home/programs/community-economic-development-initiative/participating-communities/participating-communities-2013-2016.htm [Accessed May 14, 2018].

is a natural fit for their economic development departments to coordinate these efforts, which is recognized with a Friendship Accord. Trips to neighbouring communities to learn how they approached tourism opportunities included a Chamber of Commerce and a local park as well as a First Nations community and the local national park. They were well-informed to prepare themselves to be the gateway to a new provincial park "Opemican" in their region. Over the last three years relationship building and joint planning has built trust and resulted in a joint-tourism strategy. While the journey has brought trials and satisfaction, they have stuck with it and each partner knows more about the other partners, which has built a strong foundation for collaboration.[9]

Madawaska Maliseet First Nation and City of Edmundston, NB

With a history of little contact, the community of Madawaska (134 on-reserve, 116 off-reserve) and the city of Edmundston (22,000 pop.) came together for the CEDI needs assessment in 2013. They discovered shared interests – which they shared by educating local residents and businesses – that included ratification in a Friendship Accord. "Today we are meeting to begin discussing our shared vision for the future and how to plan for it. This is the first time in history that we have done so together," says Richard Lang of the Madawaska Maliseet Economic Development Corporation. Their long-term strategy is to preserve their distinct Acadian and Maliseet identities and cultures through promotion of local business and unique business culture, drawing in new businesses and investors and enhancing regional tourism and branding.[10]

LSFN First Nation (LSFN), Municipality of Sioux Lookout and Kichenuhmaykoosib Inninuwug (KI) Collaboration, ON

When FCM suggested a partnership, LSFN Elder Garnet Angeconeb said, "This feels like you are asking us to get married. This is only our first date."

---

[9] FCM. 2017. *First Nations Municipal Updates* (June).

[10] FCM. 2016. *First Nations-Municipal Community Economic Development Initiative.* Madawaska Maliseet First Nation and City of Edmundston, NB: www.fcm.ca/ home/programs/community-economic-development-initiative/participating-communities/new-brunswick.htm [Accessed May 14, 2018].

Starting conditions

A collaborative attitude beginning with a Friendship Agreement between LSFN First Nation (LSFN), Slate Lake and Sioux Lookout was codified five years later in a Friendship Accord in 2012. LSFN lies 40 kilometres from Sioux Lookout and is home to 860 citizens with 2,500 living off reserve.[11] As with many Indigenous communities, LSFN must deal with social disintegration that manifests as loss of culture, substance abuse, mental health issues, suicide, family breakdown, unemployment, crime and physical/sexual abuse.[12] Their strategy is to achieve social recovery that embraces their culture and traditions, creating a healthy, resilient community. This context offers a wider view of some Indigenous community issues that often fit into the rubric of economic development.

In discussions leading to the Friendship Accord, the issue of racism was raised by Chief Clifford Bull, LSFN and the question was how each partner could work together to deal with it in a good way. He noted, "We're all Canadians, we all live in the same country and we all have to live and work together."[13]

Sioux Lookout, a municipality of 5,000 people, is described as the Hub of the North with connections to healthcare and essential services for 31 remote Indigenous communities.[14] It is important to have strong relationships as their main industry is supplying goods and services to the communities in their region. On the topic of racism, Vicki Blanchard, Economic Development Manager for Sioux Lookout, notes that an anti-racism committee has been in existence for many years. In her opinion, while some people have racism embedded in them through generations, more than 70 percent of their population is Indigenous. "It is important to remember that we have no tragic events similar to those faced by other communities in Canada and, because we are the hub of services for the communities, many members feel

[11] Lac Seul First Nation. 2017. *Lac Seul First Nation.* Lac Seul First Nation, ON: http://lacseul.firstnation.ca/ [Accessed May 14, 2018].

[12] Lac Seul First Nation. 2017. *Social Recovery Strategy.* Lac Seul First Nation, ON: http://lacseul.firstnation.ca/node/86 [Accessed May 14, 2018].

[13] Quequish, C. 2015. "Friendship agreement brings communities together in respect," *Wawatay News,* p. 1. www.wawataynews.ca/home/friendship-agreement-brings-communities-together-respect [Accessed May 14, 2018].

[14] Sioux Lookout Hub of the North. 2014. *About Sioux Lookout,* www.siouxlookout.ca/en/living-here/about-sioux-lookout.asp [Accessed May 14, 2018].

welcomed as they often visit other family members who live in Sioux Lookout."[15]

The municipality of Sioux Lookout and the First Nations communities of Slate Falls and LSFN determined that formally recognizing key relationships was important to working together for the future of their communities. The Sioux Lookout Friendship Accord recognizes that the municipality's planning process includes First Nations leaders and communities and "honours our ancestors, traditions and the spirit of Sioux Lookout which first drew First Nations people together. We acknowledge and honour the long history of service to the community that continues to be embodied by the Municipality of Sioux Lookout and its employees."[16]

Further it acknowledges traditions and spirit needed to nurture a respectful and lasting relationship between the municipality and First Nations communities. Values of "honesty, respect, mutual sharing and contribution"[17] are the basis for good relationships on all levels and are marked by "accountability, transparency, inclusiveness, responsiveness and shared stewardship."[18]

The Friendship Accord is a framework for constructing agreements and addressing protocols for improved communication, acknowledging First Nations government, focusing on regional leadership, health, education and offering investment opportunities and increased participation for First Nations communities in Sioux Lookout. Blanchard uses these guiding principles in the way she conducts business dealings every day. It sets a protocol of respect that underscores her business with Indigenous communities and partners. Projects flow through her office so she regularly approaches partner communities with opportunities to participate.

LSFN was particularly interested in the Friendship Accord according to Sam Manitowabi LSFN's Director of Employment and Training,[19] as they had not been able to garner support in

[15] Blanchard, Vicki. 2017, personal communication, June 20.

[16] *Sioux Lookout Friendship Accord*. 2012. www.siouxlookout.ca/en/your-local-government/resources/Friendship-Accord,-signed-copy.pdf [Accessed May 14, 2018].

[17] *Ibid*.

[18] *Ibid*.

[19] Manitowabi, Sam. 2017, personal communication, June 9.

Sioux Lookout for an urban reserve or economic development zone. The municipality's leadership was supportive and organized open houses. The negative comments from community members were based on a lack of understanding of the shared benefits such a project would bring. Some of Sioux Lookout's citizens made comments that they didn't want reserve housing with broken windows in their town nor did they want drunk people hanging around. With that experience in mind, the timing was right to reach out to build a stronger and positive relationship. KI was interested in joining the Accord as they looked for ways to reduce all costs, including food costs, and build their community. They also took the lead in applying to be part of CEDI in 2013, on their own, with LSFN and Sioux Lookout eventually becoming partners too.

Institutional design

Each of the partners to CEDI brought an interest in drawing on each other's strengths to benefit their own communities. Sioux Lookout plays a central role in the region as providing needed goods and services for Indigenous communities is their leading industry, while LSFN and Kitchenuhmaykoosib Inninuwug (KI) want to improve their communities economically and socially with opportunities that could not be accomplished without partners committed to developing the region. LSFN brings business sensitivity resulting from work on forestry, hydro dams and impact benefit agreements from resource development while KI brings the knowledge of living on the land, traditions and needs arising from isolation.

After the CEDI partners of LSFN, Sioux Lookout and KI, completed a needs assessment, the partnership focused on a food distribution centre that would decrease the cost of shipping food to the North. All partners agreed that it should go to a consulting firm to assess the feasibility of such an undertaking. The report set out project costs that were beyond the abilities of the collaboration. A new building would be built at the airport but leasing costs and taxes were very expensive.

While LSFN has withdrawn from the project, KI and Sioux Lookout are working to put a much larger partnership together. New partners include Health Canada, the Ministry of Health and Long Term Care and universities of Toronto, Guelph and Lakehead. It is a labour of love according to Blanchard as it is a social enterprise that will not bring in a lot of revenue but will give northern communities needed support. This includes northern entrepreneurs who want to buy bulk and then sell the food in their communities. Blanchard shared projections of 40 percent savings based on full planes to the north.

Their competitor is Northwest Company who rejected an offer to partner on this project, according to Blanchard but instead Northwest Company announced a similar project with a newly purchased small airline. Blanchard suggests that part of their project will require ground transportation, which is a potential opportunity for LSFN who want to grow that business. This move is indicative of respect and a healthy partnership where differences in goals are recognized so a partner can withdraw participation with other project possibilities still open to all the partners.

Other projects under discussion by the CEDI working committee include a medicinal marijuana factory and important issues involving food security. There is a familiarity with each partner's needs and wants with meetings characterized by camaraderie, open, respectful discussions, interspersed with humour leading to decisions based on consensus. This respectful and trusting environment allows for tough discussions that might not have been broached or settled in different circumstances.

It is clear that the benefits of investing in relationships outweigh the costs. As players change on the committee, the Friendship Accord is the anchor that brings new people up to speed on the vision and guiding principles. There have been several changes in leadership that continue to support the Accord and partnership.

Collaborative process

The Friendship Accord offers a context for understanding why community leadership embraced the CEDI partnership opportunity. An attitude of trust favouring partnership had been set in the Friendship Agreement that preceded the Accord. In 2013, Cat Lake First Nation joined the Accord followed by Kitchenuhmaykoosib Inninuwug (KI) in 2014 with a trust-building process characterized by participating in meetings for several years by invitation. Ideally, all the northern communities will join the Accord in the future, according to Manitowabi.[20]

[20] Manitowabi, Sam. 2017, personal communication, June 9.

Further, a Shared Territory Protocol (STP) between LSFN, Cat Lake and Slate Falls, signed in 2017, brings these communities together as potential gold deposits are explored in their area. Decision protocols outlined in the STP will strengthen the process of project development and benefit distribution for affected communities.[21]

Newly elected Mayor, Lawrance of Sioux Lookout, is working with his Chief Administrative Officer and Blanchard, to breathe new life into the Friendship Accord by organizing regular meetings and bringing partners to the table. A new First Nations Economic Development Office allows KI and LSFN to use desk space when they come to town. There is now meeting space available that underlines Sioux Lookout's effort to offer infrastructure and a welcoming atmosphere as part of the collaboration.

Sioux Lookout took the positive and bold step of declaring 2017 the Year of Reconciliation after the Calls to Action from the Truth and Reconciliation Commission focusing on municipalities. A series of events to raise awareness have been undertaken, including an animated film entitled *The Secret Path*, based on the life and death of a 12-year old boy, Chanie Wenjack, who died after he ran away from a residential school in Ontario. The topic brings hard questions forward which allows community members to go beyond a superficial, feel-good experience. Manitowabi recalls that when asked by a Sioux Lookout committee as to how LSFN citizens could be made to feel more welcome in their community, a request was made and acquiesced to that the local *Sioux Bulletin* refrain from printing a column called "Courts and Briefs" that named individuals who were in court. A large majority were Indigenous names which did not leave positive feelings. These small gestures are indicative of a shift in the paradigm that could be very meaningful to all concerned.

What further impacts have blossomed from the collaboration and investment in relationships? There are a number of promising projects and events that continue to reinforce relationships and build new ones. Reaching out to communities has value so Sioux Lookout has reached out to the township of Pickle Lake and, according to Blanchard, is providing opportunity and support

[21] Aiken, M. 2017. "Sioux Lookout expands Friendship Accord," *Kenora Online* (March 4): www.kenoraonline.com/local/sioux-lookout-expands-friendship-accord [Accessed May 14, 2018].

by involving them with the Shared Territory Protocol, framework agreements with mining corporations and First Nations. Sioux Lookout is the facilitator in the process and Blanchard is the 'glue-stick' interested in assisting in capacity building.

An annual regional mayor/chief gathering is held in LSFN each fall. Manitowabi notes that it is a great opportunity for chiefs to sit down with mayors for the first time or to renew acquaintances at a neutral gathering with no agenda. Questions can be asked without repercussion which increases comfort levels over time. Making a space for these things to happen is very rewarding for all participants.

When communities come forward that say they want to know the best way to create a Friendship Accord, Blanchard advises that they begin by mapping their history, recognizing and owning it. Next, present it to the other communities and that will escalate the next conversation to where the relationship building begins. Blanchard observes that the government is now encouraging a regional lens and the old way of working one-on-one doesn't work anymore with so much to do. Essential to success is having someone in the municipality that can facilitate, understand and build on those relationships with the strong support of the mayor and CAO or no progress will occur.

The Calls to Action under the Truth and Reconciliation Commission are another reason to consider the role of collaborations. Blanchard notes that Sioux Lookout has formed a Truth and Reconciliation Committee that took the Calls to Action focusing on municipalities and broke them down into pillars such as economic streams, health and education streams etc. They are being studied and committees are tasked to carry out sections of the work. This effort supports the overarching Friendship Accord, with the CEDI project acting as a springboard to relationship building and business activity. The Shared Territories Protocol is more regionally inclusive and the exploration framework agreement will guide all resource development. Truth and Reconciliation efforts will be one of many underlying influences.

Facilitative leadership

Leader perspectives on collaboration are captured in the following quotations, with similar sentiments echoed in the Ontario partnerships examined thus far as well as the Manitoba partnership that is examined in the next section:

"With a representation of First Nations and municipal governments, you have a stronger voice at Queen's Park, at the federal buildings in Ottawa, and you're apt to be listened to more." – Chief Clifford Bull, LSFN First Nation, ON[22]

"You're trying to keep score all the time and you can't do that... Everything we do as an individual project is not going to benefit us all equally – it never will. And if we're trying to do that, we'll never get anything done. But collectively as a whole, all those projects can be a benefit for all of us." – Mayor Tyler Warman, Town of Slave Lake[23]

"Muster your courage; take that leap of faith. The other levels of government aren't actually the enemy – they can become your best allies." – Chief Roland Twinn, Saw Ridge First Nation[24]

"We didn't just learn to work together, we became friends, and that's what was missing before." – Reeve Murray Kerik, M.D. of Lesser Slave Lake

"This project is more than a feasibility study. It is a coming together of our Municipality and regional First Nations to work on an initiative of mutual interest with support from Cando and the FCM. We look forward to working on this project and it is our hope to work on many more initiatives such as this." – Mayor Doug Lawrance, Municipality of Sioux Lookout[25]

Community champions are Manitowabi, Brian King in LSFN, Bruce Sakakeep in KI and Blanchard in Sioux Lookout and have been part of the process from the beginning, forming the core group. This is a critical element for success; but, in addition, they have the respect of the chiefs who are all respectful of the staff. The core brings stability and brings an understanding of relationship building for new partners. Blanchard's passion for

[22] Cando. 2017. *CEDI First Nations – Municipal Community Economic Development Initiative*, www.edo.ca/cedi [Accessed May 14, 2018].

[23] FCM. 2016. *First Nations-Municipal Community Economic Development Initiative*. Sawridge First Nation, Town of Slave Lake and Municipal District of Lesser Slave River, AB: www.fcm.ca/home/programs/community-economic-development-initiative/participating-communities/alberta.htm [Accessed May 14, 2018].

[24] *Ibid*.

[25] FCM. 2016. *First Nations-Municipal Community Economic Development Initiative*. Lac Seul First Nation, Municipality of Sioux Lookout, and Kitchenuhmaykoosib Inninuwug, ON: www.fcm.ca/home/programs/community-economic-development-initiative/participating-communities/ontario.htm [Accessed May 14, 2018].

the success of these partnerships leads her to "live it, eat it and drink it every day." She acknowledges that gratitude is regularly expressed for her efforts at all levels.

Sioux Lookout's commitment is extraordinary in offering the needed funding and infrastructure to enable partnerships to move forward. Blanchard provides funds for all meeting travel by leveraging CEDI funds of $5,000, for example, into a large enough portfolio that allows communication with northern communities. When the first meeting brought the KI leader and staff, that cost the first $5,000. Blanchard applies for funding that includes taking partner members to an annual Prospectors and Developers Association of Canada meeting, which is the largest mining conference in the world. Nine members went last year and 12 attended this year's conference. Blanchard manages the funds and completes the conference expense reports.

Blanchard states that their municipality is the only municipality with the ability to make funding applications for the collaboration because the province of Ontario recognizes the Friendship Accord as a treaty. A Shared Territory agreement between LSFN, Cat Lake and Slate Falls now means they have one territory with one trap line and can move about it without asking permission. They all come to the table to make large decisions about resource development. Mining companies all come through Blanchard's office so she completes all the travel arrangements for the Shared Territory protocol members, sends one bill to the mining company and then she reimburses the communities. The first exploration framework agreement will be signed in July with the First Nations Mining Corporation. She works at setting other meetings up for the Chiefs in addition to their meetings with First Nations Mining Corporation that covers the cost of travel and makes good use of the First Nation leaders' time.

Opaskwayak Cree Nation (OCN), town of The Pas and Rural Municipality of Kelsey, Manitoba

Starting conditions

These communities have come together despite a history of independence and some animosity. On behalf of The Pas, a community of 5,500 people, a municipal employee took up FCM's offer of applying to be part of CEDI. They then were required to have surrounding communities send letters of support to the application. Both OCN (3,198 on-reserve and 2,099 off-reserve) and the RM of Kelsey (2,272 pop.) determined that it was a great opportunity with possibilities of mutual benefit. The Pas and OCN play roles in meeting the needs of communities in the northern region. Recent struggles have resulted from the closure of Tolko's paper and lumber mill, the IGA store and the possibility of other business closures. The Pas is land-locked with the RM and OCN on three sides; as well, OCN is across the river, so if The Pas wants to expand, they must work with both partners.

The CEDI process brought a brainstorm of ideas to the table that were narrowed to ways to attract investors and joint strategies to attend to infrastructure issues. Without a clearly framed relationship, the brainstorming process got bogged down. A suggestion was made to consider a Friendship Accord which was agreed to and was eventually signed in 2014 by the parties. The Accord's (*Three Communities, One Heart*) key terms include a desire to strengthen the social, spiritual and economic ties that support mutual respect of interests that are beneficial to all communities, including the signatories and neighbours. This agreement acknowledges government to government relations, where wisdom can be shared for a better future for children and grandchildren. It also commits to building mutual trust and respect while acknowledging their history, past experiences and differences that impact current perspectives and opinions. These communities agree to come together twice a year for open dialogue and to agree on priorities.

OCN member and Special Projects officer, Paskwayak Business Development Corporation, Duncan Lathlin,[26] calls the Friendship Accord a strong foundation in the partnership that opened needed dialogue. Town councillor, Brian Roque, notes "There has always been a need to help each other but bad feelings from the past, got in the way," but the Friendship Accord turned the page and allowed each partner to move forward.[27] Lathlin points out that the OCN and The Pas high schools studied their community Friendship Accord and then created their own Friendship Accord that was signed by students in both communities as they met on a symbolic walk to the middle of the

[26] Lathlin, Duncan. 2017, personal communication, June 9.
[27] Roque, Brian. 2017, personal communication, June 9.

bridge that divides the two communities.[28] They are developing relationships through joint activities and as future leaders this step is remarkable. This is also very exciting for the town, according to Roque.[29] A recent Reeve report shed some light on the shifting young family demographics where an equal number live in The Pas and work in OCN and vice versa. This ties the two communities together in a newly recognized way. Roque concludes that the Friendship Accord is moving forward, but not in the ways that everyone might have expected.[30]

Institutional design

The collaborative attitude launched quarterly meetings under the purview of a Tri-Council in 2015. The Tri-Council's main CEDI-supported projects were an investor-focused brochure and website. At the Tri-Council launch of these efforts, Town Counselor Brian Roque[31] noted, "It has been a learning process, but I found it exciting and have enjoyed the networking and the connections I've made with other participants. You learn more about them and how they feel. There is a positive energy here. Tonight is called a launch because it's just a beginning. Now, with what we learned today, we can move forward and continue on with the process. The ultimate goal is let's make a better community; let the Tri-Council region become stronger because of working together and sharing our resources and situations."

Duncan Lathlin[32] shared further benefits from the collaboration. He characterized the initial relationship with The Pas and the RM as neighbourly from a distance and one where you really didn't know each other well. That has been improved from feeling like OCN was operating in a 'bubble,' as described by Lathlin, to one where they knew more about the way their neighbours did business, their organizational structure and their operating environment. Despite the differences, the partnership has greatly expanded what OCN factors into decision making that might impact one or the other of their partners. For example, if they have a large project, they will ask questions around the capacity of The Pas to handle the

[28] Lathlin, Duncan. 2017, personal communication, June 9.
[29] Roque, Brian. 2017, personal communication, June 9.
[30] *Ibid.*
[31] 2016. "Tri-Council.ca Launched," *Opaskwayak Times* (April 1): p 1.
[32] Lathlin, Duncan. 2017, personal communication, June 9.

project and are prepared to help improve needed changes to the infrastructure.

Unfortunately the change in economic climate, referred to earlier, made some of their efforts obsolete. The brochures were archived and the website removed. There is an example of a communication issue around the website at the time of these interviews. Lathlin[33] said that an agreement existed where OCN was to pay for the website in the first year which was honoured, The Pas was to bear the financial costs in the second year and the RM agreed to carry the costs in the third year. Unfortunately, OCN does not know why the website was not continued after the first year as there has not been any communication with The Pas on this decision. Lathlin[34] hypothesizes that the reason might include recent economic impacts with the mill and other businesses closing.

The lack of communication about the website will not impact Lathlin's "to do list" which includes a call to the appropriate person at The Pas. In the past, this lack of communication could be chalked up to something potentially more detrimental, but the strength of the relationship keeps the doors of communication open.[35] According to Roque, another example of the collaboration having impact is on the way they do business. For example, The Pas' community development corporation (CDC), which focuses on municipal business, was resurrected but didn't stop there. Discussions are occurring with an eye to ways to bring OCN to broaden the scope of CDC's work.[36]

The Tri-Council identified a landfill as a critical project as the landfills in the area aged out and alternatives that were up to code were needed. When the partners discussed the mutual issue, it was determined that OCN had an appropriate parcel of land that would be the best option for a regional landfill and that expanded the area of concern to approximately 20 other communities. Roque outlines the steep learning curves that occur.[37] He points to relationships with other governments, including the federal government relationship with OCN and the municipal government relationship with the provincial

[33] *Ibid.*

[34] *Ibid.*

[35] *Ibid.*

[36] Roque, Brian. 2017, personal communication, June 9.

[37] *Ibid.*

government. For this project, that means OCN can work with the federal government and the town will work with the provincial government so that a master plan is developed that works most effectively for all involved.

Collaborative process

The Tri-Council meetings are attended by general managers from each community where relevant issues are discussed and recommendations passed to the leadership. Once a consensus is reached, then recommendations are ratified by the respective leadership. If there are such things as bylaws or government permits involved, then the leadership makes final decisions. Lathlin reveals that each person's commitment is strong in doing the best they could and "what we got out of it was a really great relationship."[38] A leadership approach that is most effective, according to Roque, is to listen. While it is easy to talk about one's own issues, it is more valuable to listen to what the other person wants first. The partnership is strengthened as independent decisions disappear in situations that are more suited to the collaboration. As the relationships are strengthened, identifying where overlaps occur will be streamlined.

An important part of the relationship is the RM of Kelsey. OCN now has a more complete idea of where mutual interests lie. They thought that the RM was only involved in agriculture that occurred on land that was quite removed from OCN. They were surprised to find out that the RM owns land close to OCN. They are now working on coordinating commercial development on contiguous land that each was developing separately until the partnership opened up discussions. Lathlin notes "We have similar goals that we had no idea of before." [39]

Facilitative leadership

Lathlin[40] states that change in leadership does impact the success of the Tri-Council. A challenge to the collaboration's health, is how new leaders are brought up to speed on the partnership. Some perceptions of change in leadership, for example, occurred when an eager champion that connected well with the partners changed to a new leader who has a more "hands off" style. This is

[38] Lathlin, Duncan. 2017, personal communication, June 9.
[39] *Ibid.*
[40] *Ibid.*

not a deal breaker so long as the lines of communication are open. There are always pressures that are hidden to outsiders and as Lathlin states, "Because we are friendly, doesn't mean that I can poke my nose in their business."[41]

Roque adds that changes in leadership do not stop the momentum because each partner has goals to accomplish that drive the process. The different methods of communication can cause issues when setting meetings. For example, if an effort to schedule a meeting is not successful because there was no response to the email invitation, Roque states "call me old-fashioned but there is such a thing called the telephone. Problems occur when assumptions are made that others prefer to do things the same way that I do. It is better to realize that some people might do things a little differently."[42]

Both Lathlin and Roque are collaboration champions. They work hard to inspire others and bring their experience to the table to help the Tri-Council move forward. Roque thought a meet and greet after the new chief of OCN was recently elected made sense. He organized it himself despite the inability to set Tri-Council meetings successfully. Fifteen out of 22 leaders showed up across the three partnerships. The new chief met the mayor and many useful contacts were made for the benefit of all concerned.[43]

At OCN, Lathlin and another employee were enthusiastic and passionate about building relationships so they modeled their behaviour to others in various departments. As the value became clear, this was picked up so that now it is a common means of doing business and people feel comfortable to include the town in the process. This is done independently without leadership having to give directions.[44]

According to Lathlin and Roque, the collaboration future looks promising as it can only improve, grow and become stronger. The inevitable shift as young people step into leadership roles will require space for the wisdom of the experienced, older citizens who have much to offer. It makes sense to access all assets, even while generational practices, communication and use of technology may stretch older people's abilities. It is a work in progress that will adapt from generation to generation.

[41] *Ibid.*

[42] Roque, Brian, personal communication, June 9.

[43] *Ibid.*

[44] Lathlin, Duncan. 2017, personal communication, June 9.

Roque's[45]advice to municipalities interested in developing collaborations is to know their list of projects well enough so that opportunities for working together are quickly identified. This is a collaborative process that relies on relationship building and not going in with a demanding attitude where the focus is on venting with the purpose of winning disagreements. Speaking up quickly without the facts or bringing gossip into the picture are injurious.

Lathlin's[46] advice to First Nations communities interested in this type of partnership is to pursue it persistently. "You will find common interests and goals. The paths that lead to achieving those goals will be vastly improved with collaboration. No one has lost anything from collaboration. Instead it is multiplied for the better."

Summary

First Nations and municipality collaborations in the furtherance of community goals is of interest for many reasons. The variety of similar goals are apparent in the CEDI project profiles. Targeted projects include tourism, support for business development and meeting local needs, and sometimes reach to regional challenges. Developing relationships prior to important decisions were important in the Lac Seul and KI collaboration with Sioux Lookout and was visible in the OCN, The Pas and Kelsey collaboration. Both of these collaborations were formed after a history of some negativity. It was clear in these collaborations that knowing how to work with each other for mutual benefit was important.

The CEDI Final Report surveyed participants and one key finding reinforced the need to build trust-based relationships as these were "key sustainable outcomes, building a foundation for long-term success in this work."[47] The overall strength of these relationships was described as an unintended outcome by CEDI, but cannot be highlighted enough in these collaborations that lead to a "shared sense of unification, while working to reconciliation."[48]

[45] Roque, Brian. 2017, personal communication, June 9.
[46] Lathlin, Duncan. 2017, personal communication, June 9.
[47] FCM and Cando. 2016. Community Economic Development Initiative. "Evaluation Report" (unpublished, May 10), p 5.
[48] *Ibid.*

In both the Manitoba and Ontario examples discussed here, the way of doing business is much different; with open communication and opportunities to get to know each other beyond their jobs, it is possible to construct a framework to complete the work. The OCN collaboration with Kelsey and The Pas has a Friendship Accord as the basis for working together in a Tri-Council arrangement. For the Lac Seul, KI and Sioux Lookout collaboration, a Friendship Accord is the basis for a variety of partnerships with membership depending on specific goals. For example, the Shared Territory Protocol focuses on resource development, while the CEDI partnership is still looking at projects with shared interest. The distribution centre has expanded to include a number of new partners with one original partner withdrawing.

The CEDI Final Evaluation Report notes that CEDI had helped increase capacity in developing joint economic strategies both for organizations and for elected officials in the first capacity-building support of this sort.[49] In reflecting on the types of agreements developed in the Manitoba and Ontario collaborations discussed here, their ability to seek out joint efforts has flourished.

Leadership is critical to both these collaborations despite some players changing with elections. Useful collaboration characteristics include consistency in the level of interest despite change, open attitudes, curiosity and the ability to listen and observe when it is clear that groups do business differently. Relationships need attention so that robust business decisions can be made from a strong foundation. Building consensus needs time and an understanding that the big picture is important, including individual issues. Consensus means impactful decision-making with all partners equally committed.

The CEDI Final Evaluation Report noted that champions had increased knowledge of governance models, structures and cultural practices about their partners. Better understanding of issues impacting First Nations partners was a "valuable, yet unintended, outcome."[50] This outcome offsets initial capacity limitations that might have stalled the new relationships.

---

[49] *Ibid.*

[50] FCM and Cando. 2016. Community Economic Development Initiative. "Evaluation Report" (unpublished, May 10), p 5.

Champions are evident in both collaborations and bring their own levels of commitment. All are supportive of the collaborations and work hard to support success. The Ontario collaboration has a municipality and champion that consistently funds travel to meetings, handles many administration details and provides a strong level of coordination with bringing in new business and levels of government to support collaboration at a regional level. One important finding in the *CEDI Final Evaluation Report* was that insufficient support staff challenged critical supportive communication between the Phase One collaboration partners, which impeded work on resolving key partnership issues.

At a recent Cando conference, the Ontario collaboration was presented to an audience that included economic development officers from across Canada. Members of the audience indicated that they were ready for collaborations with neighbouring municipalities but had met with rejection. With the growing number of success stories across the country from CEDI and those that occur without outside attention, it is possible that more partnerships will form for the benefit of all. Getting all levels of government on board to support and sustain growing relationships between communities as they encourage a regional focus will have decided impact, especially with communities that have unused capacity to become more self-sustaining in partnership.

For the second phase of CEDI projects, the *CEDI Final Evaluation Report* recommended mentors to share their experiences and success. There may be phase one CEDI partners, who could reach out beyond the CEDI group, as peer mentoring might overcome problems mentioned at the Cando Conference. The CEDI application process acted as initiator for many of the collaborations that were highlighted here. The role of a support that has resources, training and relevant information in the initial and continuing stages of these partnerings would add value to the process that FCM and Cando has begun in building strength upon strength.

CHAPTER 6

Co-management of Fisheries Resources in the Western Canadian Arctic

By Burton Ayles,* Redmond Clarke, Kristin Hynes,
Robert Bell, John Noksana

Introduction

C anadian Arctic governance, in the broad sense of social systems and institutions, has been defined by modern comprehensive land settlement agreements, or treaties, between the original peoples of the Arctic and the governments of Canada, provinces and territories (INAC 2017).

In this chapter, we describe a particular form of collaborative governance referred to as co-management. Co-management is about the sharing of power and responsibility between governments and local resource users; see Pinkerton (1989) for descriptions of a range of co-management ventures in North America, and Berkes (2009) for a discussion of how co-management is evolving. Specifically we discuss how fisheries co-management, established under the *Inuvialuit Final Agreement* (IFA) (1984), operates in the western Canadian Arctic, providing local people with significant responsibilities and decision-making opportunities for present and future management (utilization and protection) of fish and marine mammals in the area.

* Corresponding author, Burton Ayles, Fisheries Joint Management Committee, 255 Egerton Road, Winnipeg, MB, R2M 2X3. aylesb@mts.net

In Canada, the Department of Fisheries and Oceans (DFO) has constitutional authority for "sea, coast and inland fisheries."[1] This authority is exercised primarily through the *Fisheries Act* (1985), the *Oceans Act* (1996) and the *Species at Risk Act* (SARA) (2002) and their associated regulations and policies.[2] In the Inuvialuit Settlement Region (ISR) (Figure 1), the region established by the IFA, some of the DFO governance responsibilities are now shared with the Fisheries Joint Management Committee (FJMC) (2017a), the body established under the IFA to provide recommendations and advice to the Minister of Fisheries and Oceans.

FIGURE 1. Map of the Western Canadian Arctic showing the Inuvialuit Settlement Region

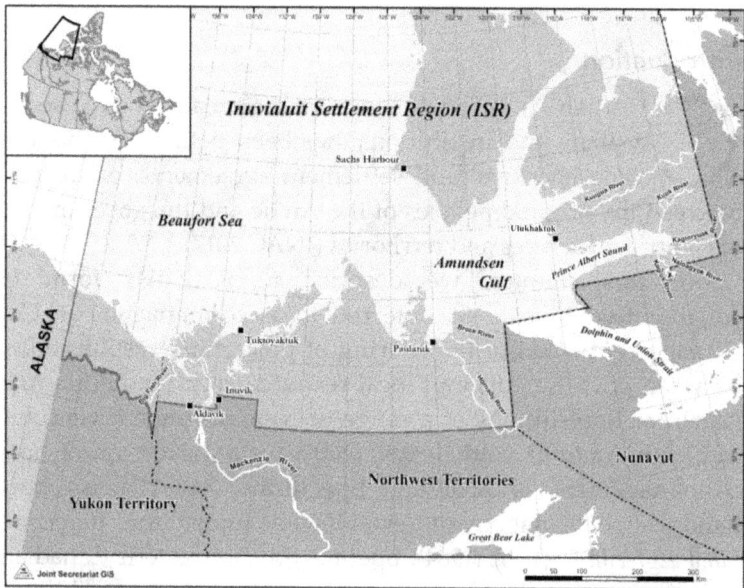

---

[1] Inland fisheries are managed primarily by provincial governments through their constitutional responsibilities for private property and through regulatory arrangements with the federal government. See Thompson (1974) for a full discussion.

[2] See DFO (2017) for a summary of policies related to fisheries management.

Scope

In this chapter we discuss aspects of the co-management processes of the FJMC. We summarize the environmental and social context leading to the IFA, the conditions at the establishment of the FJMC, institutions that it employs, and the importance of leadership. We then discuss two examples of its collaborative processes that enhance its role as a bridge between Inuvialuit communities and the government. First, we discuss the annual community/government consultation process to identify and address community and government concerns and issues, and second, the adaptive co-management process by which it handles major specific tasks. We conclude with a brief summary of some outcomes from the history of fisheries co-management in the western Arctic that gives us confidence that there are elements of these processes that are relevant for resource management elsewhere in Canada and in the world where local communities seek to control more of their own future.

Methodology

For our presentation, we follow the framework provided by Ansell and Gash (2008). Our analysis is based on material from minutes of committee meetings, FJMC presentations at scientific and community meetings, published reports, interviews with seven individuals intimately involved in the starting conditions of the FJMC, and the direct experience of the five co-authors. The phone and email interviews were semi-structured, and focused on the elements of the starting conditions highlighted by Ansell and Gash and our own understanding at the time.

The interviewees included the senior negotiator for the Inuvialuit, the negotiator for Tuktoyaktuk who became Premier of the Northwest Territories, the fisheries negotiator for the federal government who also became the first chair of the FJMC, the Regional Director of Fisheries Management for the DFO, DFO's Western Arctic Area Manager immediately after signing, and the first permanent resource biologist for the FJMC. Of the co-authors, the first was a DFO senior Regional Director for the Central and Arctic Region, the region responsible for the western Arctic, who after retiring began service as a Canada member of the FJMC; the second was also a senior Regional Director who since retirement has worked with the FJMC on a number of projects; the third is currently the senior resource biologist with the FJMC; the fourth was a long-term chair of the FJMC from shortly after its inception; and, the fifth is a current Inuvialuit member of the FJMC. This direct experience brings intimate knowledge and understanding, but it could also lead to biased interpretations of the results of actions and events and charges of a view through 'rose-coloured' glasses. The authors alone accept responsibility for any misinterpretation.

Context/background

The Mackenzie Delta, Beaufort Sea, Amundsen Gulf and associated coastal areas of the western Canadian Arctic are the homeland of the Inuvialuit. These are Inuit people, biologically, culturally and historically related to other Inuit living in northeastern Russia, Alaska, throughout the Canadian high Arctic and Greenland.[3] While related to other Inuit, and most closely related to the Alaskan Inupiat, they have maintained a separate identity as reflected in their land claim. To southerners, the land is cold and forbidding with long harsh winters and short cool summers. But it is also rich and varied with many geographically distinct areas. The most significant feature is perhaps the delta of the Mackenzie River, the largest north flowing river in North America, but there are also high mountains, lowland plains, islands and coastal areas (Western Arctic Handbook Committee 2002).

Prior to contact with Euro-Canadians the Inuvialuit were, thanks to the diverse and rich resource base of their homeland, perhaps the richest people in the Canadian Arctic because of their access to land, freshwater and marine resources (Alunik *et al.* 2003). The Inuvialuit continue to make use of those resources (Usher 2002) and the fish and marine mammals of the rivers, lakes and the marine areas are particularly important. Beluga whales (*Delphinapterus leucas*), bowhead whales (*Balaena mysticetus*), ringed seals (*Pusa hispida*), Arctic char (*Salvelinus alpinus*), Dolly Varden char (*Salvelinus malma*) and various species of whitefish (*Coregonus spp.*), as well as other country foods such as caribou (*Rangifer tarandus*), musk ox (*Ovibos moschatus*) and waterfowl (*Anatidae*) provide sustenance and historical and cultural links to their ancestors (McGhee 1974; Department of Education 1991; Alunik 1998; Alunik *et al.* 2003).

---

[3] See ITK (2017) for general discussions of the history of the Inuit in Canada, and IRC (2017) for general discussions of the Inuvialuit and their homeland.

The first Europeans to arrive in the region were with Alexander Mackenzie in 1789 in his search for the Pacific Ocean. There was only periodic contact over the next 60 years but then the Hudson's Bay Company opened a post on the Peel River in the Mackenzie Delta in the middle of the 19th century, and trading with the outside world became commonplace for the Inuvialuit. Missionaries arrived at the end of the century, whalers from California in 1889 and police in 1903. The interactions opened up additional opportunities for trade in skins and meat; trading muskrat and fox furs made many Inuvialuit families wealthy. The southerners also brought the near destruction of the bowhead whales and periodic disease epidemics that decimated the Inuvialuit population. Schools and other aspects of commercial life arrived in the first half of the 20th century, and government offices and military (the Distant Early Warning (DEW) line) by the middle of the century. The economy periodically expanded, but, as with many northern regions, it was boom or bust and few of the benefits went to the Inuvialuit (Alunik *et al.* 2003).

In the late 1950s, oil exploration work started in the Mackenzie Delta, and in 1968 there was a major oil find in northern Alaska. In 1970, in response to the hydrocarbon exploration, the Inuvialuit established the Committee for Original People's Entitlement (COPE) to represent the interests of the indigenous people of the western Arctic. They wanted to ensure that they would have input into resource development and that they, not just southerners, would benefit from any development (IRC 2009). Negotiations between COPE and the Government of Canada began in 1974 and lasted over the course of 10 years. They were given additional impetus with the March 1974 initiation of the Mackenzie Valley Pipeline Inquiry, the Berger Commission (Berger 1977), to investigate the social, environmental and economic impacts of a proposed gas pipeline though the Yukon and along the Mackenzie River to southern Canada.

Commissioner Berger recognized the Inuvialuit concerns about loss of control. At the first community hearing, he visited Archie Headpoint's small log cabin hunting and fishing camp north of Aklavik on the West Channel of the Mackenzie Delta and observed a landscape crisscrossed by seismic trails and vehicle tracks that seemed to come from nowhere and to go nowhere. He heard from the Headpoints how seismic trails extending across the Delta and into the foothills of the Richardson Mountains were affecting the productivity of the land by blocking streams and polluting ponds. And out on the ice-covered river, not half a mile away, he could see a series of bright orange trailers on runners, a Shell seismic exploration camp. He asked "Can these two Norths coexist in the Mackenzie Delta and the Beaufort Sea? Or must one recede into the past, while the other commands the future?" (*Ibid.*: 52). In 1977 the Berger Commission report recommended a 10-year moratorium on the building of the pipeline, stating "postponement will allow sufficient time for native claims to be settled" (*Ibid.*).

On June 5, 1984, the Inuvialuit and the Government of Canada, supported by the governments of the Northwest Territories and Yukon, signed the IFA. It was the first comprehensive land claim agreement signed north of the 60th parallel, and the second in Canada.[4] The IFA established the ISR, and set out goals that reflect the desire of the Inuvialuit to protect their homeland and its resources and to participate in the modern economy:

- "to preserve Inuvialuit cultural identity and values within a changing northern society;
- to enable Inuvialuit to be equal and meaningful participants in the northern and national economy and society; and,
- to protect and preserve Arctic wildlife, environment and biological productivity" (IFA 1984).

The ISR covers an area of about 435,000 square kilometres, extending over 750 km from the Canada/Alaska border east to the border between Nunavut and the Northwest Territories, and 1,300 km north from the Mackenzie Delta to well north of the Parry Islands in the Canadian Archipelago (approximately 141° W to 110° W and 68° N to 80° N). There are six small communities in the area – Inuvik, Aklavik and Tuktoyaktuk in the Mackenzie Delta, and Sachs Harbour, Ulukhaktok and Paulatuk in remote coastal areas – with a population of about 6,000 (about 4,000 are Inuvialuit, the rest primarily Gwich'in and Euro-Canadian). The ISR is connected via gravel highway to the Alaska Highway in southern Yukon and via river barge and towboat north on the Mackenzie River in summer, but only one community, Inuvik, has all season road connections. Of the five other communities, the three in the remote coastal areas are only accessible by aircraft or boat, whereas the two Mackenzie Delta communities are also

---

[4] See IRC (2009) for a perspective on the negotiating process, and INAC (2017) for a description of the modern land claims process.

accessible via winter ice road. An all-weather road between Inuvik and Tuktoyaktuk on the Arctic coast is under construction.

The IFA established a number of bodies to support its implementation. They include the Inuvialuit Regional Corporation (IRC) to represent the collective Inuvialuit interest in economic and social development (there are individual corporations in each community), the Inuvialuit Game Council (IGC) to represent the collective Inuvialuit interest in wildlife and wildlife habitat, and Hunters and Trappers Committees (HTC) in each community. The IFA also established five co-management bodies that have broad legislated responsibilities and ongoing funding and that bring together the Inuvialuit and various levels of government for integrated resource co-management:

- Inuvialuit Environmental Impact Screening Committee (EISC) – reviews proposed industrial projects for potential impact on wildlife and the environment in the ISR;
- Inuvialuit Environmental Impact Review Board (EIRB) – leads public reviews and makes recommendations on projects that the EISC deems to have potential for significant environmental impacts;
- Wildlife Management Advisory Council – Northwest Territories (WMAC-NWT) – wildlife co-management in the ISR within the Northwest Territories;
- Wildlife Management Advisory Council – North Slope (WMAC-NS) – wildlife co-management in the ISR within Yukon; and,
- Fisheries Joint Management Committee FJMC) – co-management of fisheries, including marine mammals, and their habitats in the ISR.

The Joint Secretariat – Inuvialuit Settlement Region (IJS) was established separately in 1986 to provide technical and administrative support to the Inuvialuit Game Council and the four co-management boards headquartered in Inuvik. The WMAC-NS is headquartered in Whitehorse and has its own administrative support.

Under the IFA, fisheries and marine mammals in the ISR are jointly managed by the Inuvialuit and the Government of Canada (DFO) through the FJMC co-management body (IFA 1984; Doubleday 1989). The FJMC reports to the Minister of Fisheries and Oceans. It also provides quarterly updates to the IGC. It comprises two members appointed by Canada (the Minister of

Fisheries and Oceans), two members appointed by the IGC, and an independent chair appointed by the members. The FJMC has decision-making responsibilities, such as allocating subsistence quotas among communities and setting conservation limits on total catch. It also has responsibilities to advise and to make recommendations to the Minister of Fisheries and Oceans on sport and commercial fishing, fisheries management, fisheries research and international issues that might be relevant to Inuvialuit fisheries.[5] In order to carry out its responsibilities, the FJMC receives annual funding from the federal government to support its operations and to support fisheries and marine mammal management actions and research activities of others.

Starting conditions

Fisheries co-management in many jurisdictions has started with a crisis or search for a solution for a single set of problems such as over fishing or inequities in sharing of harvests (Linke and Bruckmeir 2015). This is often not an easy path. See for example von der Porten *et al.*'s discussion of the long struggle that indigenous peoples on the Pacific Coast of Canada had with DFO trying to establish some sort of joint management of the herring fishery (von der Porten *et al.* 2016).

In the 1980s, the Central and Arctic Region of the DFO had started along a similar path of co-management for the fisheries of Great Bear Lake and Great Slave Lake, but these committees were primarily advisory. Fishers participated and provided effective advice for the management of the fish stocks but responsibility, power and financial resources remained with the department. There had been no such initiative in the Mackenzie Delta Beaufort Sea Area[6] and the Inuvialuit had to advocate strongly during negotiations for the co-management with DFO of fish and marine mammal resources in the ISR.[7] The Inuvialuit considered that co-management of marine fish and marine mammals, such as beluga and bowhead in the Beaufort Sea, would help ensure Inuvialuit rights and responsibilities for the management and protection of marine areas of the ISR.[8] The signing of the IFA brought a new process of fisheries co-management to the Canadian Arctic over

---

[5] See Section 14 of the Agreement (IFA 1984).
[6] R. Josephson, personal communications, May 2017.
[7] N. Cournoyea, personal communication, May 2017.
[8] *Ibid.*

night; it gave real power to the Inuvialuit stakeholders[9] and set the FJMC, and the other co-management bodies, on the path to what now functions at what Pinkerton (2003) calls "complete co-management" and what Berkes *et al.* (2007) refer to as a "mature stage" co-management relationship between the FJMC, the Inuvialuit and the government.

In this section we examine the relationship between the three parties, the Inuvialuit, the DFO and the FJMC at the beginning of the path to complete co-management. We do not discuss the negotiations leading up to the IFA, except as they relate to the fisheries component.[10] Following Ansell and Gash's (2008) model, we will address the prehistory of cooperation/conflict on fisheries issues, power/resource knowledge asymmetries at the time of the IFA signing and in the early meetings of FJMC, incentives for/constraints on participation by the Inuvialuit and by DFO employees and common/conflicting objectives of the parties.

There had been relatively few conflicts between the Inuvialuit and the federal government with respect to fisheries issues but little cooperation either. Conflicts were generally restricted to relatively small fisheries enforcement issues, such as fishing without a licence, not major policy issues. One problem was that nationally the DFO's focus was primarily on the east and west coast commercial fisheries and the issues of the north were related to subsistence indigenous fisheries. From the perspective of the Inuvialuit, the initial negotiations were impeded by a negotiator who was a retired fishery officer from the Pacific Region with little sympathy or understanding of the negotiating process or the fisheries of the Arctic. The negotiations improved when the original DFO negotiator was replaced with a regional fisheries biologist.

"If I had to rank the problems we had with wildlife and wildlife management, fisheries was about the last of the pressing issues... ... Fisheries wasn't a stumbling block for us".[11] While there was no real history of conflict between the DFO and the Inuvialuit, conflict did arise within the DFO research community

[9] See Jentoft (2005) for a discussion of empowerment and fisheries co-management.

[10] Readers should see Puxley (2002) for an informal perspective of the Berger Commission, and IRC (2009) for an Inuvialuit perspective on the negotiation of the IFA.

[11] R. DeLury, personal communication, May 2017.

after the signing of the IFA and the transfer of power to the local HTCs. Some scientific staff refused to accept that conditions had changed and that they could not carry out research in the ISR without consulting with the FJMC and the communities beforehand. "I lost some good biologist friends over that. They did not think that anybody could tell them where they could work in the Arctic and refused to work in the ISR again".[12] Those attitudes faded over time and some 25-30 years on community consultation before and after projects has long been the standard, helping to build trust and understanding between the scientific community and local hunters and fishers.

One might expect that there were significant power imbalances between the government(s) and the Inuvialuit, and it is certainly correct that the government had the jurisdiction and the formal power, but the Inuvialuit were far from powerless. This was the case both during the negotiations of the IFA and the early days of the FJMC. One has to remember that from the government perspective one of the driving forces was Berger's recommendations; the government and the oil and gas industry needed an agreement before further development could proceed and there was a sense of political and economic urgency. The Inuvialuit had been trading with the Hudson Bay Company and with American whalers for fur and goods for decades and had experience with government operations during the Cold War and with the oil and gas industry. They were not naïve negotiators; they had already rejected earlier government proposals for a treaty (IRC 2009).

The governments were also disadvantaged in the number and conflicting roles that had to be balanced. As well as several federal departments – INAC, DFO, Environment and others – there were the governments of the Northwest Territories and Yukon, each with their different attitudes and priorities. The Inuvialuit, on the other hand, were a relatively cohesive negotiating force.

There was also a knowledge imbalance. When it came to the establishment of the terms of reference for the co-management bodies such as the FJMC, a major advantage for the Inuvialuit, recognized by all, was that they had a much better understanding of the fish and wildlife in the western Arctic. They had the personal experience of the community negotiators, many of whom were experienced on the land, and centuries of traditional

[12] V. Gillman, personal communication, May 2017.

Inuvialuit knowledge of spatial and temporal distributions of critical species, factors that affect their health, behaviours, how the species inter-related and how those resources contributed to their own sustenance and culture. The governments had access to some recent but limited scientific studies on the distribution of some species but only preliminary knowledge of such critical information as annual variability and habitat use, and no idea of local systems of management or of the Inuvialuit view of the world. Another common source of power imbalance between government and other agencies can be disparities in financial resources, but the IFA provided funds for the operation of the co-management bodies that included resources for community involvement and capacity building.

A major incentive for the DFO staff to participate in this new system of co-management was that the regional DFO managers had been handed a new set of responsibilities. They were from a biological/science background, not an enforcement background, and they realized that they would be unable to manage the fisheries effectively without the cooperation of the communities. As important for individual researchers was that the FJMC had IFA implementation funds to support its responsibilities to recommend to the Minister on research and management actions. Those funds allowed the FJMC to 'buy' research from government, university and environmental consultants. The researchers could use the FJMC support to gain additional support from within a department seeking to build relevant positive relationships with 'clients.'

The Inuvialuit fishers and hunters were eager to participate in co-management of freshwater and marine fishery resources and their habitats. They had seen the impact of the oil and gas exploration on their lands and waters and experienced the lack of say or influence over government decisions about their resources. Now they were empowered and ready to take on their responsibilities. One of the first resource biologists serving the FJMC, L. Harwood, summed it up as follows, "What I remember from those days was very positive. ...The Inuvialuit members, particularly Alex Aviugana, Nelson Green and Billy Day, supported by Canada member Don Dowler and the Chair Bob Bell, were active and prominent elders, well respected and well known, and seemed to me to have great pride, dedication and a fundamental desire to make co-management work. This was in part an outcome of their COPE involvement (in the IFA negotiations), their long-term vision, altruism, and the active keepers of traditional knowledge of their ancestors. There were bumps in the road, of course, but generally everyone was working steadfastly toward conservation for the greater good."[13]

Early on after its establishment, the FJMC faced three major issues, namely: opportunities for new commercial fisheries in the ISR; the management of beluga whales; and a potential harvest of a bowhead whale. The federal government had previously supported the establishment of new commercial char and whitefish fisheries as a potential driver of economic development. These initiatives were advanced without understanding of the biological productivity of the harvested stocks; none of them resulted in a new successful venture, and several ended in virtual collapse of the stocks, thus impacting on subsistence harvests for many years (Porta and Ayles 2015). Nevertheless, Inuvialuit were interested in the opportunities that new fisheries might provide and in response the FJMC funded a number of basic biological assessments of possible harvestable stocks. The general results of the assessments were that new opportunities were very limited (Stewart *et al.* 1993). These negative assessments were accepted by the Inuvialuit fishers and the DFO. Interestingly in later years, as concerns about climate change and foreign overfishing grew and the interrelationships between potential stocks of marine fish and the dependence of beluga whales and seals on those stocks became better understood, the HTCs asked for, and helped develop, a fisheries framework that placed significant restrictions on new offshore commercial fisheries (Fisheries and Oceans Canada *et al.* 2014).

Beluga whale harvests have been part of the Inuvialuit culture for centuries (McGhee 1974). They had self-managed the harvests and were very concerned that these harvests should continue without government intervention. The regional fisheries managers felt pressured to establish a quota-based management system, similar to that employed for harvested fish stocks in southern Canada. The FJMC, the Inuvialuit and DFO worked together to resolve the conflicts and in 1991 a Beaufort Sea Beluga Management Plan was completed (FJMC 2017b). The plan addressed objectives for conservation and protection and sustainable harvests (supported by community bylaws and

[13] L. Harwood, personal communication, May 2017.

by the HTCs but without quotas), and established protection zones that provided guidelines for industry (primarily oil and gas, shipping and tourism). The plan has been updated several times but perhaps more important it was the basis for further cooperation between the FJMC, the Inuvialuit and DFO, leading to two federal Marine Protected Areas in the Beaufort Sea and a Large Ocean Management Plan for the Beaufort Sea.[14]

The Inuvialuit had harvested small numbers of bowhead pre-contact, but American commercial whalers had virtually destroyed the western Arctic bowhead population by the second decade of the last century and the last Inuvialuit bowhead harvest was probably in the 1920s (Stoker and Krupnick 1993). The Alaskan Inupiat had continued a small subsistence hunt of bowhead after the end of the commercial whaling industry and the population had recovered significantly. With the signing of the IFA there were Inuvialuit hunters who felt that it was time to re-establish their cultural traditions. Canada had banned commercial whaling in 1972 and withdrawn from the International Whaling Commission. There were pressures on Canada from animal rights groups to reject any application for a bowhead whale hunt, and there were pressures from the United States to rejoin the International Whaling Commission to support their Alaskan harvests. It was a priority for regional DFO managers to demonstrate that Canada was prepared to live up to its commitments under the IFA despite the conflicting pressures and to demonstrate that Canada was managing whale populations responsibly. The outcome of the FJMC-led negotiations was a legal bowhead whale harvest in 1991, the first in 70 years (see Freeman *et al.* 1992, for an assessment of the importance of the harvest for the rights of the Inuvialuit). Commenting on the role of DFO in the negotiations, the chief IFA negotiator stated "For bowhead, after the IFA Fisheries (i.e., DFO) was very cooperative. They tried very hard to get it (i.e., the licence to harvest a bowhead) approved".[15]

With respect to the starting conditions for fisheries co-management in the western Arctic, our assessment is that conditions were favourable for establishing a successful system of collaboration. There was no history of significant conflict between the DFO and the Inuvialuit. There were asymmetries

[14] See BSP (2017) for descriptions of Oceans programs of the Inuvialuit, Canada and other partners.
[15] R. DeLury, personal communication, May 2017.

in the power structure between the parties, but no one party had overwhelming power. There were incentives for both parties to participate and to make co-management work. Finally, the three potential areas of conflict were resolved satisfactorily in fairly short order, helping to establish trust between the parties and the FJMC, and confidence that this system could work well in the future for the conservation and management of fish and marine mammal stocks in the Western Canadian Arctic.

Institutional design

Co-management in the western Arctic started with a strong legislative mandate that provided a basis for its initial institutional design and for further institutional development. The IFA provides the framework for the FJMC's fisheries co-management activities by defining its organizational structure and core responsibilities, and the Agreement also provided federal funding for implementation. These responsibilities are discharged in the context of the IFA and relevant federal requirements, of which the *Fisheries Act* and its associated regulations and policies are most important to fisheries management.

The overall goals of the IFA, namely Inuvialuit cultural preservation, economic participation and protection of Arctic wildlife (see above), underlie all the FJMC's co-management actions and decisions. Core functions include: decision-making responsibilities – e.g., allocating subsistence fisheries quotas among communities and regulating fisheries on Inuvialuit lands; advising and recommending responsibilities – e.g., research, environmental protection and commercial fishing; and operational responsibilities – e.g., conducting harvest assessments and coordinating between government agencies and Inuvialuit communities. The IFA also gave to the community Hunting and Trapping committees (HTCs) fisheries-related responsibilities to sub-allocate quotas of fish and marine mammals and to make local harvest by-laws (IFA 1984).

Federal legislation and policies are critical to the work of the FJMC. Since its formation in 1986, the FJMC has had to work within the framework provided by federal legislation (as well as the IFA), and to adapt its activities to reflect changes in legislation and policies. Its institutional design and its leadership have enabled this to be accomplished successfully. Over the 30 years since the IFA was signed, the *Fisheries Act* has been modified and new regulations and policies changed in many ways (Bailey *et al.* 2016). As well two other important acts have come into force: the *Oceans Act* and the *Species at Risk Act* (SARA).

While these changes were not anticipated in 1986, the mandate of the FJMC is broad and the federal government has recognized the need to involve Indigenous and co-management bodies. For example, the SARA makes specific reference to the involvement of Indigenous co-management plans, and the DFO Integrated Aboriginal Policy Framework (DFO 2017) provides guidance to DFO employees in building respectful and mutually beneficial relations with Aboriginal groups. As a result, the FJMC has been able to adjust to the changes in the *Fisheries Act* and has assumed the lead role for the new *Oceans Act* and SARA responsibilities in the ISR (Ayles *et al.* 2016). To help face evolving legislation and government policies and emerging issues, the FJMC adopted a strategic planning process and practices that encompass many of the strategies that Berkes has identified to improve co-management, including the bridging of knowledge, the co-production of knowledge, participatory research, collaborative monitoring and participatory scenario building, strategies that contribute to power sharing, institution building, creation of social capital, and governance (Berkes 2009).

In the early 2000s, the FJMC developed a formal statement of a "Vision", "Principles" and goals or targets for the upcoming 5-10 year period to further guide committee actions. The vision statement, now in its third iteration, is as follows:

"The FJMC Vision for the future is that all marine, anadromous and freshwater fish and marine mammal stocks of the Inuvialuit Settlement Region will be managed and conserved for the wise use and benefit of present and future generations. We interpret this to mean that stocks and habitats will remain healthy with respect to contaminants and population size and ecosystem structure, and that harvests are sustainable and managed cooperatively with the harvesters" (FJMC 2017b).

The statement is then followed by mechanisms by which this vision will be accomplished. The vision is supported by the following principles:

- incorporate the "precautionary principle" and the "precautionary approach," as information and knowledge become available, in its approach to the management of the renewable freshwater and marine resources of the ISR;

- support the goals of the Inuvialuit Final Agreement;
- support the spirit and principles of "adaptive co-management" in its approach to the management of the fish and marine mammals of the ISR and their supporting ecosystems and as a means for continuous learning from the past to improve actions in the future;
- support the traditions, beliefs and activities of the Inuvialuit, and be respectful and considerate of the traditions and beliefs of all people; and,
- endeavour to ensure that fish and marine mammals are treated with respect during any harvesting, scientific studies or other use of the resource.

Specific targets/milestones for the upcoming 5-10 year period are outlined. The Collaborative Processes section of this chapter discusses the FJMC annual planning processes that support this overall strategic plan.

The FJMC also has instituted practices that foster further collaboration. They include:

- FJMC formal annual planning, consultation and project funding cycle (see Collaborative Processes section).
- Specific task groups of FJMC members and partners are established to address individual issues (described under Collaborative Processes section).
- Operating procedures for day-to-day operations of the FJMC (FJMC 2017a). The Operating procedures address roles of the chair and members (see Leadership section for examples), development of communication plans amongst others, and annual calendar of events amongst others.
- Electronic newsletter, Facebook Page (FJMC Facebook 2017) and website (FJMC 2017a).
- Shared positions on fisheries and environmental issues between Inuvialuit, FJMC and DFO (e.g., MGP-JRP 2009).
- Cooperative community/science workshops and meetings (e.g., Rosenberg 2003; FJMC Newsletter 2013).
- Formal meetings with the Minister of Fisheries and Oceans, DFO senior managers, Inuvialuit leaders and federal politicians (e.g., SSCFO 2010).
- Active participation of FJMC members at national and international meetings on resource co-management and Arctic resources.

- Active participation in the Beaufort Sea Regional Coordinating Committee, the overarching planning body that promotes integrated resource management in the Beaufort Sea Large Ocean Management Area (LOMA) (BSP 2017) and with DFO science planning for LOMA (e.g., Paulic *et al.* 2009).

From an institutional design perspective, a key result is that the strong and broad mandate provided by the IFA and federal legislation and policies have allowed the FJMC to expand beyond the original responsibilities as circumstances have changed. This evolution has increased the control and influence of the Inuvialuit with respect to fisheries and marine mammal management and environmental protection in the ISR.[16]

In summary, the institutional design of the FJMC is based on a legislated mandate and developed practices that provide the framework that permit it to fulfil its responsibilities successfully and to adapt to address emerging issues. In doing so, it used many of Berkes strategies that improve co-management, especially the bridging of knowledge, participatory research and collaborative monitoring (Berkes 2009). The result is true sharing of power between the Inuvialuit and the Government of Canada (see Collaborative Processes section), with the FJMC having a major role in the ISR as a bridging organization.

Facilitative leadership

Ansell and Gash (2008) have emphasized the critical nature of leadership in the initiation and maintenance of the collaborative process. Fisheries co-management in the western Canadian Arctic has benefited significantly from the leadership of the Inuvialuit, primarily through the Inuvialuit Game Council, but also the Inuvialuit Regional Corporation, and from the leadership of regional senior managers of the Department of Fisheries and Oceans. Freeman *et al.* described the aspirations, actions and patience but also the persistence of the Inuvialuit while attempting to re-establish their rights to harvest a bowhead whale. He also described the changes in the DFO approach that eventually led to the 1991 harvest (Freeman *et al.* 1992). Since that event the

---

[16] See, for example, papers in Berkes *et al.* (2005) and BSP (2017) for changes related to the *Oceans Act*, and Ayles *et al.* (2016) for planning for new commercial fisheries with future climate change.

Inuvialuit patience and persistence and support has continued and the regional DFO management has been very supportive of co-management initiatives; this support makes it clear to community members, and to DFO scientific and management staff, that co-management is fully accepted in the ISR. This is further exemplified through the establishment of the Beaufort Sea Regional Coordinating Committee (BSP 2017) and the development of the Integrated Fisheries Management Framework for the Beaufort Sea (Ayles *et al.* 2016).

New leadership can energize an organization and bring new ideas to the table, but it can also be disruptive and counterproductive when priorities and personalities shift too frequently. Working together cooperatively on fisheries resource issues brings together different world views, fosters trust and respect, develops networks, and uses both science and traditional knowledge to facilitate decision making (Berkes *et al.* 2007). This takes time and continuity, not just a forceful and innovative leader.

Fisheries co-management in the ISR has benefited from strong and stable leadership of the chairs and members of the FJMC, of the IGC and the IJS. The chair of the FJMC is not appointed by the government or by the Inuvialuit, but is independently selected by its appointed members. The chair is on a one-year contract that must be specifically renewed annually. In its 30-year history, the FJMC has had only three chairs. The first chair had been the primary fisheries negotiator for the federal government and was a DFO employee. The fact that he was selected by the initial members of the committee speaks to the confidence that the Inuvialuit had in the negotiating process. The second chair, who served for 23 years, had been a school teacher in Aklavik and a resource manager with the GNWT. The third chair had been a DFO field biologist in the western Arctic and then local DFO manager in the early years of the FJMC, before moving on to other senior managerial roles in the regional DFO structure. The three brought a clear understanding and support of the changes that co-management brought to both the Inuvialuit and the DFO – i.e., power sharing and the need to work together for the management and protection of the fish and marine mammal resources. The latter two also brought years of personal involvement with the area and with individuals. This familiarity facilitated the trust with community members that helped to establish the credibility of the committee.

This credibility was further enhanced by two Inuvialuit elders, Alex Aviugana and Billy Day, both original signers of the IFA for their communities. They were experienced on the land and with government operations and each served for nine years on the committee, providing stability and an understanding of Inuvialuit resource use, culture and traditional ecological knowledge. Two long serving Canada members, one for 19 years and the other 18 years and still serving, were both former senior regional managers within DFO and brought experience knowledge and familiarity with fisheries research, management and protection, and with government operations and policies in general. The long-term appointees helped ensure committee memory, and their personal relationships helped to stabilize committee operations during critical periods. All were very supportive of advancing fishery co-management in the ISR.

The Inuvialuit Game Council, the group that represents the collective interest of the HTCs and appoints the Inuvialuit members to the co-management bodies, provides strong rules and guidelines for Inuvialuit members, and in so doing provides guidance for respectful behaviour of both government and Inuvialuit appointees to the committees. Co-management has also benefited from the stability of the IJS, the organization that provides technical and administrative support to the IGC, the FJMC and the other co-management boards. Its Executive Director, an environmental scientist, served for nearly 30 years, providing leadership, corporate memory and history, and strategic guidance for regional, national and international involvements of the IGC and the co-management committees.

One leadership role that the FJMC sees for itself is that of a bridging or boundary organization (Guston 2001) between government and Inuvialuit fishers. Berkes (2009) and Armitage *et al.* (2011) have identified bridging as an important strategy for improving co-management. The FJMC has responsibilities in the worlds of both the government and Inuvialuit communities: it has both government and Inuvialuit appointees, it is accountable to both the government and to the Inuvialuit and it works with both western scientific knowledge and the traditional knowledge of the Inuvialuit. Through its practices and procedures (see section on Institutional Design), it attempts to bridge the gap between the two different worlds by bringing together fishers, community members, biologists and government managers to address common issues. Ayles *et al.* have described one such initiative, the development of an integrated fisheries co-management framework for new and emerging fisheries in the Beaufort Sea (Ayles *et al.* 2016). The section on Collaborative Processes describes two other initiatives: one the annual process of setting research and management priorities and funding scientific and traditional knowledge based projects, and the second, the development of a Dolly Varden char management plan.

The FJMC has explicitly recognized this bridging function in its operating procedure for member responsibilities:

"In general the expectation is that Committee meetings will be informal vs. formal and that member interactions and decisions will be based on consensus building, incorporating a spirit of collegiality and respect for the beliefs, opinions and knowledge of others both within and outside the Committee. These procedures are guided by the belief that the FJMC is an organization with responsibilities to interpret and explain issues of resource management between fishers/hunters, government, and local, national and international communities. The FJMC has an important role in interpreting and explaining issues of resource management between fishers/hunters, government, and local, national and international communities. The Committee members come from diverse backgrounds, formal and informal education and experience and part of the responsibility of individual Committee members is to better understand that diversity so that diversity can be fully considered when decisions are made within the Committee and when Committee members represent the Committee in other meetings or venues. For example within Committee meetings an experienced Inuvialuit elder on the Committee would be expected to explain Inuvialuit traditional values to other committee members while a Canada member with regulatory experience would be expected to explain the problems/opportunities associated with regulatory change vs. policy initiatives. Conversely when interacting with federal policy officials the Canada member might well take the lead in explaining the importance of traditional knowledge while Inuvialuit members might take the lead in explaining decisions related to funding of scientific projects when the Committee meets with local fishers" (FJMC 2017a).

This approach was reaffirmed by a Japanese researcher who wrote:

"The author has observed FJMC meetings since 1998 and analyzed the interaction during the meetings. As a result, characteristics of the FJMC became apparent. Members of FJMC make the utmost effort to achieve their difficult task while respecting different experiences and values of each other... FJMC members are aware of the improvement in the relationship between the local people and the government since the formation of FJMC. They recognize the important role that FJMC plays in resolving the conflicts in resource management between the hunters and the government" (Iwasaki-Goodman 2005).

From a leadership and bridging perspective, the FJMC has been served well by the ongoing support of its two partners and the stability and knowledge provided by its chairs and members. The FJMC perceives its primary leadership role is to be a bridge between the two worlds of government and the Inuvialuit community. The FJMC has benefited from the commitment of its members to co-management and from its stability which has helped build trust and understanding (Ansell and Gash 2008). Certainly, the leadership style of the FJMC is consistent with coordinated, non-hierarchical and non-authoritarian decision making that Rocan considers essential for successful collaborative management (Rocan 2009).

Collaborative processes

In this section, we discuss two examples of collaborative processes. First, we discuss the annual consultative cycle the FJMC uses to identify research and fisheries/environmental management priorities from the joint perspective of the communities, the DFO and the FJMC. This is the process by which the FJMC makes overall funding decisions for the support of scientific proposals, community proposals and committee operations. Second, we discuss the process used to address a specific community issue, Dolly Varden char management, as a model of how similar issues are addressed.

Planning and consultation cycle

Importantly, the Agreement provided funding (ongoing) to address the responsibilities of the FJMC and the other co-management bodies. The broad objectives of the Inuvialuit were identified in the negotiating process, and the general management objectives of the DFO were known. But how were those to be refined and differences reconciled? The DFO District Manager and the Chair realized that this would not be done wholly within a small co-management committee and one of the first sets of activities of the FJMC was to begin a community consultation process through annual visits to each of the communities in the ISR. Over the years, these community visits have evolved into the annual core FJMC process for planning and budgeting and for bridging the two different worlds of community fishers and hunters and of western science, management and bureaucratic requirements of the federal government.

The committee meets quarterly to address its administrative, planning and budgeting responsibilities. Communication with the communities and with DFO is now built into those regular meetings and other events as well. The annual cycle has changed over time, but now it is as follows:

- June, September, October and March – FJMC provides updates on its activities to the IGC at IGC meetings. The FJMC Chair, one Inuvialuit member and/or one FJMC resource biologist attend. Other regional stakeholders (e.g., industry, researchers, non-governmental organizations) also attend. This is a useful meeting for information exchange as the other co-management bodies give updates at the same time.

- June – visits by the full FJMC Committee to three of the six ISR communities, visiting each community on alternate years, to hear and discuss community, FJMC and DFO programs, plans, issues, problems, priorities and desires for the near future. Normally, as well as the FJMC members and a resource biologist, representatives attend from different DFO programs (e.g., science, enforcement, and operations programs). The meetings are with each community's HTC, but they are open, and depending on the local issues or interests, other Inuvialuit hunters and fishers, elders, youth and community members may attend. The meetings are relatively informal and wide-ranging, and include presentations, and questions and answers. The FJMC and DFO participants describe results of past activities and plans for the summer field season, but mostly their role is to listen and explain if questioned. Depending on the circumstances there may be a community feast, lunch, or other activities such as an opportunity to go out on the land. Because of the remoteness of the communities, travel is by small charter aircraft and meetings may involve overnight stays in the communities; the costs are substantial. However, these visits are important to help to build and maintain good relationships between the various parties, to help to educate community members about the resource and government management, and to educate FJMC and DFO staff about local knowledge and issues.

• September – meeting in Inuvik with the six HTC presidents. The purpose of this meeting is to identify regional and local issues and priorities relating to fish and marine mammals in the ISR. The six HTC presidents meet first in-camera, and then meet for open discussions with FJMC members. The HTC presidents are expected to provide feedback on these discussions to their communities. The FJMC normally hosts a dinner for the HTC presidents, FJMC members and other guests at the meeting. As the HTC presidents change fairly regularly, this meeting helps to identify the broad ISR issues and to build collegial relationships.

• October – following the June and September meetings and the sessions with the IGC, the FJMC prepares an annual consolidated statement of issues and priorities for fisheries and marine mammal research and management activities. This document is informed by the community consultations, but it also considers other initiatives regionally, nationally or internationally, e.g. input from workshops, conferences, scientific studies, media etc., that the committee feels are relevant to its responsibilities. The statement invites DFO staff, universities, non-government organizations and the HTCs to submit proposals for consideration by the committee for funding for the coming fiscal year and the longer term.

• January – the committee meets at the DFO Central and Arctic regional headquarters in Winnipeg with senior regional management and with scientific staff that have or hope to have research projects in the ISR in the coming year. Discussions with the senior regional managers are primarily about operational issues, such as the lack of departmental staff in the ISR, habitat or enforcement issues, and ongoing unfulfilled needs to address science questions that the committee considers to be a priority. It is also an opportunity to address with the DFO managers common issues, such as the regional and Inuvialuit roles with respect to international Arctic fisheries agreements or concerns about changes to federal legislation (e.g., Bailey *et al.* 2016). These could be issues that the FJMC can raise separately with the Minister or Deputy Minister but that can support regional perspectives. Part of this meeting are presentations by scientific staff on their past year's results and new proposals for FJMC consideration and funding. In recent years, with the establishment of two new Marine Protected Areas (MPAs) in the ISR (BSP 2017), the meetings have been expanded to enable additional Inuvialuit participants to attend and discuss MPA issues with the DFO Oceans program staff. These meetings provide opportunities for face-to-face dialogue to expand Inuvialuit understanding of the roles of government science and management, and to enhance DFO staff's understanding of local knowledge and priorities. At the end of the meeting, the committee reviews the projects proposed for the coming year, assigns interim funding and gives approval-in-principle to individual projects. The Chair of the FJMC confirms with the DFO Regional Director General the committee's understanding of decisions and actions resulting from the discussions. The committee's resource biologist then informs individual project proponents of the FJMC's interim decision, and requests a full proposal for final approval before the start of the upcoming fiscal year.

- March-April – the FJMC meets in a convenient location to review and approve budget allocations for scientific and management projects for the coming year and to address other committee operations. Subsequently, individual project proponents are informed and budgets are allocated through the normal DFO financial process. Community members are informed of the project approvals through the FJMC Newsletter (see Institutional Design section).
- Periodic – under the IFA, the FJMC is responsible for the provision of advice and recommendations to the Minister of Fisheries and Oceans. Most interactions are with regional

and headquarter DFO staff. However, the FJMC endeavours to meet with each Minister shortly after his or her initial appointment. The purpose of these meetings is to introduce the Minister to co-management, Arctic fisheries issues and the Inuvialuit. The meetings are informal and collegial and the discussions can range from Canada's position on international fisheries agreements, to the high cost of food in the Arctic, or to the cultural and symbolic importance of subsistence whaling. The face-to-face meetings with the Minister not only enhance the credibility of the FJMC in the communities, but they also enhance the attention given to the Committee by senior departmental officials.

The process for consultation, planning and budgeting is in place but that does not mean that everything is always positive. Generally, the work that the FJMC, the DFO and the communities consider important is being addressed. However, although funding is provided for FJMC operations and for support of scientific and community projects, as with most agencies, the participants consider the funding to be inadequate given the responsibilities and the issues, and that funding requests each year usually are greater than the available funds. There are limited funds available and not all problems can be managed with money, hard work and goodwill. The IFA calls for meaningful Inuvialuit participation in resource management, and that means including the use of traditional ecological knowledge as well as scientific knowledge in decision making related to the management of fish and marine mammals and their ecosystems. The Inuvialuit and co-management bodies in the ISR have collected significant traditional ecological knowledge, and are addressing the issues of collection, storage and ownership (North Slope Conference 2015). A significant issue that remains is how to incorporate that knowledge into a management decision-making system that is rules-based, bureaucratic and biased towards western science. This remains an ongoing issue for the committee.

Community members have a more holistic view of the world than does a co-management committee with a mandate limited by the IFA and the Canadian *Constitution*. Community members have frequently come to open meetings with real problems that are water-related but are beyond the mandate of the FJMC. Recent examples are concerns about sewage lagoons and about the recent arrival of beavers into small streams and lakes in the

Mackenzie Delta. A simple response that this is not an issue for the committee is not acceptable, and ways must be found to help the communities address those issues.

More problematic for the FJMC is that the Inuvialuit have ongoing concerns with changes in their environment, particularly known and unknown contaminants levels and the implications for the health of the wildlife and for their own health as consumers. In 1984, when the IFA was signed, DFO in the Central and Arctic Region had a significant contaminants program, and over the years the FJMC helped to fund some contaminant research studies in the ISR. However, DFO priorities have changed significantly over the years and now the Region does not have the mandate or capacity to address community-identified contaminant concerns. The FJMC has not been able to resolve this issue and may need to develop new relationships with another department or with university researchers, but that is not straightforward as the funds to support FJMC projects flow through the DFO.

The cost of this comprehensive consultation and communication is significant. Travel to and from the western Arctic and southern Canada is more expensive than travel from southern Canada to Europe or Asia, and travel within the ISR, often by charter flight, is even more costly. The travel by small plane is also subject to significant uncertainties in terms of weather and availability of equipment. The timing and effort for the actual work is also significant, and for hunters and fishers who live by the season and the weather, participation in meetings with 'bureaucrats' can also be problematic. However, the long-term experience is that the linkages between the different members of the two worlds of the government and the communities, the knowledge and understanding exchanged, the power shared and the level of trust that has developed make the process worthwhile and improve the management of fish and marine mammals.

In summary, the FJMC's planning and consultation cycle is based on bridging the worlds of the Inuvialuit and government which is necessary to fulfil successfully its legislated fisheries co-management mandate. The community visits, the meetings with DFO managers and science staff and meetings with the Minister of Fisheries and Oceans are of particular importance as bridging activities. They lay the groundwork for building trust and understanding between the Inuvialuit and government (e.g., Ansell and Gash 2008). The January meetings with DFO science staff are part of advancing the co-production of knowledge and participatory research and monitoring by the Inuvialuit and DFO, a key to successful co-management (Berkes 2009). The actual conduct of participatory research and monitoring projects (*Ibid.*) involving Inuvialuit and DFO is, of course, vital as well. Generally, the work that the FJMC, the DFO and the communities consider important is being addressed.

Single-issue task group –
Dolly Varden Char Management

In this section, we discuss the management of the Dolly Varden fishery in the ISR as an illustration of the establishment of a working group to address a single issue. A working group enables DFO, the FJMC, an HTC and other stakeholders to work closely together to address an issue and to fulfill their responsibilities within the context of the IFA, *Fisheries Act* and other legislation or policy requirements.

The FJMC vision statement calls for an adaptive co-management process for the management of fish and marine mammals and their environments. The adaptive co-management process focuses on: establishing clear decisions and rationales for proposed actions; implementing those decisions; documenting and evaluating the results on fish stocks and fisheries; and responding to the evaluation by confirming, modifying or changing decisions for future years (Armitage *et al.* 2007; Holling 1978). In simple terms, it means "learning by doing" (Berkes 2009). In the ISR, the establishment of a working group, now the cornerstone of implementing the adaptive co-management process, began much more simply.

It began in the early 1990s with the concern of a local DFO biologist that a short exposition at the Paulatuk HTC general monthly meeting on the results of a year's collection of biological data on the local fish and marine harvests was inadequate to inform the hunters and fishers about the stocks or to receive informed feedback on potential management actions. The solution was separate meetings with a small number of fishers to examine the results and discuss the implications. The meetings were chaired by a local fisher, and the FJMC biologist and an FJMC member provided support. The fishers became comfortable with the process and strong advocates for the group decisions on management actions – e.g., increases or decreases in harvest levels based on biological data or more access to fish for some groups such as elders. Similar procedures were established in other communities and the concept has expanded to cover tasks beyond local fish harvest management and to include other jurisdictions. For example, in recent years working groups have been established to consider the possibility of additional MPAs in the Beaufort Sea and to develop fisheries management plans for newly accessible fishing areas along the soon to be opened Inuvik to Tuktoyaktuk Highway.

A working group usually follows this process: it assesses the issue, evaluates pertinent scientific, traditional and local information and knowledge, revisits community concerns, and develops by consensus proposed management actions to address the initial concerns; it consults with affected communities on any recommendations from its assessment; and it presents proposed management actions to the community, and ensures they are reviewed formally by all relevant stakeholders (Ayles *et al.* 2007). The FJMC, DFO, the appropriate HTC and others as necessary would ratify the final plan. The process is then repeated each year to incorporate results from management actions and harvesting, and new information.

In the western Arctic, Dolly Varden is an important subsistence species of Inuvialuit and the neighbouring Gwich'in. It occurs in six river systems (from west to east the Fish, Malcolm, Firth, Babbage, Big Fish, Rat and Vittrekwa) draining into the Beaufort Sea. The rivers occur in areas co-managed by DFO, Gwich'in, Inuvialuit and Parks Canada (the western part of the range is in Ivvavik National Park). The main traditional Dolly Varden fisheries for the Inuvialuit are on the Big Fish River, including spawning and overwintering areas (the "fish holes"), and along the Beaufort Sea coast (DFO 2003, 2013). The coastal fishery is a mixed stock fishery, harvesting fish from the Big Fish River and from other river systems. During the 1970s, an unsuccessful commercial fishery operated on the Big Fish River.

The development of a management plan for Dolly Varden resulted from the collapse of the subsistence fishery. Significant decreases occurred in the harvests and estimated population levels of Dolly Varden in the Big Fish River in the 1970s, with harvests decreasing from 8,000-12,000 in 1972 to 94 in 1980

(Fisheries and Oceans Canada *et al.* 2010; DFO 2013). The population has not returned to pre-collapse levels. It was thought that the decline in harvests and estimated population levels was due to overharvesting, changes to the spawning and overwintering habitat, or a combination of both (DFO 2013).

By 1987, Aklavik residents, having observed the decline in abundance and size of Big Fish River Dolly Varden over a number of years, requested and agreed to a legislated closure of the river, including the "fish holes," for five years. The FJMC was supportive, and asked DFO to close the fishery for five years. DFO agreed; the Big Fish River was closed to all fishing, and the mouth of the Big Fish River and some adjacent channels were closed to gill nets in August. The mixed-stock coastal fishery was allowed to continue. The Big Fish River fishery was reopened in 1992, but catches continued to be poor, never exceeding 300 fish in total over the next five years, and the size of the fish did not increase (Ayles *et al.* 2007).

In 2000, the FJMC proposed to DFO that the Aklavik community should be responsible for the management of the Dolly Varden. The Minister of Fisheries and Oceans agreed, contingent upon completion of a satisfactory management plan approved by DFO and the FJMC. In 2001, the West Side Working Group (WSWG) was established to develop a management plan for Dolly Varden in the ISR, especially the Big Fish River. Members of the WSWG were from the Aklavik HTC and Elders Committee, DFO, FJMC and Parks Canada. An initial success for the WSWG was the explicit recognition by DFO and fishers in 2003 that habitat changes were limiting the abundance of Dolly Varden in the Big Fish River. However, by 2005, there was no evidence of the recovery of the stock and no formal management plan, and the WSWG was shifting its focus to promoting environmental monitoring by the community.

At the start of the process, there was a significant learning curve for WSWG members, the need to build trust among themselves, and the need to reconcile traditional knowledge and scientific knowledge. Although there was commitment to the process by the participants, trust did not exist at the start. For instance, the community was unhappy that the fishery was not recovering despite the initial statements from DFO that only a five-year closure would be necessary, and that local knowledge that Big Fish River habitat had changed was not acknowledged by

DFO until 2003. Also, there were several instances of interpersonal conflicts (e.g., between DFO staff and HTC staff, between DFO staff and FJMC staff, and between FJMC members), partly a result of parochial outlooks. The WSWG's initial emphasis was on scientific knowledge at the expense of traditional knowledge, and this also helped split some community members along those lines. Another issue was inconsistency in HTC participation, as HTC members had jobs and needed to be hunting and fishing, which affected availability to serve on the WSWG and other committees. The varying HTC membership, and other WSWG membership changes slowed the building of commitment and trust. Consequently, little progress was made initially on developing a fishing plan for Big Fish River Dolly Varden.

During this initial phase of its activities, the WSWG enabled its members to work closely together to fulfil their responsibilities for managing the Dolly Varden fisheries and stocks. However, the WSWG's initial slow progress reflects that many of Ansell and Gash's (2008) requirements (e.g., the need for face-to-face dialogue, building trust, having a commitment to the process, and developing shared understanding) were partially lacking.

In 2009, an assessment of the health of Dolly Varden stocks began that could result in Dolly Varden being listed under the SARA, and consequently might impose conditions on the Inuvialuit in managing Dolly Varden stocks and fisheries (DFO 2013). The process for developing a Dolly Varden management plan expanded to include the neighbouring Gwich'in. The Gwich'in also were concerned about the implications of Dolly Varden being listed under SARA, and faced a decline in the Rat River Dolly Varden population, similar to the Big Fish River Dolly Varden decline.

As a result of the SARA concern, the Gwich'in and Inuvialuit led the establishment of a steering committee of DFO, the Gwich'in Renewable Resources Board (GRRB), the FJMC and Parks Canada Agency to oversee the development of an Integrated Fisheries Management Plan (IFMP) for Dolly Varden in the Gwich'in Settlement Area and ISR. The IFMP would identify measures necessary to conserve the stocks and manage the fisheries. The WSWG and its Gwich'in counterpart, the Rat River Working Group (RRWG), memberships expanded to include cross-representation. The WSWG and RRWG were crucial in the development of the IFMP. The work went smoothly under the leadership of the

Steering Committee even though it involved meetings of people with many differing backgrounds. There was acceptance of the process, face-to-face meetings, common goals and mutual trust – not to say there weren't disagreements on the details! The IFMP was completed in 2010 (Fisheries and Oceans Canada *et al.* 2010). In short, it was a successful cooperative process that demonstrated the strengths of co-management and that good results can occur when Ansell and Gash's (2008) requirements are met.

The contents of the IFMP do reflect that the Gwich'in and Inuvialuit had (and continue to have) major roles in defining what is important for the management of their Dolly Varden fisheries and the conservation of the Dolly Varden stocks. Through the WSWG, the RRWG and the Steering Committee, the Gwich'in and Inuvialuit communities, DFO and Parks Canada Agency were able to identify and agree on objectives, strategies, management requirements, fishing plans and research and monitoring needs for the Dolly Varden stocks (Fisheries and Oceans Canada *et al.* 2010).

After the completion of the IFMP, Aklavik fishers, particularly elders, had repeatedly raised the issue of harvesting in the over-wintering/spawning area of a main tributary of the Big Fish River. This area they called the "fish holes," which had been important harvest sites before the stock collapse in the 1980s and the subsequent closure of the Big Fish River to fishing. The possibility of reopening the "fish holes" had been discouraged by fisheries biologists, citing the potential for over-harvest and for disruption of spawning fish and their habitats. The elders argued that this was part of their cultural traditions and that fishing in that area and at that time was efficient and inexpensive compared to fishing along the coast.

In the fall of 2013, the Aklavik HTC raised the issue more strongly, and, in response, the WSWG submitted to the Steering Committee four goals for the management of the stock, namely: to ensure the long-term sustainability of the stock; to ensure a small allowable annual harvest for cultural and sustenance purposes; to make future changes in the harvest level based on agreed biological indicators; and to permit fishing in the "fish holes" following an agreement on harvest methods. In a meeting at the end of February 2014, the Steering Committee accepted the first three goals but reserved decision on the fourth pending further review and citing concerns about historical population status, historical harvest practices, harvesting locations, potential risks, benefits, and regulatory requirements. But the HTC was already moving forward independently.

In mid-January 2014, the HTC had written to the Minister of Fisheries and Oceans describing the years of cooperative work on the fishery, the current stable, if depleted, status of the stock, the monitoring and research programs, and their rights under the IFA, and requesting specifically to go back to their old fishing practices. The Minister, advised by the FJMC and regional DFO staff, replied positively to the HTC, commending the collaboration between the parties and agreeing to allow fishing in the "fish holes" following the development of an agreed upon harvest plan that would ensure protection of the stock and the spawning habitat. The FJMC and local DFO staff worked with the HTC to develop a harvest plan, and in the fall of 2014 the community harvest at the "fish holes" was allowed to proceed and has proceeded in subsequent years.

The community harvest plan for the "fish holes" that has been approved since 2014 was a substantial accomplishment for co-management in the ISR. However, the plan represents a compromise between some interests of the Aklavik HTC, DFO and the FJMC. The Big Fish River and its tributaries remains closed to all fishing under DFO regulations, with the annual harvest program being approved through a DFO Aboriginal Communal Fishing Licence that contains conditions regarding when, where and how the harvest may occur. Traditionally Inuvialuit from Aklavik would travel to the "fish holes" soon after the first snowfall in late fall or early winter when they could travel by snow machines (historically by dog team) when the Dolly Varden would be best for eating and less ice would have formed over the area of the river used for fishing. The current fishery occurs somewhat later, ensuring that the harvest occurs after the Dolly Varden have had the opportunity to spawn. The timing also is coordinated to help ensure that DFO staff are available to participate in the program. Most of the traditional "fish holes" are included in the program, but a few are excluded.

The harvest method is one of the larger compromises for the harvest program. The methods used by DFO in a pre-existing mark-recapture program have been adopted to ensure concerns about disturbing Dolly Varden habitat were addressed. Now seine nets are used instead of the traditionally used gill nets.

Lastly, biological information is recorded for each fish harvested in the program, with most harvested fish being sampled to provide further information on the stock to support its ongoing co-management. Traditionally as well as today, biological sampling of fish is not always preferred by the Inuvialuit; while they are very interested in learning more about fisheries stocks, many enjoy eating Dolly Varden raw and frozen, and the taste is compromised after biological sampling occurs. A small portion of the annual harvest does not include sampling, enabling those Dolly Varden to be provided to elders from Aklavik. Despite these compromises, Aklavik and its HTC remain very pleased with and supportive of the harvest program. However, they would like the closure of the Big Fish River and its tributaries to be lifted, allowing community members to harvest Dolly Varden from the "fish holes" using their traditional methods at times of their choosing, and to have a stronger leadership role in the management of this resource.

There are three points to draw from these events. First, they demonstrate the empowerment that the Inuvialuit have gained through the IFA; it is extremely unlikely that a fishing community outside a co-management area would be able to receive such a favourable response to a letter to the Minister. Second, they also demonstrate a potential problem; HTCs may see an opportunity to interact directly with the Minister if they think that the FJMC and DFO are not doing enough to address community priorities, and in doing so inadvertently damage the co-management process and the trust that has been established. Third, the advice and actions of the FJMC, with the support of DFO staff, enabled DFO and the Inuvialuit to reach an agreement that should ensure the conservation of the Big Fish River Dolly Varden stock and enable the Inuvialuit to resume their traditional harvest. And, of course, compromise is necessary.

Finally, the WSWG, now including membership form Yukon Territorial Parks, continues to play a successful role in the management of Dolly Varden in the ISR. Also, Dolly Varden was identified as a species of special concern in 2010, and was listed as a species of special concern under SARA in 2017, thus requiring the preparation of a SARA management plan. The Dolly Varden IFMP now is being updated by DFO, GRRB, FJMC and Parks Canada to better meet the SARA requirements and to incorporate new information. It is hoped, therefore, that no new management requirements would be imposed on the Gwich'in and Inuvialuit through SARA.

In summary co-management in the ISR, as implemented by the FJMC, was successful in the advancing management of Dolly Varden. It demonstrated the importance of commitment, building trust, a shared understanding and positive inter-personal relationships (Ansell and Gash 2008; Rocan 2009). Face-to-face meetings also were beneficial in enabling the process to proceed. It demonstrated the importance of the FJMC as a leader and a bridging organization in a situation with multiple stakeholders (Ayles *et al.* 2016), and that the WSWG (and other working groups) is a successful bridging organization too. Also, it demonstrated the need to reconcile traditional knowledge and scientific knowledge, and the benefit of continuity in membership – tempered by the benefit of new perspectives. Perhaps the initial slow progress in the work of the WSWG can be attributed to some deficiencies in meeting Ansell and Gash's requirements, and, perhaps, to the lack of any defined intermediate outcomes.

Conclusions

Co-management, a form of collaborative governance, of fishery resources in the ISR has enabled the Inuvialuit to have a meaningful and effective voice in the management of fishery resources in the western Arctic. Favourable starting conditions set the co-management process on a positive track. There was no history of real conflict, both sides were predisposed to work cooperatively and there were some big initial wins that encouraged further developments. There was a strong institutional base in the IFA and in DFO statutes, regulations, policies and funding and the FJMC built on this base with a range of practices that enhanced communication and cooperation between the government and the community members. Leadership from the members was strong and stable, especially at the start, and the DFO Regional and District staff and the Inuvialuit organizations provided ongoing and effective support. Collaborative processes have followed an adaptive co-management process – i.e., "learning by doing" – with an emphasis on bringing community and government staff together to address issues collaboratively.

Like all organizations, there was a learning curve. However, the stability of the organization and of committee membership, strong leadership, a common commitment to and vision of co-management, teamwork and its bridging activities enabled the FJMC to build trust with the Inuvialuit communities and between the Inuvialuit and DFO. Now, the FJMC is considered to represent the mature stage of co-management. Some particular features of its activities are the efforts blending traditional knowledge and scientific knowledge so there is shared understanding, making decisions by consensus, holding face-to-face meetings involving Inuvialuit and DFO, involving the Inuvialuit in the identification and development of research projects, promoting and conducting collaborative research and monitoring, and participating jointly in the development of fisheries management objectives, fishing plans, management measures and data needs. None of this would have been possible without the leadership of the FJMC and the participation and support of the Inuvialuit and DFO staff.

As with most organizations, constraints exist on the activities of the FJMC. Its activities are framed within the context and details of the IFA. In fulfilling its responsibilities, it has to work within the framework of government legislation and policies; but government does have to consult with Aboriginal groups on changes to legislation and policies, and the FJMC has been able to influence changes. Money, of course, is a constraint, and, as with most organizations, perceived needs outweigh the financial and personnel resources available.

Our description of fisheries co-management in the western Canadian Arctic has been fairly positive, but we do recognize the possibility of confirmatory bias in this single example. We should note that not every commentator is as enamored of co-management as are we. Others have argued that co-management can perpetuate colonial-style relations by concentrating power in administrative centres rather than in the hands of the local people, and that co-management can subvert traditional knowledge and the Aboriginal worldview by incorporation into conventional – i.e., "western based science and decision practices" – environmental and management decision making (e.g., Nadasdy 2007; Stevenson 2004; White 2006).

Based on our experience we disagree with such comments and consider this example of collaborative governance to be positive for both the Inuvialuit and the federal government and to be preferable to the usual hierarchical practices of fisheries and environmental management. Working together has enabled the co-management partners to address both simple and complex issues and work together to achieve effective solutions. We do caution that while there are many elements of this case study of co-management that support Ansel and Gash's (2008) criteria for successful collaborative management, it is problematic to say which, if any, of the identified elements are more important than the others. Were the early wins, or the leadership, or the personalities, or the mandate, or the funding, or the face-to-face meetings, or the particular mix of community, fisheries and environmental issues all essential? And possibly more important, which elements are essential to continue success into the future? We can't say.

Although the fisheries co-management model described in this chapter is specific to the western Arctic, an area where there is a settled land claim, the authors believe that the general approach to fisheries co-management in the ISR is applicable elsewhere in Canada and the world, where local people should and need to be involved in making decisions about the fisheries resources upon which they depend.

Acknowledgements

We would like to thank the individuals who provided the information and insights from the negotiations leading up to the IFA and the starting conditions for the FJMC. More importantly, we thank them for the decisions they made and the actions that they took which led to the subsequent success of fisheries co-management in the western Canadian Arctic. Specifically, we would like to thank, in alphabetical order, N. Cournoyea, R. DeLury, V. Gillman, L. Harwood, R. Josephson, and G. Yaremchuk.

References

Alunik, I. 1998. *Call Me Ishmael: Memories of Ismael Alunik, an Inuvialuit Elder.* Inuvik, NWT: Kolausok Ublaaq Enterprises.

Alunik, E., D. Kolausok, and D. Morrison. 2003. *Across Time and Tundra: The Inuvialuit of the Western Arctic.* Vancouver, BC: Raincoast Books.

Ansell, C., and A. Gash. 2008. "Collaborative Governance in Theory and Practice," *Journal of Public Administration Research and Theory,* 18(4): 543-571.

Armitage, D., F. Berkes, A. Dale, E. Kocho-Schellenberg and E. Patton. 2011. "Co-management and the Co-production of Knowledge: Learning to Adapt in Canada's Arctic," *Global Environmental Change*, 2: 995-1,004.

Armitage, D., F. Berkes, and N. Doubleday (eds.). 2007. *Adaptive Co-management: Collaboration, Learning and Multi-level Governance.* Vancouver, BC: UBC Press.

Ayles, B., R. Bell and A. Hoyt. 2007. "Adaptive Fisheries Co-management in the Western Canadian Arctic," in D. Armitage, F. Berkes, and N. Doubleday (eds.). *Adaptive Co-management: Collaboration, Learning and Multi-level Governance.* Vancouver, BC: UBC Press, p. 125-150.

Ayles, B., L. Porta, and R. McV. Clarke. 2016. "Development of an Integrated Fisheries Co-management Framework for New and Emerging Commercial Fisheries in the Canadian Beaufort Sea," *Marine Policy*, 22: 246-254, https://www.researchgate.net/publication/301832015_Development_of_an_integrated_fisheries_co-management_framework_for_new_and_emerging_commercial_fisheries_in_the_Canadian_Beaufort_Sea [Accessed May 15, 2018].

Bailey, M., B. Favaro, S.P. Otto, A. Charles, R. Devillers, A. Metaxas, P. Tyedmers, N.C. Ban, T. Mason, C. Hoover, T.J. Duck, L., Fanning, C. Milley, A.N. Cisneros- Montemayor, D. Pauly, W.W.L. Cheung, S. Cullis-Suzuki, L. The, and U.R. Sumaila. 2016. "Canada at a Crossroad: The Imperative for Realigning Ocean Policy with Ocean Science," *Marine Policy*, 63: 53-60.

Berger, T. 1977. *Northern Frontier, Northern Homeland. The Report of the Mackenzie Pipeline Inquiry, Volume One.* Ottawa, ON: Department of Supply and Services, www.pwnhc.ca/extras/berger/report/BergerV1_complete_e.pdf [Accessed May 15, 2018].

Berkes, F. 2009. "Evolution of Co-management: Role of Knowledge Generation, Bridging Organizations and Social Learning," *Journal of Environmental Management*, 90: 1,692-1,702.

Berkes, F., D. Armitage and N. Doubleday. 2007. "Synthesis: Adapting, Innovating and Evolving," in D. Armitage, D., F. Berkes, and N. Doubleday (eds.). *Adaptive Co-management: Collaboration, Learning and Multi-level Governance.* Vancouver, BC: University of British Columbia Press, p. 308-327.

Berkes, F., R. Huebert, H. Fast, M. Manseau and A. Diduck (eds.). 2005. *Breaking Ice: Renewable resource and ocean management in the Canadian North*. Calgary, AB: University of Calgary Press.

BSP (Beaufort Sea Partnership). 2017. www.beaufortseapartnership. ca [Accessed May 15, 2018].

Department of Education. 1991. *Inuvialuit Pitquisiit: The Culture of the Inuvialuit*. Government of the Northwest Territories, NWT: Department of Education.

DFO (Fisheries and Oceans Canada). 2003. "Big Fish River Dolly Varden." *DFO Science Stock Status Report*, Ottawa, ON: Fisheries and Oceans Canada, D5-60.

DFO (Fisheries and Oceans Canada). 2011. "Identification of Ecologically and Biologically Significant Areas (EBSA) in the Canadian Arctic." *DFO Canadian Scientific Advisory Secretariat Scientific Advisory Report 2011/055*. Ottawa, ON: Fisheries and Oceans Canada.

DFO (Fisheries and Oceans Canada). 2013. "Assessment of Dolly Varden from the Big Fish River, NT 2009-2011." *DFO Canadian Science Advisory Secretariat Advisory Report 2012/065*. Ottawa, ON: Fisheries and Oceans Canada.

DFO (Fisheries and Oceans Canada). 2017. "Fisheries policies and frameworks," www.dfo-mpo.gc.ca/reports-rapports/regs/policies-politiques-eng.htm [Accessed May 15, 2018].

Doubleday, N. 1989. "Co-management Provisions of the Inuvialuit Final Agreement," in E. Pinkerton (ed.). *Co-operative Management of Local Fisheries: New Directions for Improved Management and Community Development*. Vancouver, BC: University of British Columbia Press, p. 209-227.

Fisheries Act. 1985. http://laws-lois.justice.gc.ca/eng/acts/F-14/ [Accessed May 15, 2018].

Fisheries and Oceans Canada, Fisheries Joint Management Committee, Inuvialuit Game Council, and Inuvialuit Regional Corporation. 2014. "Beaufort Sea Integrated Fisheries Management Framework for the Inuvialuit Settlement Region, Canada: 2013-2017." *Canada/Inuvialuit Fisheries Joint Management Committee Report 2014-1*, https://fjmc.ca/wp-content/uploads/2016/08/Beaufort-Sea-Integrated-Fisheries-Management-Framework-2014-FINAL-version.pdf [Accessed May 15, 2018].

Fisheries and Oceans Canada, Gwich'in Renewables Resources Board, Fisheries Joint Management Committee, and Parks Canada Agency. 2010. *Integrated fisheries management plan for Dolly Varden (Salvelinus malma malma) of the Gwich'in Settlement Area and Inuvialuit Settlement Region, Northwest Territories and Yukon North Slope, 2011-2015.* www.grrb.nt.ca/pdf/fisheries/ DV%20IFMP%20Volume%202 [Accessed May 15, 2018].

FJMC (Fisheries Joint Management Committee). 2017a. "Operating Procedure OP-12: Role of chair, vice-chair and members," www.fjmc.ca/about-us [Accessed May 15, 2018].

FJMC (Fisheries Joint Management Committee). 2017b. https:// fjmc.ca/about-us/fjmc-vision/ [Accessed May 15, 2018].

FJMC Facebook (Fisheries Joint Management Committee). 2017. https://www.facebook.com/ISR.FJMC/?ref=hl [Accessed May 15, 2018].

FJMC Quarterly Newsletter (Fisheries Joint Management Committee). 2013. https://fjmc.ca/wp-content/uploads/2015/07/ FJMC-Newsletter-Issue-9-Spring-2013.pdf [Accessed May 15, 2018].

Freeman, M.R., E.E. Wein, and D.E. Keith. 1992. *Recovering Rights: Bowhead Whales and Inuvialuit Subsistence in the Western Canadian Arctic.* Calgary, AB: University of Alberta Press, Occasional publication series, Canadian Circumpolar Institute, 31: 154, http://www.uap.ualberta.ca/titles/288-9780919058798-recovering-rights [Accessed May 15, 2018].

Guston, D.H. 2001. "Boundary Organizations in Environmental Policy and Science: An Introduction," *Science Technology and Human Values,* 26: 399-408, http://journals.sagepub.com/doi/ abs/10.1177/016224390102600401 [Accessed May 15, 2018].

Holling, C.S. (ed.). 1978. *Adaptive Environmental Assessment and Management. International Institute for Applied Systems Analysis.* Chichester, UK: J. Wiley & Sons.

IFA (Inuvialuit Final Agreement). 1984. *The Western Arctic Claim: The Inuvialuit Final Agreement.* http://webarchive.bac-lac. gc.ca:8080/wayback/20060205004956/http://www.ainc-inac. gc.ca/pr/agr/inu/wesar_e.pdf [Accessed May 15, 2018].

INAC (Indigenous and Northern Affairs Canada). 2017. "General Briefing Note on Canada's Self-Government and Comprehensive Land Claims Policies and the Status of Negotiations." Ottawa, ON: Indigenous and Northern Affairs Canada, https://www.aadnc-aandc.gc.ca/eng/1373385502190/1373385561540 [Accessed May 15, 2018].

IRC (Inuvialuit Regional Corporation). 2009. *COPE: An Original Voice for Aboriginal Rights.* http://irc.inuvialuit.com/sites/default/files/COPE-Original%20Voice%20for%20Inuvialuit%20Rights.pdf [Accessed May 15, 2018].

IRC (Inuvialuit Regional Corporation). 2017. *Inuvialuit Regional Corporation.* www.irc.inuvialuit.com [Accessed May 15, 2018].

ITK (Inuit Tapiriit Kanatami). 2017. *Inuit Tapiriit Kanatami, the National Representational Organization Protecting and Advancing the Rights and Interests of Inuit in Canada.* www.itk.ca [Accessed May 15, 2018].

Iwasaki-Goodman, M. 2005. "Resource Management for the Next Generation: Co-management of Fishery Resources in the Western Canadian Arctic Region," in N. Kishigami and J.M. Savelle (eds.). *Indigenous Use and Management of Marine Resources.* Osaka, Japan: National Museum of Ethnology and Senri Ethnological Studies, 67: 101-20.

Jentoft, S. 2005. "Fisheries Co-management as Empowerment," *Marine Policy,* 29: 1-7, (doi:10.1016/j.marpol.2004.01.003).

Linke, S., and K. Bruckmeir. 2015. "Co-management in Fisheries – Experiences and Changing Approaches in Europe," *Oceans and Coastal Management,* 104: 170-181, http://dx.doi.org/10.1016/j.ocecoaman.2014.11.017 [Accessed May 15, 2018].

McGhee, R. 1974. *Beluga Hunters: An Archaeological Reconstruction of the History and Culture of the Mackenzie Delta Kittegaryumiut.* Toronto, ON: Canadian Museum of Civilization and University of Toronto Press.

MGP-JRP. 2009. "Foundation for a Sustainable Northern Future." *Report of the Joint Review Panel for the Mackenzie Gas Project Volume I – Chapters 1 to 10,* http://www.reviewboard.ca/upload/project_document/EIR0405-001_JRP_Report_of_Environmental_Review_Executive_Volume_I.PDF [Accessed May 15, 2018].

Nadasdy, P. 2007. "Adaptive Fisheries Co-management and the Gospel of Resilience," in Armitage, D., F. Berkes and N. Doubleday (eds.). *Adaptive Co-management: Collaboration, Learning and Multi-level Governance*. Vancouver, BC: University of British Columbia Press, p. 208-227.

North Slope Conference. 2015. *Best Practices in the Use of Aboriginal Traditional Knowledge. Wildlife Management Advisory Council (North Slope)*, www.wmacns.ca [Accessed May 15, 2018].

Oceans Act. 1996. http://laws-lois.justice.gc.ca/eng/acts/O-2.4/ [Accessed May 15, 2018].

Paulic, J.E., M.H. Papst and D.G. Cobb. 2009. "Proceedings for the Identification of Ecologically and Biologically Significant Areas in the Beaufort Sea Large Ocean Management Area," *Canadian Manuscript Report for Fisheries and Aquatic Science*, http://www.beaufortseapartnership.ca/wp-content/uploads/2015/04/ebsa-report-2009.pdf [Accessed May 15, 2018].

Pinkerton, E. (ed.). 1989. *Co-operative Management of Local Fisheries*. Vancouver, BC: University of British Columbia Press.

Pinkerton, E. 2003. "Towards Specificity in Complexity: Understanding Co-management from a Social Science Perspective," in Wilson, D.C., J.R. Nielson and P. Pegnbol (eds.). *The Fisheries Co-management Experience: Accomplishments, Challenges and Prospects*. Dordrecht, Netherlands: Kluwer Academic Publishers, p. 61-77.

Porta, L. and B. Ayles. 2015. "A History and Context of Commercial Fishing in the Canadian Beaufort Sea." *Canada/Inuvialuit Fisheries Joint Management Committee Technical Report, 2015-01*: vi + 21 p. https://fjmc.ca/resources/publications/.

Puxley, P. 2002. *A Model of Engagement: Reflections on the 25th Anniversary of the Berger Report*. Ottawa, ON: Canadian Policy Research Networks Inc.

Rocan, C. 2009. "Multi-Level Collaborative Governance: The Canadian Heart Health Initiative," *Optimum Online*, 39(4): 1-10.

Rosenberg, D.M. 2003. "Mercury in Beluga Whales in the Canadian Beaufort Sea: Causes, Consequences, and Potential Research." *Fisheries Joint Management Committee Report 2003-2*, http://fishfp.sasktelwebhosting.com/publications/FJMC%20Report%20Series/Mercury%20in%20Beluga%20e-copy.pdf [Accessed May 15, 2018].

Species at Risk Act. 2002. http://laws-lois.justice.gc.ca/eng/acts/s-15.3/ [Accessed May 15, 2018].

SSCFO (Senate Standing Committee on Fisheries and Oceans). 2010. *The Management of Fisheries and Oceans in Canada's Western Arctic.* Ottawa, ON: Senate of Canada, https://sencanada.ca/content/sen/Committee/403/fish/rep/rep04may10-e.pdf [Accessed May 15, 2018].

Stevenson, M.G. 2004. "De-colonizing Co-management in Northern Canada," *Cultural Survival Quarterly,* 28(1): 68-71.

Stewart, D.B., R.A. Ratynski, L.M.J. Bernier and D.J. Ramsey. 1993. "A Fishery Development Strategy for the Canadian Beaufort Sea-Amundsen Gulf Area," *Canadian Technical Report for Fisheries Aquatic Sciences, 1910,* http://publications.gc.ca/collections/collection_2012/mpo-dfo/Fs97-6-1910-eng.pdf [Accessed May 15, 2018].

Stoker, S., and I. Krupnik. 1993. "Subsistence Whaling," in Burns, J.J., J.J. Montague and C.J. Cowles (eds.). *The Bowhead Whale.* Lawrence, KS: Special Publication Number 2, The Society for Marine Mammalogy, p. 579-629.

Thompson, P. 1974. "Institutional constraints in fisheries management," *Journal of the Fisheries Research Board of Canada,* 31. 1965-1981. 10.1139/f74-260, https://www.researchgate.net/publication/237179699_Institutional_Constraints_in_Fisheries_Management [Accessed May 15, 2018].

Usher, P.J. 2002. "Inuvialuit Use of the Beaufort Sea and Its Resources, 1960-2000," *Arctic* 55 (Supp. I): 18-28.

Von der Porten, S., D. Lepofsky, D. McGregor and J. Silver. 2016. "Recommendations for marine herring policy change in Canada: Aligning with indigenous legal and inherent rights," *Marine Policy,* 74: 68-76, http://dx.doi.org/10.1016/j.marpol.2016.09.007 [Accessed May 15, 2018].

Western Arctic Handbook Committee. 2002. *Natural History of the Western Arctic.* Inuvik, NT: Western Arctic Handbook Project, distributed by Gordon Soules Book Publishers Ltd, www.gordonsoules.com.

White, G. 2006. "Cultures in Collision: Traditional Knowledge and Euro-Canadian Governance Processes in Northern Land Claims Boards," *Arctic,* 59(4): 401-414.

CONCLUSION

Walker, there is no path. The path is made by walking.

– Antonio Machado, Spanish poet

The authors of the case studies in this book have described with clarity, precision and honesty the collaborative approaches taken to deal with a particular 'wicked' problem. In so doing, they have provided important insights on actions that have been taken, and their consequences. The description and analysis of the Calgary Poverty Reduction Initiative (CPRI) by Cook and Mahoney illustrates the impact of power relations within an ambitious and innovative attempt to address the multi-dimensional and multi-faceted issue of poverty in that city.

Dryden describes how the Gang Action Interagency Network (GAIN), a broad network focusing on the problem of the criminal gangs plaguing the City of Winnipeg, helped to educate provincial government departments and agencies about the interconnections between gang activities and other areas of public policy. Moreover, the experience and expertise gained by network members were instrumental in the development of a gang exit strategy, which provides members with short-term and longer-term supports.

Krantzberg shows the significance of place-based types of restoration initiatives and shows how technological measures were married to collaborative structures to lead to significant improvements in the environment of that area. Beyond the immediate benefits of improved water quality for Collingwood Harbour, Krantzberg points out that the collaboration led to "cooperative learning" and improved community capacity, which will help prepare the community to face environmental threats in the future.

From Paris and Garon, we learn of Quebec's attempt to improve and apply the model from the WHO Global Network for Age-Friendly Cities and Communities to make municipal structures and services more suitable and accessible for older people. In this case, the Quebec government took the initiative, but the planning and implementation took place at the local level involving a range of actors who became "the true masters" of the initiatives.

Wuttunee's case studies on economic development underscore the need to invest the time for relationship-building, particularly where different cultures are involved, and where there has been a history of isolation and even animosity between the communities involved. Ayles *et al.* describe a co-management model – a form of collaborative governance – to manage fisheries in the western Arctic. Beyond the formal provisions of the Inuvialuit Final Agreement, the authors describe the steps taken to bridge cultural differences by building strong and continuing relationships between representatives of the Department of Fisheries and Oceans and the Inuvialuit. Of particular importance in this respect was finding ways to incorporate both scientific and traditional knowledge relating to the fisheries.

The authors do not suggest that the steps taken to address the particular problem in question settle the issue for all time. In all these cases, one expects that these will be continuing challenges. This is entirely consistent with wicked problems, which, as stated in the Introduction, are never truly "fixed." However, they represent positive contributions, and each in its own way helps to put into place some pieces for the enormous puzzles that confront modern society.

There is no generic approach to a wicked problem. Each is unique, and needs to be treated as such (Rittel and Webber 1973; Head 2008). Furthermore, the attempts to deal with a wicked problem through collaboration will also be unique. No two situations will ever be identical. History, personalities, policy domain, resources and so on will play a major role in determining the governance of the initiatives at play. To a large extent, the specific shape of the governance structures that emerge reflect the overall factors that surround the particular initiative in question.

It follows, therefore, that making generalizations about specific factors that determine the success or failure of a collaborative 'enterprise' is a risky undertaking. No such attempt will be made here. That stated, certain common themes emerge from the case studies presented here, and it is worthwhile to highlight some of the more prominent ones using the categories from our analytical framework. The attentive reader will no doubt be able to identify others of significance.

Starting conditions

It is noteworthy, though not surprising, that in none of the case studies was the decision to collaborate on a joint initiative made in a vacuum. In other words, pre-conditions for the application of collaborative governance were in place. Having a previous history of working together clearly made a positive difference. Dryden, for example, reports that many of the participants in the GAIN had established relationships as a result of previously working together on related issues. Cook and Mahoney point out that although members of the Stewardship Group did not have a great deal of experience in working together, the CPRI was preceded by a number of initiatives that had related objectives and had been organized on a collaborative basis. These earlier experiences had led the players to an appreciation of the complexity of the issue of poverty, and no doubt a common recognition that no one organization could achieve significant change on its own.

Furthermore, having a common vision, and the *process* of developing such, emerged as an important unifying factor. Paris and Garon observe that working together to define clear objectives helped to motivate the players involved in the Age-Friendly Cities and Communities process in Quebec. A similar point is made by Krantzberg who indicates that developing clear and meaningful goals early in the process had a unifying effect on the team involved in the Collingwood Harbour Remedial Action Plan (RAP).

Another theme that emerges strongly from the case studies is the importance of having a foundational document. In the case of the co-management of fisheries in the western Arctic, Ayles *et al.* highlight the importance that the Inuvialuit Final Agreement (IFA), a modern-day treaty, has had in framing and defining the co-management process. Wuttunee points out the importance of the Friendship Accords for the two case studies she presents in detail. Although somewhat less formal than the IFA, Wuttunee observes that these accords helped to build a platform for the activities that ensued. At the same time, the author makes the point that while similar in concept, the two accords differed from each other in content, as they sought to reflect the particular circumstances in their respective communities. Other case studies also included a core document, whether in the form of a report (GAIN), an international agreement (RAP), or a global framework combined with a local action plan (Age-Friendly Cities and Communities).

Institutional design

From the perspective of institutional design, one sees, as expected, a number of different ways such initiatives can be structured. Looking at the range of experiences, a few broad observations can be hazarded. The first is that the case studies all seem to reflect a deliberate attempt to be inclusive of the wide range of parties having an interest in the issue at hand. This can be a bigger challenge for some initiatives than for others, depending on the number of such interested parties that need to be included in order to encompass the broad and inter-connected aspects of an issue. If there are numerous such parties, the challenge is to find a way to encourage meaningful participation of a large number, while at the same time having a manageable process. To address this, the CPRI established a number of "Constellation Groups," each assigned to a particular topic, and reporting to the "Stewardship Group." The GAIN, for its part, makes extensive use of temporary working groups, reporting to the GAIN executive, which, in turn, reports to the Leadership Advisory Board.

What we also see is the commitment in these cases to consensus-based decision making; in no case is there a decision-making 'formula,' or a formal mechanism to allow for majoritarian decision making. In her description of the economic development collaborations, Wuttunee states that consensus means "impactful decision-making with all parties equally committed." Although often implicit, one infers from all cases that the imposition of decisions by one or several parties on the others would be seen as inconsistent with the spirit of collaboration. Still, this does raise the question about how differences can be resolved when entrenched interests differ. A partial answer to this may be found in the RAP experience, where, as Krantzberg recounts, the process of defining clear goals at the outset helped to deal with disputes when they arose.

How power differentials between the participants were managed in these cases is also significant. In all instances, government representatives were part of the network, and therefore had access to formal and mandated authority in a way that representatives of civil society did not. Technically, this would form an uneven playing field. This is not unusual, as networks often exist "within the shadow of hierarchy" (Scharpf 1994: 37). Generally, however, the use of this authority was deliberately constrained and efforts were made to level the playing field. This is illustrated in the case of the Collingwood Harbour RAP, where, as Kranzberg notes, the federal and provincial government representatives acted, not as decision makers, but rather as a "resource offered to the community," with the officials taking the role of technical advisers.

In the case of the co-management of Western Arctic Fisheries, formal authority had a stronger presence. As Ayles *et al.* indicate, federal legislation sets the framework for the Fisheries Joint Management Committee (FJMC) and the government still retains jurisdiction and formal power, which would allow it to make decisions unilaterally. However, power differentials here are mitigated, among other ways, in the learning process involved in reconciling traditional knowledge and scientific knowledge. The effect of merging these two streams of knowledge is such that Ayles *et al.* refer to the "true sharing of power" between the Inuvialuit and the Government of Canada. Similarly, in the economic development initiatives described by Wuttunee, the heightened understanding on the part of the other partners (towns and rural municipalities) of the issues faced by First Nations, achieved through dialogue and relationship-building, helped to offset "initial capacity limitations" that might otherwise have been damaging to the functioning of the network.

More problematic power differentials are seen in two cases. Cook and Mahoney point to inequalities that were present among the members of the participants in the CPRI, both at the levels of the Stewardship Group and the Constellation Groups. As these authors point out, those selected to take part in the CPRI tended to be prominent leaders from their respective fields, whether private industry, civil society, or political circles. This led to a certain élite-level over-representation in the network. Only reluctantly did the parties agree to involve individuals living in poverty, and even when these individuals did become involved, their voice tended to be over-shadowed by the others. Along similar lines, Paris and Garon point to inequality of resources between groups participating in the steering committees as well as between individuals. Such issues of power inequalities, while not necessarily crippling, if left unresolved, have the potential to compromise the effectiveness of a collaboration, (Huxham and Vangen 2005: 166) and there is a suggestion, particularly with the CPRI, that this was indeed the case.

Collaborative process

The importance of trust for a successful collaboration can hardly be over-stated. As stated in the Introduction, this factor is repeatedly mentioned in the scholarly literature and is perhaps the strongest theme to come out of the case studies presented here. Where the parties had a previous history of working together on projects of a similar nature, for example, in the case of the GAIN, an element of trust was present from the beginning which helped in getting on with the project at hand. Where no prior culture of collaboration existed, on the other hand, progress was more challenging. Paris and Garon describe cases where some members of the Steering Committee, particularly elected municipal officials, did not have a history of working together, and were in fact distrustful of doing so, thereby causing difficulties in the development of a regional municipal plan.

In cases where the parties did not know each other well but seemed open to doing so, trust-building can be achieved through various means. Cook and Mahoney indicate that one of the first steps of the CPRI was to build trust and a common vision among members of the Stewardship Group, who otherwise represented competing interests. As mentioned earlier, the process of arriving at an agreement on the collaboration's vision, goals and objectives, and at negotiating a foundational document, is an important trust-building activity. Also, as Paris and Garon note, achieving small gains can help the participants build confidence in each other and in the process, a point similarly raised by Krantzberg.

Perhaps more challenging are the cases where deep cultural barriers had to be overcome before trust could develop. Ayles *et al.* and Wuttunee argue forcefully about the importance of building trust-based relationships in these instances and stress the importance of investing the *time* necessary to allow trust to build. Describing the case of the participants in the LSFN First Nation (LSFN), Municipality of Sioux Lookout and Kichenuhmaykoosib Inninuwug (KI) Collaboration, Wuttunee reports that participants met by invitation for several years in a trust-building process. Ayles *et al.* reflect that although there was no particular history of conflict between the Inuvialuit and the DFO, "comprehensive consultation and communication," while costly, helped to establish the groundwork for trust and understanding. Moreover, as both Wuttunee and Ayles *et al.* show, trust-building across cultural barriers is not a one-off activity. This is an area that requires a sustained and ongoing commitment. Ayles *et al.* explain how DFO officials conduct annual visits to each one of the communities in the Inuvialuit Settlement Region, and that these visits have become an integral part of the planning and budgeting process and a way to bridge traditional and scientific knowledge. What helps to build and sustain trust and respect in this case is the stability in the tenure of the participants in the process, with individuals from both the DFO and Inuvialuit teams remaining in their roles for long periods of time. Wuttunee gives examples of imaginative steps that were taken to bring communities together before transactions around economic development could even begin, such as a canoe trip for leaders of a collaboration and their families, and a "blanket exercise" following the tragic death of a young First Nations man.

What is clear from all the case studies is that trust and trust-building is essential for a collaboration to be able to function effectively and make progress towards achieving the group's objectives. How one builds and maintains trust in a partnership no doubt varies greatly depending on the personalities of the players and the circumstances surrounding the initiative. In addition to working together on a foundational document and of achieving small gains together, what can also be seen in these cases is the importance of joint learning, in which partners solidify their relationships by deepening their understanding of each other's interests and perspectives and their knowledge of the various aspects of the issue they are attempting to address. This point is reflected in the importance of incorporating knowledge and expertise from the various partners (GAIN, CPRI) and of "cooperative learning" (RAP), in addition to the cases mentioned above where participants share traditional and scientific knowledge.

Facilitative leadership

As mentioned in the Introduction, leadership is the most commonly listed factor in the success of a collaboration. Much has been written about the type of leadership that is most appropriate in a network. What makes leadership in this context particularly challenging is the fact that networks are often composed of individuals, or of representatives from autonomous organizations, each with their own decision-making structures. As we have seen, members of a network often represent organizations or sectors that have competing interests. In this context, the leader of such a network does not exercise authority over the members, at least not in a conventional sense. Indeed, in these cases, a leader has very limited leverage over the others. So what is the type of leadership appropriate in these circumstances, and what are the skills the "leader" must bring to the table?

Although the application differs from case to case, what emerges clearly from these case studies are forms of what might be called "distributive leadership," in which many share in the decision-making process. For instance, Dryden points out that while an important leadership function is invested in the position of the GAIN chair, a considerable amount of leadership comes from the individuals who participate in the working groups. Moreover, with GAIN, all major decisions are discussed at the network level as opposed to being taken by the executive.

In a similar way, Cook and Mahoney point out that while the CPRI was headed by the Steering Group selected by the Mayor and United Way of Calgary and Area, much of the impetus in the process emanated from the Constellation Groups formed around particular topics, and that it was the dialogue across Constellation Groups that allowed the network to be flexible and adaptive.

Paris and Garon mention that while the elected officials on the steering committees of the Age-Friendly Cities and Communities projects had power by virtue of their role in deciding commitment of resources, this power was counter-balanced by other players on the committee based on their personal and professional competencies and the respect these individuals enjoyed from other steering committee members.

The authors also make the important observation that the leadership roles evolved with the different stages of a project: in one case going from a 'selling' role at the planning stage, to a 'watch-dog' role at the implementation stage.

The economic development initiatives documented by Wuttunee are also characterized by a distributive style of leadership. The economic development manager for the LSFN, Sioux Lookout, and KI Collaboration is described as the 'glue stick' to the process, one of her main roles being to build relationships and capacities among the participants. In the case of the Opaskwayak Cree Nation, The Pas, and R.M. of Kelsey Manitoba Collaboration, two of the participants, one a Reeve for the RM, the other the economic development manager, play the role of "collaboration champions," whose work is focussed on building relationships and ensuring open lines of communication.

Overall, rather than strong leadership in the conventional sense, what one sees through these case studies is reflective of what some have called *stewardship* (Paquet 2008), where leaders devote their energies primarily to motivating, facilitating, negotiating, and coordinating. The role of the leader in a collaborative governance initiative to "nurture, nurture, nurture" (Huxham and Vangen 2005: 42) finds its reflection in the statement from the economic development manager cited by Wuttunee, that her commitment to the success of the partnership leads her to "live it, eat it, drink it every day."

Taking the next step

The case studies in this book are all situated in some sense at the community level. In some cases, notably the high Arctic, community is defined somewhat broadly, but even here, the case examined involves a geographically specific area, though admittedly quite expansive, and an identifiable group of actors. The question remains, however, how does this model of governance translate at the "macro" level, if indeed it does at all? In other words, does collaborative governance, as seen in these specific instances, apply at the broader societal level? Is the political system we have in Canada open to or ready for such a radical transformation, and if so, under what specific conditions?

The answer to these questions is far from clear. What we do know is that there are significant challenges on the road to collaborative governance at the national level in Canada. We will look at a few.

Since the focus in this book is on the Canadian context, let's begin by asking about the readiness of the federal government to enter into these arrangements. The trend toward the concentration of power within the Canadian government has been documented in some detail (Savoie 1999), and as Dutil has shown, has roots deeper than many might have expected (Dutil 2017). Decision making at the federal government level is increasingly made by the Prime Minister and a narrow circle around him/her mostly situated in the Prime Minister's Office or the Privy Council Office. Is it realistic to think that those inside this tight circle will ever be open to allowing outsiders to participate in decision making when even, as Donald Savoie and many others have reported, individual Ministers and Cabinet itself are often marginalized when important decisions are made? Compounded within this is the tendency of the federal bureaucracy – perhaps any bureaucracy – to be control-oriented, risk-averse and resistant to change (Hubbard and Paquet 2010: 59; Goldsmith and Eggers 2004: 160). One of the four guiding principles of *Blueprint 2020*, positioned as the federal government's bold new plan for Public Service Renewal, is: "An open and networked environment that engages citizens and partners for the public good" (Canada 2013: 4). This plan openly acknowledges that much remains to be done in this area. Yet while the need for change is recognized, it is an open question whether the federal bureaucracy has the capacity, the tools, and the organizational culture, to achieve it. We will return to this point later.

Admittedly, there are occasions where collaboration in decision making may not be realistic. To begin with, collaboration becomes more difficult to achieve in the upper reaches of government (Armstrong and Lenihan 1999: 30; Peters 1998: 307). As the cliché goes, it really does get lonely at the top. There are instances where, for reasons good and bad, top decision-makers feel the need to put distance between themselves and the many competing voices around an issue in order to make a crucial decision.

A second and partially overlapping instance is in the area of what sometimes has been called "summit politics," (Dupré 1985) where federal and provincial/territorial governments are involved in high-stakes negotiations on issues such as transfer payments, tax-sharing, jurisdiction, or constitutional reform. Whereas consultations can take place in the early stages of such talks, when the level of intensity increases, outside forces tend to be pushed to the side. Third, as Bakvis and Juillet have shown, the level of difficulty around collaborative approaches increases at the strategic level, as opposed to the administrative/program areas (Bakvis and Juillet 2004). This is to be expected, since strategic discussions tend to take place in closed settings, whereas programs often include outside stakeholders and partners in the delivery that can more easily be invited into the conversation. Finally, there are times when the federal government must assume "high state" functions involving international diplomacy, defence and internal security matters, where matters must be discussed in great confidence.

Looking at the issue through a broader lens, collaborative governance presents a challenge, not just for Canada but for liberal democracies, because it implies a re-definition – but not necessarily a reduction – of the role for the state (Kooiman 2000: 144). This model implies that while governments will continue to have a special role in collaborations because of their public mandate, their legal position and their access to financial and other resources, they would now have to contend with the reality that they must share the playing field with others. Increasingly there are instances where government – in this case the federal government – will be only one voice amid a number voices, including voluntary sector organizations, private sector bodies, and other levels of government. This point is explicitly acknowledged in *Blueprint 2020*. The significance of this transformation in practice can hardly be overstated. In many cases, it would mean that the role of the government would become more like that of a referee or facilitator, ensuring a degree of inclusion so that as many viewpoints and interests on a particular part of public policy are brought into the discussion, and then to pro-actively act as a broker to help reach a consensus around a particular outcome (Denhardt and Denhardt 2000: 553). A part of the government's role in cases like these may be to take steps to level the playing field as much as possible so that under-resourced groups have an opportunity to participate effectively in the process. In the end, these changes amount to a shift to what some observers have called "substantive democracy," in which the state has the courage "to share rather than control knowledge and administrative processes," and to create broader fora for meaningful discussion and decision making (Box *et al.* 2001: 616).

Transformation of the role of the state along these lines will require the tools and competencies necessary to take on these roles, which in turn implies a major cultural change within the federal bureaucracy and, for that matter, in government bureaucracies in general. It will be important to have actors in government, both at the political and bureaucratic levels, who have developed skills in negotiations, facilitation, and facilitative leadership, as well as the more conventional skills of management in a hierarchical organization (Moore 2009: 206; Rhodes 1997: 56). Public servants will need to become "bi-cultural" in an organizational sense, meaning they would need the ability to move from a more conventional hierarchical model of decision making – which, as noted, will still be needed in some instances – to one that is more flexible, inclusive, and collaborative. It also means that public servants, and indeed other players in a collaboration, will essentially have two sets of loyalties: on the one hand, to the organization of which they are formally a part, that is, their employer, and on the other, to the other members of the network (Hertting 2007: 56). (This touches on the issue of accountability, which we will discuss below.)

Yet even this understates the challenge. The reality is that in many cases, individuals will be participants in not just one, but a number of networks simultaneously, as was this author in his role with Health Canada/the Public Health Agency of Canada (see Introduction). So indeed, what is involved is not simply *dual* loyalties, but *multiple* loyalties. As a consequence, governments will need, not just to adjust to this reality, but to also pro-actively develop the incentives for public servants to participate effectively in networks, something which appears to be lacking in the current context. When these pieces related to the role of government are seen in their totality, one sees what O'Toole has referred to as "intriguingly complicated terrain" (O'Toole 2010: 8). It is exactly that! Yet facing up to these issues is necessary if, as a society, we are to deal more effectively with the wicked problems that confront and confound us.

A related challenge lies in the area of accountability. It has been pointed out that the standard instruments of accountability are inconsistent with the very purpose of a network, which is "to provide decentralized, flexible, individualized and creative responses to a public problem" (Goldsmith and Eggers 2004: 123). The difficulty rests in the fact that under a governance model many hands are involved in the decision-making process. At the end of the day, who then is ultimately accountable? In reality, the linear accountability model that rigidly follows the chain of command is basically a fiction in a context where no one is completely in charge. Worse, this model can be quite misleading in that it can ascribe responsibility to officials who, in a complex and inter-connected world, may have very little control over the area or program for which they are putatively responsible. Clearly there is a need to broaden the notion of accountability so that it is more reflective of real-life circumstances. The exact accountability lines vary according to the specific context, but the key point here is the development of a model of accountability – what Hubbard and Paquet and others have referred to as "360-degree accountability" (Hubbard and Paquet 2010: 140) – that is broader, more multi-faceted and more flexible than the linear model associated with a command-and-control hierarchical system. This will also require the development of indicators and measures that go beyond outputs, and include broader measures related, among others, to learning, fairness, inclusion and participation (Denhardt and Denhardt 2002: 133; Stein 2009: 165; Stoker 2006: 53; Kettl 2002: 494) Moreover, as Anna De Hart points out in her chapter (see Annex), collaborative governance calls for models of evaluation and impact assessment that take into account, not just the direct consequences, but also the collateral impact that both primary and secondary players have on an initiative.

Yet another challenge to be addressed is in the area of dispute resolution. As with accountability, we have not yet developed a general approach to conflict resolution in the context of collaborative governance (Pierre 2000: 245). On the one hand, it is to be expected, and is indeed probably inevitable, that conflict will occur within a collaboration. It is simply in the nature of human beings that differences in style, content, even personalities will occur as people strive to achieve a common objective. Moreover, properly managed, conflict can have a positive and creative effect on a collaboration (Imperial 2005: 311). Unfortunately, conflict is often an issue that participants feel uncomfortable addressing directly when the basic structures of a collaboration are being put in place. It may be the case that participants in a network starting out feel that relations with their new associates are still too fragile to risk discussing how to resolve conflicts that could arise in the future. Yet leaving the issue unaddressed can have its consequences. For example, we saw in another study that a lack of a consistent and effective mechanisms to deal with internal conflicts compromised somewhat the success of the Canadian Heart Health Initiative (Rocan 2012: 118). Internal conflicts in collaboration, and the lack of a mechanism to deal with them, can easily lead to break-downs and help to explain the high failure rate of collaborations.

From a research perspective, conflict resolution within a collaboration can be a difficult area to explore. Participants often find it somewhat awkward to discuss openly, perhaps because doing so might lay bare some internal tensions, or risk inflaming them. (Some of this may be reflected in the case studies included in this book.) Yet it is important to come to terms with this area in order to increase the chances of a collaboration being successful in achieving its objectives. To be clear, it is not conflict that one must attempt to avoid, since this would not be realistic or even desirable. Rather, the challenge is to anticipate that conflicts will occur, and accordingly to develop, *and use* mechanisms of conflict resolution, where required, so that obstacles can be eliminated and the process can go forward.

Acknowledging the challenges involved does not mean giving up on the concept of collaborative governance at the highest level. As stated in the Introduction, wicked problems necessitate major changes in the way society organizes itself to respond to them. It may be true, as some have suggested, that governments are not yet capable of developing and participating in genuine collaborations (Tiesman and Klijn 2002: 204). But by incorporating a strong learning component that emphasizes "reflection, lesson drawing, and continuous adaptation," governments can better equip themselves to face the new realities (Stoker 2006: 49). As stated earlier, one learns to collaborate by collaborating, and by systematically building on one's experience and the experience of others engaged in similar exercises.

Over time, collaborative governance at the community or grass-roots level can help to shape how governance is exercised at higher levels. As experience in this model of governance builds, it will hopefully become imbedded in our political culture such that there will be an expectation and an understanding of a more inclusive way of governing at all levels. The learning derived and the competencies developed from governance at the community level, in addition to its intrinsic value, can help inform and shape what takes place at more "macro" levels. In this way, it is hoped that the case studies contained in this book can be of use to present and future practitioners, and in so doing contribute to the successful application and expansion of the collaborative governance model at all levels of public policy.

References

Agranoff, Robert and Michael McGuire. 2003. "Integrating the Paradigms of Intergovernmental and Network Management," *International Journal of Public Administration*, 26(12): 1,401-1,422.

Armstrong, Jim and Donald G. Lenihan. 1999. *From Controlling to Collaborating: When Governments Want to be Partners*. Toronto, ON: Institute of Public Administration of Canada.

Bakvis, Herman and Luc Juillet. 2004. *The Horizontal Challenge: Line Departments, Central Agencies, and Leadership*. Ottawa, ON: Canada School of Public Service.

Box, Richard C., Gary S. Marshall, B.J. Reed, and Christine M. Reed. 2001. "New Public Management and Substantive Democracy," *Public Administration Review*, 61(5): 608-619.

Canada. 2013. *Blueprint 2020 – Getting Started – Getting Your Views: Building Tomorrow's Public Service Together*. Ottawa, ON: www.canada.ca/en/privy-council/topics/blueprint-2020-public-service-renewal.html [Accessed May 15, 2018].

Denhardt Janet V. and Robert B. Denhardt. 2002. *The New Public Service: Serving, Not Steering*. Armonk, NY: M.E. Sharpe.

Denhardt, Robert B. and Janet Vinzant Denhardt. 2000. "The New Public Service: Serving Rather than Steering," *Public Administration Review*, 60(6): 549-559.

Dupré, J. Stefan. 1985. "Reflections on the Workability of Executive Federalism," *Intergovernmental Relations*, 63: 1-32.

Dutil, Patrice. 2017. *Prime Ministerial Power in Canada: Its Origins under Macdonald, Laurier and Borden*. Vancouver, BC: UBC Press.

Goldsmith, Stephen and William D. Eggers. 2004. *Governing by Network*. Washington, DC: Brookings Institution Press.

Head, Brian W. 2008. "Wicked Problems in Public Policy," *Public Policy*, 3(2): 101-118.

Hertting, Nils. 2007. "Mechanisms of Governance Network Formation – A Contextual Rational Choice Perspective," in Sorenson, Eva and Jacob Torfing (eds.). *Theories of Democratic Network Governance*. New York, NY: Palgrave Macmillan, p. 43-60.

Hubbard, Ruth and Gilles Paquet. 2010. *The Black Hole of Public Administration*. Ottawa, ON: University of Ottawa Press.

Huxham, Chris and Siv Vangen. 2005. *Managing to Collaborate: The Theory and Practice of Collaborative Advantage*. London and New York: Routledge.

Imperial, Mark T. 2005. "Using Collaboration as a Governance Strategy: Lessons from Six Watershed Management Programs," *Administration & Society*, 37(3): 281-320.

Kettl, Donald F. 2002. "Managing Indirect Government," in Lester M. Salamon (ed.). *The Tools of Government: A Guide to the New Government*. Oxford, UK: Oxford University Press, p. 490-511.

Kooiman, Jan. 2000. "Social Governance: Levels, Modes, and Orders of Social-Political Interaction," in Jon Pierre (ed.). *Debating Governance: Authority, Steering, and Democracy*. Oxford, UK: Oxford University Press, p. 138-166.

Moore, Mark. H. 2009. "Networked Government: Survey of Rationales, Forms, and Techniques," in Goldsmith, Stephen and Donald F. Kettl (eds.). *Unlocking the Power of Networks: Keys to High-Performance Government*. Washington, DC: Brookings University Press, p. 190-228.

O'Toole, Laurence J. Jr. 2010. "The Ties That Bind? Networks, Public Administration, and Political Science," *PS: Political Science and Politics*, 43(1): 7-14.

Paquet, Gilles. 2008. "Governance as Stewardship," *www. optimumonline*, 38(4): 14-46.

Peters, B. Guy. 1998. *Managing Horizontal Government: The Politics of Coordination*. Ottawa, ON: Canadian Centre for Management Development, Research Paper no. 21.

Pierre, Jon (ed.). 2000. *Debating Governance: Authority, Steering, and Democracy*. Oxford, UK: Oxford University Press.

Pierre, Jon and B. Guy Peters (eds.). 2000. *Governance, Politics, and the State*. New York, NY: St. Martin's Press.

Pierre, Jon and B. Guy Peters. 2005. *Governing Complex Societies: Trajectories and Scenarios*. Hampshire and New York: Palgrave.

Rocan, Claude. 2012. *Challenges in Public Health Governance: The Canadian Experience*. Ottawa, ON: Invenire Books.

Rhodes, R.A.W. 1997. *Understanding Governance: Reflexivity and Accountability*. Buckingham, UK: Open University Press.

Rittel, Horst W.J. and Melvin M. Webber. 1973. "Dilemmas in a General Theory of Planning," *Policy Sciences*, 4(2): 155-169.

Savoie, Donald J. 1999. *Governing from the Centre: The Concentration of Power in Canadian Politics*. Toronto, ON: University of Toronto Press.

Scharpf, F.W. 1994. "Games Real Actors Could Play: Positive and Negative Coodination in Embedded Negotiations," *Journal of Theoretical Politics*, 6(1): 27-53.

Sorensen, Eva and Jacob Torfing. 2007. "Theoretical Approaches to Governance Network Failure," in Sorensen, E. and J. Torfing (eds.). *Theories of Democratic Network Governance*. Hampshire, UK: Palgrave Macmillan, p. 95-110.

Stein, Janice G. 2009. "The Politics and Power of Networks: The Accountability of Humanitarian Organizations," in Miles Kahler (ed.). *Networked Politics: Agency, Power, and Governance*. Ithaca and London: Cornell University Press, p. 151-170.

Stoker, Gerry. 2006. "Public Value Management: A New Narrative for Networked Governance?" *American Review of Public Administration*, 36(1): 41-57.

Teisman, Geert R. and Erik-Hans Klijn. 2002. "Partnership Arrangements: Governmental Rhetoric or Governance Scheme?" *Public Administration Review*, 62(2): 197-205.

ANNEX

Assessing Collateral Impact within a Collaborative Governance Framework

By Anna J. De Hart

Why assess collateral impact in collaborative governance initiatives?

Traditional evaluation frameworks have been criticized because they tend to centre on readily observable elements or those that can be defined in clear, concrete terms. This careful selection of criteria has tended to narrow the focus of any evaluation process. By narrowing the focus of the evaluation, the potential of missing some critical core data increases. And given that this relates to efforts of core stakeholders, it virtually eliminates data from secondary sources. And, yet it is this secondary data that could derail an otherwise positive initiative.

It is possible, if not probable that these secondary aspects are coming from stakeholders or clients that were not considered as part of the initial evaluation because they were not defined as being in the core group. And yet, the influence that these secondary stakeholders and clients could have on the core group could quite likely determine the project's success. They could represent an organization's management, secondary funding sources, competing groups or other interested parties as well as an auxiliary group of clients.

Not being part of the core groups has left them on the fringe of a project but that does not mean they have no influence. Consider the multiplicity of influencers within any collaborative governance project. Here we have multi-stakeholders who are engaging with each other within multiple layers of governance. It is a dynamic and fluid process. Any one stakeholder's influence could rise or fall depending on those stakeholders' influencers. It is challenging if not impossible for any formal, traditional evaluation framework to capture the full impact picture within such a dynamic process. Impact from such influencers as secondary stakeholders, and even clients, I will call *collateral impact*.

Although core stakeholders' influence can rise and ebb throughout the project and could at times be considered to be collateral, the full collateral impact would more likely come from sources outside the core participants. Within any multi-dimensional and fluid initiative using the collaborative governance model, the influencing nature of these impacts could indeed determine the extent of the success of the project as a whole. We can see how this might work when a project, labelled as a success through the formal evaluation framework, is perceived as not working for the stakeholders or their clients.

It is because of this quandary that evaluators have been puzzling over the failure of any one formal evaluation framework's inability to capture the full impact of a project. Sometimes professional evaluators have turned to elaborate computer and mathematical algorithms to find a better tracking framework. While this has satisfied some aspects of project evaluation, I suggest that the continuing gap in the data could be attributed to the failure to take into account collateral impact. By leaving the reality of collateral impact out of the picture, the influence that comes from secondary stakeholders and clients is not fully accounted for. Essentially it eliminates the possibility of achieving a complete and valid picture of the project as a whole.

By stretching the formal evaluation paradigm to include collateral impacts, it becomes possible to obtain a more complete picture of the initiative, its working environment and the impact it has had on the core participants, as well as those groups and individuals who were not identified as part of the initial project.

When one considers the complexity of multi-stakeholder or multi-level projects as in the case of collaborative projects, the potential for *collateral impact* is multiplied. In multi-stakeholder and multi-level initiatives, the interaction between partners is both dynamic and constantly changing. As such there is always the possibility of both positive and negative impacts. And, given that traditional evaluation frameworks do not focus on any subtle changes in relationships, these secondary impacts or collateral impact could be missed. Not recognizing this impact could put the project on an unexpected path that could ultimately derail the initiative.

Traditionally the key stakeholder is the funding agent. Often this stakeholder has been identified through some agreement of a hierarchy of stakeholders. However within collaborative governance, we can have multiple funding sources and various levels of "in-kind" contributions. Therefore the hierarchy model no longer works. We now need an evaluation process that not only identifies the dynamic interaction of key stakeholders but also recognizes the impact exerted by secondary sources.

Essentially, the formal, traditional approaches to evaluation do not encompass the probability of collateral impact within collaborative governance, and that the collateral impact will increase as many projects involve multiple organizations who most likely cover a broad network of stakeholders and clients.

Also within a collaborative governance initiative, we know that any time a stakeholder is added or leaves the project the internal dynamics of the project changes. And as any of the active partners' knowledge and skills evolve over time, their influence or impact also evolves. Traditional evaluation approaches struggle to encapsulate the impact of this fluidity and therefore this continual evolution and its collateral impact can go undocumented.

While it is critical to track collateral impact, recognizing and tracking its impact need not require a completely new evaluation paradigm. In fact, collateral impact can be a valuable additional management tool that can be integrated into most existing approaches to evaluation.

For instance, within the domain of international humanitarian projects, such multi-stakeholder, multi-government projects are invariably the operational norm. Modern evaluators are looking for approaches to the assessment of these projects that embrace partners and clients who were not before considered because they were not essential to the core group. While some essential governing or funding organizations within the field of international humanitarian initiatives have expressed concern with these apparent gaps in data, it has become increasingly apparent that this missing data could be the reason for the derailment of some key projects at the local level. Projects that should be a success are found to be floundering. This raises the concern that this may have contributed to wasteful spending. With funding becoming increasingly scarce, these assessment gaps must be closed.

One way to remedy this has been the promotion of collecting information related to secondary sources and the impact of those sources. The international professionals who are promoting the recognition and assessment of collateral impact believe that, with projects involving multi-stakeholder networks, a full and viable assessment can be achieved by adding data related to what is essentially collateral impact.

Considering collateral impact within peace and conflict impact assessments

Projects using a collaborative governance model can be complex, involving multi-stakeholders and multi-levels of government. Each stakeholder group not only exists within its own network but it also participates in the collaborative initiative as well. As such, it is logical that any stakeholder group will participate in the collaborative project from the base of their organization's priorities and, at times, assessing progress using their own unique internal evaluation process. Balancing any one individual group's priorities with the others within a collaborative governance initiative requires dynamic, multi-level interactions between all stakeholders.

It is reasonable to assume that this complex interaction will need an assessment model that can ensure all influencers are accounted for. The assessment model must include core stakeholders and clients as well as their networks of stakeholders and clients who may not be directly involved with the project but who will still have impact on its outcome.

It is difficult for traditional evaluation models to embrace such a dynamic and fluid model of project management because they tend not to emphasize horizontal or multi-dimensional aspects of initiatives involving multi-stakeholders. As we have previously mentioned, in an attempt to address this many designers of evaluation systems have attempted to use complex formulae, even computer modelling. And yet, in the end they find that some networks, in particular auxiliary networks, simply do not fit into the formula.

The puzzle remains regarding how to obtain as true a picture as possible in any situation where there is a multi-dimensional and fluid organization of partners. And, for those working in the field of international humanitarian efforts, this includes clients and stakeholders who do not have the resources to properly use sophisticated and complex models to gather and interpret the data. It is a reality in this field that many do not have the resources or skills to access sophisticated and complex evaluation options.

In any situation where there exists a multiplicity of networks, any evaluation process must value the importance of the interactions between organizations that form the initial base of stakeholders with other seemingly outside networks that are active with any or the entire core group. These secondary stakeholders could be economic, financial and political, or even represent alternative community-based interests. All, however, have or will have perspectives to add to the understanding of a situation and the successful delivery of the proposed project.

Within the complex and multi-faceted field of international humanitarian projects, we see evidence of a search for an evaluation framework that addresses potential gaps rising from a lack of information related to influences from secondary stakeholder networks.

One example where this is occurring is within the Peace and Conflict Impact Assessment Model (PCIA).[1] Initially being based on a very traditional evaluation framework, evaluators at the field level were concerned that it was too complex for grassroots stakeholders and clients. PCIA was at that time best suited for a well-educated population with computer literacy skills. This virtually eliminated the participation of many grassroots clients and even some stakeholders. It did serve traditional organizations or government bureaucracies as it, initially, meshed with a

---

[1] PCIA is a means of anticipating/monitoring/and evaluating the ways in which an intervention in a violence-prone stetting may affect/ is affecting/ or has affected, the dynamics of peace or conflict. The term "intervention" is used in its broadest sense to include, for example, initiatives that are intended to have beneficial impacts on levels of social development, humanitarian conditions, economic development, or peace & security. PCIA is a process similar to Gender Analysis and Environmental Impact Assessment in that it is concerned with impacts beyond the stated outputs, outcomes, and objectives of an initiative.

hierarchical approach to project management. And, for most part the traditional aspects of a PCIA evaluation framework did work.

Where it did not work was when a project's clients or stakeholders did not possess the necessary technical or communication skills and knowledge to participate in a more complex evaluation framework. The result was that information from key direct or even indirect stakeholders and clients could not be effectively considered. It was extremely difficult to know if such projects were failing at the grassroots level.

Recognizing that critical information from both core and secondary networks was missing, evaluators refocused efforts to address this information gap. Because their projects use public funding, they needed to have a framework that could adequately include evaluation data from all partners within a multi-dimensional project. By not fully considering collateral impact within these multi-level projects, there were gaps in the ongoing evaluation data that had been gathered.

In part due to its formal or traditional approach to evaluation, PCIA was also criticized for being too complex and was deemed too bureaucratic and daunting for most field projects. Indeed, with the focus on providing traditional core data, the collection of information from stakeholders and clients ran the danger of missing critical data.

PCIA evolved. Professor Ken Bush was one who began to work towards a PCIA instrument that could incorporate the assessments of all clients and stakeholders who operated within a multi-dimensional governance model and whose influence has not previously been fully documented (Bush 2004). He proposed the addition of including critical data gathered from stakeholders and clients who did not have the ability to use or even understand a complex western assessment process. This facilitated the beginning of recognizing the importance of including data that came directly from collateral stakeholders in any project assessment process.

Evaluators who have included this new data in PCIA have reported that this can take additional time to establish connections with all direct and indirect stakeholders and clients. However, by accepting the existence of collateral impact and thereby embracing information from all the non-core stakeholders and clients, they have also reported that this gives management, and funding organizations yet another tool to track the success of the project.

The ongoing tracking of collateral impact does not need to be an onerous additional task. With some adaptations, the PCIA model has evolved to embrace both traditional evaluation needs for funding and accountability measures, as well as including data associated with collateral impacts. This comprehensive approach provides a more viable analysis of the project's status. Indeed, without such input, project management loses critical data on the impact that the project is having and whether that unexpected collateral impact is positive or negative.

Including collateral impact within the PCIA's evaluation framework required some 'out of the box' thinking. Stemming from some of Dr. Bush's suggestions, evaluators have even implemented a 'blank page' or pictorial process virtually eliminating language needs. This and similar adaptations have been used within some humanitarian projects situated in isolated and remote areas where communications with stakeholders cannot use traditional western forms of evaluation. These adjustments to traditional data gathering ensured information from both core and collateral sources are included in the evaluation process. Without the addition of critical information from secondary clients or stakeholders, project managers would not have been be able to fully understand the impact of their efforts on all stakeholders and clients.

While this shift to include an assessment of collateral impact is relatively new within the PCIA model, it has proven to be an additional element that complements any funding agency's requirement by integrating information from both core and non-core clients and stakeholders.

The PCIA example has shown that assessing collateral impact does not require a completely new approach to evaluation and that most evaluation models are flexible enough to accommodate the gathering and integration of additional information. Collateral impact is an additional element whereby the impact of all participants is acknowledged. The real and potential impact on the project can be acknowledged and can show both positive and negative impacts within a multi-dimensional framework. From this perspective, it meshes well with the dynamic nature of collaborative governance.

As well the PCIA example has shown that it need not be an additional bureaucratic layer. Paying more attention to the collateral impact associated with stakeholders and clients who are not directly involved with the core aspects of the project can increase the potential that the project will not be derailed and can be clearly seen to be a success. In recognizing the collateral impact secondary stakeholders and clients are having on an ongoing basis allows the project or program management to remain dynamic, fluid and responsive. And, using information gathering tools already within a project's communications management, information relating to collateral impact can always be available to complement an evolving management framework.

Examples of collateral impact within this book

Just as we have seen an increase in the appreciation of the impact of secondary sources on projects within the field of international humanitarian work, there is evidence that within many of the case studies identified in this book, there have been elements of collateral impact that were noted as having an impact on the projects cited.

Revising the traditional evaluation paradigm in order to more adequately measure the progress of projects within collaborative governance, it has been noted that very often when formal institutions are involved either as a stakeholder or as a funding agent, there is a call for "accountability." And that this request has been so broad ranging that accountability, as Hubbard and Paquet have suggested, has come to mean a variety of things ranging from true responsibility to the simple obligation of formally offering an official account of what has happened (Hubbard and Paquet 2010).

Even when significant detail is added to formal evaluation processes, those offerings do not capture all the critical data. There is a need for attention to be paid to these gaps as they increase with the multi-layered aspects of collaborative initiatives. It is within this complex and dynamic interaction of all stakeholders that critical data about the impact of the project exists. And, I would suggest that this would include the collateral impact of secondary stakeholders.

Hubbard and Paquet identify how, while it is relatively simple to define impact within strictly hierarchical organizations, it becomes much more complex in organizations where officials need to address the potentially conflicting individual goals of a variety of stakeholders. They offer *intelligent accountability* as a more realistic appreciation of the complexity found within collaborative initiatives. This concept does embrace a more dynamic situation where stakeholders vary and goals may evolve. Using such a model would likely uncover the impact on the initiative that comes from dynamic stakeholder interaction.

Compatible with this new approach would be to give some additional consideration for the collection of data related to the collateral impact of both direct and secondary stakeholders. These complementary elements would not only satisfy core agents and more effectively assess a dynamic and fluid process, but also fully embrace data from secondary stakeholders and clients.

As a core example of recognizing the importance of identifying the impact of all stakeholders and clients are the initiatives described by Wanda Wuttunee (chapter 5). This chapter highlights the benefits of ensuring that all voices are heard, that all stakeholders are identified and that all clients are considered. They have shown that such recognition promotes partnerships working well together. As well this project demonstrates the importance of recognizing history and culture as part of relationship building between stakeholders and clients – both at the core of the project as well as secondary ones. I would suggest that recognizing such impact and utilizing the information to build relationships and to off-set potential conflict in order to enhance the project's outcome is definitely encompassed within the concept of collateral impact.

We have noted that a collaborative partnership can start with a formal agreement of some nature; we have also seen that this may only serve as a starting point, a declaration of the willingness to work together. However, once the project is active, the dynamic and fluid nature of collaborative governance stakeholders emerges. Stakeholders, client populations will change or evolve. As these changes take place we begin to see how important it is to remember the impact that these changes will have on all participants involved either directly or indirectly with the project.

Cook and Mahoney in their case study (chapter 1) identified that: "Collaborative governance models offer promise to the extent that they can bring diverse interests together to forge agreement on innovative strategies." And, this project has shown that within the collaborative governance framework lays the importance of the impact brought to the project through the individual participation of all core stakeholder organizations and clients as well as their partners. This initiative recognized that to have *collective impact*, it was important that all stakeholders work towards a common agenda that offered a shared vision. And, it demonstrates that continuous critical input is needed to achieve any system change through a collaborative process. Tracking multi-stakeholder input, and impact, is essential.

Tracking the collective impact in its entirety recognizes how individual stakeholders and clients can impact the project's eventual outcome. And within the dynamic framework of collaborative governance, the complexity of this impact is compounded as new groups or stakeholders are added to or leave the initial project. As well, the goals of both core and secondary stakeholders and clients often evolve over time. And, it is within this internal framework of collective impact that there exists essential data related to collateral impact.

Not all evaluation mechanisms acknowledge either collective impact or collateral impact, but the initiatives cited in this chapter clearly demonstrate the need for evaluators to recognize these impacts due to the dynamic and fluid aspects inherent in collaborative governance.

Collateral impact evaluation – some final comments

It is becoming clear that traditional, hierarchical evaluation frameworks are not able to fully capture all the necessary evaluation data that is found within a dynamic and fluid governance model such as collaborative governance.

The search for a more effective framework that can be applied to multi-stakeholder, multi-level initiatives is ongoing. And, this evolution will continue. At the same time, it seems ineffective to attempt to create a completely new paradigm when modifying some existing frameworks could produce effective and adaptable alternatives. I would suggest that by integrating data related to collateral impact into these existing frameworks, the dynamic interaction between all stakeholders, both core and secondary, can be tracked.

By including collateral impact when assessing collaborative governance initiatives, managers and supporting agencies will have a better analytical tool for assessing the progress, and for identifying opportunities for intervention or additional input, while serving to off-set potential conflict.

References

Bush, Ken. 2004. *Hands on PCIA: A Handbook for Peace and Conflict Impact Assessment.* www.berghof-foundation.org/fileadmin/redaktion/Publications/Handbook/Dialogue_Chapters/dialogue4_bush_app.pdf [Accessed May 16, 2018].

Hubbard, R and G. Paquet, 2010. *The Black Hole of Public Administration.* Ottawa, ON: Invenire

Rocan, C. 2012. *Challenges in Public Health Governance: The Canadian Experience.* Ottawa, ON: Invenire

Tamborra, Marialuisa. 2002. "Socio-economic Tools for Sustainability Impact Assessment: Contribution of EU Research to Sustainable Development", *EU Quarterly – European Commission: Community* Research, www.Europa.eu.int/research/rtdinfo_en.html.

ABOUT
LA MAISON GOUVERNANCE

L A MAISON GOUVERNANCE is the name of the new collective which has taken over the responsibility for *Optimum, The Journal of Critical Governance Studies*, and for the publishing house, Invenire, as of July 2017.

As is well-known to readers of the *Journal* and to those familiar with the books published by Invenire, governance is a *manière de voir*, an analytical framework, a clinically useful apparatus, and a new mental toolbox. But, fundamentally, it is a subversive approach: it aims at permanently and critically analyzing all governance arrangements in place – in particular, the hierarchical and coercive ones like the state.

This interest in *critical governance studies* emerged in the National Capital Region in the 1980s. In the colloquial exchanges of the colleagues who partook in these palavers about governance since then, LA MAISON GOUVERNANCE has been the informal moniker used to refer to the virtual and shifting rally points around which most of the activities crystallized. This label has also served to identify the disparate group of hundreds of academics, technocrats, professionals and practitioners who met semi-regularly to debate problems of pathologies of governance. Colleagues from other parts of the country joined in on occasions of diverse forums organized in Ottawa.

None of these aficionados ever felt the need to formalize or patent the moniker, nor the collegium for which it stood. They felt comfortable with the openness and the continually renewed composition of the group, its evolving interests, and the organization of meetings only when it was felt useful. Its informality fit the *humeur vagabonde* of the group well, and the various projects that brought them together more or less regularly.

Some will remember the activities organized by the Canadian Higher Education Research Network, the meetings of the Lunar Society, the projects carried out under the aegis of PRIME (Program of Research in International Management and Economy), and the multiplicity of events – some relatively private, others mobilizing significant audiences – in association with the Institute for Research on Public Policy (then located in Ottawa) or the Canadian Centre for Management Development, etc. – all mobilizing moments built on impermanent arrangements to discuss issues pertaining to the governance of private, public, social or civic organizations that generated consequential results.

In the 1990s, there was a general changing of the guard on the Ottawa scene: the Economic Council of Canada and the Science Council of Canada – two poles of critical discussion at the centre of heated debates – disappeared, but other loci like the Canadian Centre for Management Development stepped in. LA MAISON GOUVERNANCE both expanded and spread out, with the result that its activities also branched out in a number of directions.

At that time, a particularly active research group in critical governance studies came together at the University of Ottawa's Faculty of Administration (now the Telfer School of Management). It was the time when *Optimum* became a flagship publication of the Faculty, when a good number of colleagues in management and elsewhere at the University began to bring in graduate students interested in governance studies, and when the University of Ottawa, at the request of Gilles Paquet and colleagues, agreed to create the Centre on Governance (COG) in 1997.

LA MAISON GOUVERNANCE then, more or less, faded away in the shadow of the Centre on Governance.

The worksite created by Gilles Paquet and his colleagues in 1997 has generated important research products, but it has also, over the years, triggered resistance in a university framework, where the progressive ideology and political correctness were becoming ever more present. The COG was and remained a privileged locus of critical thinking – as much of the excesses of the fetishism of the market, of the state, as of blind compassion. It became, over time, the target of persiflage, and less than well-tolerated in quarters where market, state or compassion are revered.

After some 20 years of enlightening but critical books and papers, some academic units – imperceptibly in certain cases, savagely in others – have been led to abandon support for these heretical activities. When the COG abruptly terminated its support for our activities, this signalled an opportune moment to resuscitate LA MAISON GOUVERNANCE, to get it to rise like the mythical Phoenix from its nominal ashes. And since we are in 2017, a website is obviously in order. It is up and running at www.lamaisongouvernance.org. In addition, interested parties can keep informed of the circumstances of this renaissance by consulting www.gouvernance.ca or www.invenire.ca.

For it must be said, loudly and clearly, that critical studies in governance will go on. Gilles Paquet, the *animateur* of LA MAISON GOUVERNANCE, remains associated with the Telfer School of Management and with the Graduate School of Public and International Affairs at the University of Ottawa, and a new team associated with other institutions from the National Capital Region have formally joined him in carrying forward activities on the critical governance studies front.

It would be tragic, however, if because of an unfortunate administrative hiatus, the body of work accomplished over the last 30 years were to disappear from sight. The spirit of LA MAISON GOUVERNANCE, invested in the ventures pursued between 1988 and 1997, and temporarily attached between 1999 and 2017 to the Centre on Governance, has left an indelible impact on the governance scene. The group of colleagues that has been the soul of the Centre since its inception has been responsible for a refereed quarterly journal on governance and public management which has profoundly permeated the public debate about governance in Canada and abroad, producing hundreds of papers and reports over the last 25 years, and publishing some 70 books, authored by colleagues from Canada and elsewhere, under different banners.

As *ground zero* of the new incarnation of LA MAISON GOUVERNANCE, it may be useful to remind the members of the *Optimum* community and those who have followed the publications of Invenire of some of the works produced in the period of incubation of governance studies of LA MAISON GOUVERNANCE from the mid-1980s to 1997. These works, listed below, may be said to be the foundation on which the Centre on Governance was built. The period from 1999 to 2017 saw critical governance studies prosper. We provide also below a list of the main books and reports that this group and their associates across Canada and elsewhere have produced since 1997, in collaboration with a number of publishing houses. Most of these books are available through www.amazon.ca.

Under diverse banners during the incubation period before 1998

B. Bazoge & G. Paquet (sld). 1986. *Administration : unité et diversité.* Ottawa, ON: University of Ottawa Press, 350 p.

G. Paquet & M. von Zur Muehlen (eds.). 1987. *Education Canada? Higher Education on the Brink.* Ottawa, ON: Canadian Higher Education Research Network, 300 p.

G. Paquet (sld). 1989. *La pensée économique au Québec français : témoignages et perspectives.* Montreal, QC: Association canadienne-française pour l'avancement des sciences, 364 p.

G. Paquet & M. von Zur Muehlen (eds.). 1989. *Edging Towards the Year 2000: Management Research and Education in Canada.* Ottawa, ON: Canadian Federation of Deans of Management and Administrative Studies, 130 p.

G. Paquet *et al.* (sld). 1990. *Éducation et formation à l'heure de la compétitivité internationale.* Montreal, QC: QC Association des économistes québécois, 217 p.

G. Paquet & O. Gélinier (sld). 1991. *Management en crise : pour une formation proche de l'action.* Paris, FR: Economica, 162 p.

C. Andrew, L. Cardinal, F. Houle & G. Paquet (sld). 1992. *L'ethnicité à l'heure de la mondialisation.* Ottawa, ON: Association canadienne-française pour l'avancement des sciences, 114 p.

J.A. Boulet, C.E. Forget, J.P. Langlois & G. Paquet (sld). 1992. *Les grands défis économiques de la fin du siècle.* Montreal, QC: Association des économistes québécois, 340 p.

G. Paquet & J.-P. Voyer (sld). 1993. *La crise des finances publiques et le désengagement de l'État.* Montreal, QC: Association des économistes québécois, 380 p.

D. Côté, G. Paquet & J.-P. Souque (sld). 1993. *Décrochage scolaire, décrochage technique : la prospérité en péril.* Ottawa, ON: ACFAS-Outaouais, 135 p.

J. de la Mothe & G. Paquet (eds.). 1995. *Technology, Trade and the New Economy*. Ottawa, ON: PRIME, 125 p.

S. Coulombe & G. Paquet (sld). 1996. *La ré-invention des institutions et le rôle de l'État*. Montreal, QC: Association des économistes québécois, 480 p.

J. de la Mothe & G. Paquet (eds.). 1996. *Evolutionary Economics and the New International Political Economy*. London, UK: Pinter, 319 p.

J. de la Mothe & G. Paquet (eds.). 1996. *Corporate Governance and the New Competition*. Ottawa, ON: PRIME, 117 p.

J. de la Mothe & G. Paquet (eds.). 1997. *Challenges Unmet in the New Production of Knowledge*. Ottawa, ON: PRIME, 112 p.

J. de la Mothe & G. Paquet (eds.). 1998. *Local and Regional Systems of Innovation*. Boston, MA: Kluwer Academic Publishers, 341 p.

J. de la Mothe & G. Paquet (eds.). 1999. *Information, Innovation and Impacts*. Boston, MA: Kluwer Academic Publishers, 339 p.

Under the banner of the University of Ottawa Press (1999-2010)

D. McInnes. 1999. *Taking it to the Hill – The Complete Guide to Appearing before Parliamentary Committees*

G. Paquet. 1999. *Governance through Social Learning*

L. Cardinal & C. Andrew (sld). 2001. *La démocratie à l'épreuve de la gouvernance*

L. Cardinal & D. Headon (eds.). 2002. *Shaping Nations – Constitutionalism and Society in Australia and Canada*

P. Boyer *et al.* (eds.). 2004. *From Subjects to Citizens – A hundred years of citizenship in Australia and Canada*

C. Andrew *et al.* (eds.). 2005. *Accounting for Culture – Thinking though Cultural Citizenship*

G. Paquet. 2005. *The New Geo-Governance: A Baroque Approach*

J. Roy. 2005. *E-government in Canada*

C. Rouillard *et al.* 2006. *Re-engineering the State – Toward an Impoverishment of Quebec Governance*

E. Brunet-Jailly (ed.). 2007. *Borderlands – Comparing Border Security in North America and Europe*

R. Hubbard & G. Paquet. 2007. *Gomery's Blinders and Canadian Federalism*

N. Brown & L. Cardinal (eds.). 2007. *Managing Diversity – Practices of Citizenship*

J. Roy. 2007. *Business and Government in Canada*

T. Brzustowski. 2008. *The Way Ahead – Meeting Canada's Productivity Challenge*

G. Paquet. 2008. *Tableau d'avancement – Petite ethnographie interprétative d'un certain Canada français*

P. Schafer. 2008. *Revolution or Renaissance – Making the transition from an economic age to a cultural age*

G. Paquet. 2008. *Deep Cultural Diversity – A Governance Challenge*

L. Juillet & K. Rasmussen. 2008. *A la défense d'un idéal contesté – le principe de mérite et la CFP 1908-2008*

L. Juillet & K. Rasmussen. 2008. *Defending a Contested Ideal – Merit and the Public Service Commission 1908-2008*

C. Andrew *et al.* (eds.). *Gilles Paquet – Homo Hereticus*

O.P. Dvivedi *et al.* (eds.). 2009. *The Evolving Physiology of Government – Canadian Public Administration in Transition*

G. Paquet. 2009. *Crippling Epistemologies and Governance Failures – A Plea for Experimentalism*

M. Small. 2009. *The Forgotten Peace – Mediation at Niagara Falls 1914*

R. Hubbard & G. Paquet. 2010. *The Black Hole of Public Administration*

P. Dutil *et al.* 2010. *The Service State: Rhetoric, Reality, and Promises*

G. DiGiacomo & M. Flumian (eds.). 2010. *The Case for Centralized Federalism*

R. Hubbard & G. Paquet (eds.). 2010. *The Case for Decentralized Federalism*

Under the banner of Invenire (2009-)

R. Higham. 2009. *Who do we think we are: Canada's reasonable (and less reasonable) accommodation debates*

R. Hubbard. 2009. *Profession: Public Servant*

G. Paquet. 2009. *Scheming Virtuously: The Road to Collaborative Governance*

J. Bowen (ed.). 2009. *The Entrepreneurial Effect: Ottawa*

F. Lapointe. 2011. *Cities as Crucibles: Reflections on Canada's Urban Future*

J. Bowen. 2011. *The Entrepreneurial Effect: Waterloo*

G. Paquet. 2011. *Tableau d'avancement II – Essais exploratoires sur la gouvernance d'un certain Canada français*

R. Chattopadhyay & G. Paquet (eds.). 2011. *The Unimagined Canadian Capital – Challenges for the Federal Capital Region*

P. Camu. 2011. *La Flotte Blanche – Histoire de la Compagnie de la navigation du Richelieu et d'Ontario 1845-1913*

M. Behiels & F. Rocher (eds.). 2011. *The State in Transition – Challenges for Canadian Federalism*

R. Clément & C. Andrew (eds.). 2012. *Cities and Languages: Governance and Policy – International Symposium*

R. Clément & C. Andrew (sld). 2012. *Villes et langues : gouvernance et politiques – Symposium international*

C.M. Rocan. 2012. *Challenges in Public Health Governance: The Canadian Experience*

T. Brzustowski. 2012. *Why we need more innovation in Canada and what we must do to get it*

C. Andrew *et al.* 2012. *Gouvernance comunautaire : innovations dans le Canada français hors Québec*

M. Gervais. 2012. *Challenges of Minority Governments in Canada*

R. Hubbard *et al.* (eds.). 2012. *Stewardship: Collaborative decentred metagovernance and inquiring systems*

G. Paquet. 2012. *Moderato cantabile: Toward principled governance for Canada's immigration policy*

G. Paquet & T. Ragan. 2012. *Through the Detox Prism: Exploring organizational failures and design responses*

G. Paquet. 2013. *Tackling Wicked Policy Problems: Equality, Diversity and Sustainability*

G. Paquet. 2013. *Gouvernance corporative : une entrée en matières*

G. Paquet. 2014. *Tableau d'avancement III – Pour une diaspora canadienne-française antifragile*

R. Clément & P. Foucher. 2014. *50 years of official bilingualism: challenges, analyses and testimonies*

R. Clément & P. Foucher. 2014. *50 ans de bilinguisme official : défis,analyses et témoignages*

R. Hubbard & G. Paquet. 2014. *Probing the Bureaucratic Mind: About Canadian Federal Executives*

G. Paquet. 2014. *Unusual Suspects: Essays on Social Learning Disabilities*

R. Hubbard & G. Paquet. 2015. *Irregular Governance: A Plea for Bold Organizational Experimentation*

L. Cardinal & P. Devette (sld). 2015. *Autour de Chantal Mouffe – Le politique en conflit*

R. Higham. 2015. *What would you say? ... as guest speaker at the next Canadian citizenship ceremony*

D. Gordon. 2015. *Town and Crown – An Illustrated History of Canada's Capital*

G. Paquet & R.A. Perrault. 2016. *The Tainted-Blood Tragedy in Canada: A Cascade of Governance Failures*

G. Paquet & C. Wilson. 2016. *Intelligent Governance: A Prototype for Social Coordination*

R. Hubbard & G. Paquet. 2016. *Driving the Fake Out of Public Administration: Detoxing HR in the Canadian Federal Public Sector*

C. Maule (ed.). 2017. *A Future for Economics – more encompassing, more institutional, more practical*

G. Paquet. 2017. *Tableau d'avancement IV : un Canada français à ré-inventer.*

G. Paquet. 2017. *Pasquinades in E – Slaughtering Some Sacred Cows*

G. Paquet. 2018. *Pasquinades en F – Essais à rebrousse-poil*

C.M. Rocan (ed.). 2018. *Building Bridges: Case Studies in Collaborative Governance in Canada*

With other publishing houses

Éditions Liber

G. Paquet. 1999. *Oublier la Révolution tranquille – Pour une nouvelle socialité*

G. Paquet. 2004. *Pathologies de gouvernance – Essais de technologie sociale*

G. Paquet. 2005. *Gouvernance : une invitation à la subversion*

G. Paquet. 2008. *Gouvernance : mode d'emploi*

G. Paquet. 2011. *Gouvernance collaborative : un anti-manuel*

Éditions Vrin

P. Laurent & G. Paquet. 1998. *Épistémologie et économie de la relation – coordination et gouvernance distribuée*

Éditions H.M.H.

G. Paquet & J.P. Wallot. 2007. *Un Québec moderne 1760-1840 : Essai d'histoire économique et sociale*

Government of Canada

G. Paquet. 2006 (en collaboration). *The National Capital Commission: Charting a New Course*

Report of the NCC Mandate Review Panel

A selection of the main research reports

J. Roy & C. Wilson. 1998. *Strategic Localism and Competitive Advantage*

COG. 1999. *Corporate Governance & Spin-in Ventures*

COG. 1999. *The Borough Model: Municipal Restructuring for Ottawa*

COG. 2000. *Governance in the 21st Century* (The Royal Society of Canada)

COG. 2000. *The Governance of the Ethical Process for Research – A study for the Tri-council*

G. Paquet. 2001. *Si Montfort m'était conté ... Essais de pathologie administrative et de rétroprospective*

Talentworks Project (under the supervision of Christopher Wilson)

COG. 2001. *Evaluating TalentWorks: Creating a Foundation for Successful Collaboration*

COG. 2002. *Ottawa's Workforce Environment, Report I of Ottawa Works: A Mosaic of Ottawa's Economic and Workforce Landscape*

COG. 2002. *Profiling Ottawa's Workforce, Report II of Ottawa Works: A Mosaic of Ottawa's Economic and Workforce Landscape*

COG. 2002. *Ottawa's Workforce Development Strategy, Report III of Ottawa Works: A Mosaic of Ottawa's Economic and Workforce Landscape*

A. Chaiton & G. Paquet (eds.). 2002. *Ottawa 2020 – A synthesis of the Smart Growth Summit*

G. Paquet & Kevin Wilkins. 2002. *Ocean governance ... An inquiry into stakeholding*

B. Collins *et al.* 2003. *Assessment of Public Internet Access in Ottawa: Report of Key Findings*

COG. 2003. *SmartCapital Evaluation Guidelines Report*

COG. 2003. *SmartCapital Baseline Assessment*

R. Hubbard, G. Paquet & C. Wilson. 2004. *CIPO: Reaching the World of SMEs*

COG. 2004. *SmartCapital: A Smart Community Assessment*

G. Paquet & J. Roy. 2005. *CIPO as an Innovation Catalyst*

Printed in June 2022
at Imprimerie Gauvin,
Gatineau (Quebec), Canada.

www.ingramcontent.com/pod-product-compliance
Lightning Source LLC
Chambersburg PA
CBHW071739270326
41928CB00013B/2732